Hampshire and the Isle of Wight

THE
ORIGINAL
HOTEL

ORDNANCE SURVEY HISTORICAL GUIDES

Hampshire and the Isle of Wight

David A Hinton
and Dr A N Insole

GEORGE PHILIP
ORDNANCE SURVEY

First published in Great Britain in 1988 by
George Philip & Son Ltd,
27A Floral Street,
London WC2E 9DP
and Ordnance Survey,
Romsey Road
Southampton SO9 4DH

British Library Cataloguing in Publication Data

Hinton, David A.
Hampshire and the Isle of Wight.—
(Ordnance survey historic county guides).
1. Hampshire—Historical geography
2. Isle of Wight—Historical geography
I. Title II. Insole, Allan N. III. Series
911'.4227 DA670.H2

ISBN 0-540-01137-1

Filmset by Tameside Filmsetting Ltd,
Ashton-under-Lyne, Lancashire
Printed by BAS Printers Ltd,
Over Wallop, Hampshire
Bound by Robert Hartnoll Ltd
Bodmin, Cornwall

Picture acknowledgements

The illustrations in this book are reproduced by kind permission of the following:
BBC Hulton Picture Library: pp 1, 31, 114–115
Cultural Services Department, Isle of Wight County Council: endpapers, pp 21, 127, 131 (top), 134–135, 136–137, 141 (top), 145, 146–147, 149, 150
Hampshire County Museum Service: pp 2, 7, 9, 38 (top), 41, 44, 50 (lower), 53, 54 (top), 58–59, 64, 71, 74, 78–79, 86 (top), 94–95, 97 (top), 102 (top), 106 (top), 110, 118 (top), 119 (top), 122–123
A. N. Insole: p 144
W. I. McMahon: pp 131 (lower), 134 (lower), 136, 141 (lower)
Christine Wevill: pp 38 (lower), 50 (top), 51, 54 (lower), 59 (lower), 65, 67, 68, 73, 75, 80, 86 (lower), 97 (lower), 100, 102 (lower), 106 (lower), 116, 117, 118 (lower), 119 (lower), 126

Endpapers: *The Broadway, Sandown, in about 1875.*
Half title: *The City Bridge, Winchester, in 1910.*
Frontispiece: *Market day at Ringwood in about 1890.*

Contents

Hampshire

Basingstoke in the early morning in 1866 (see page 51).

'HAMPSHIRE' IS ANGLO-SAXON. The name comes from two Old English words, *Hamtum* and *scir*, and means the district governed from the town which is now called Southampton. This district may not have been as big as the modern county, but at any rate by the time of the Domesday Book survey in 1086, *Hantescire* was much as it is today, except that Christchurch was removed from it in 1974 and there have been some earlier changes, such as the addition to it of Martin in the west towards the end of the nineteenth century.

It is a county of chalk and heath. Gravels, sands and clays lie in an arc around Southampton Water, and dominate the north and north-east. The rest is chalk, cut through and drained by a series of streams and rivers. The chalk even manages to climb above the clays to create the spine-like Portsdown Hill, which looms over Portsmouth harbour. To farmers, the chalk soils provide the best opportunities: grazing for sheep, ploughlands for grain. The rest is for market gardening or rough pasture: hence, of course, the New Forest with its unique combination of woodlands, open heaths and mires, deer, cattle and ponies.

Hampshire is also a coastal county. It has two great, often competing, ports at Southampton and Portsmouth, and many harbours for smaller boats. The coastline is relatively modern: the Isle of Wight did not become an island until 8000 years ago, long after *Homo sapiens* first began to hunt and to fish in the area. Because of sea-level changes, many of the sites used by early peoples are now under water, but traces of their activity can be found in raised beaches along the shore, just as their flint tools can be found inland. They may have been the first to make an impact on Hampshire's natural environment, cutting and burning woodland clearings for their settlements.

Around 7000 years ago, the first farmers appeared in the Hampshire landscape, further reducing the forests and creating fields mainly for cattle and wheat, other stock and crops being less important to them. Conditions were ideal: the climate was warm but not too dry, and the woods had created a deep cover of rich soil not only in the valleys, but on the hills and over the clays. Consequently the population could grow quickly: Hampshire has some forty of the long barrows that these people used for burial and which probably served as landmarks to show their tribal centres, although curiously there are none of their other well-known monuments such as henges. The influence of the farmers still survives, for by the middle of the third millennium BC they had cleared the forest from most of the chalkland, creating a landscape that is basically that of today.

The cutting down of the woods continued during the second millennium BC, when round barrows replaced long barrows as the favoured burial-places. Well over a thousand of these are known in Hampshire, many now ploughed flat but many still visible, particularly in the New Forest where their occurrence shows that the land was being used for agriculture, as it was also in the north and north-east. Denuded of trees, however, the soils quickly lost their fertility, and further stress was caused by erosion of soil, not only on the clays but also on the chalk hills. It is scarcely exaggeration to talk about ecological disaster, aggravated by a change in the climate to wetter and colder conditions. There are remains of field systems of this period which suggest that people were forced to adopt new farming methods to meet the changed circumstances.

The appearance of hill-forts in the landscape could be a sign of the strains that these problems created, with communities having to compete against each other for land that was still usable. The river valleys may have been particularly important, and it seems that some of the hill-forts, like Danebury near Stockbridge, were built to control such resources. Not all the forts are on the chalk, however, and Buckland Rings, near Lymington, shows that at least the coastal fringes of the New Forest were still important, and there are traces of field systems that prove that some agriculture was being practised there.

The boundary changes of 1974 deprived Hampshire of one of its most important sites, Hengistbury Head in Christchurch harbour. This was an industrial and trading centre protected by a great rampart and ditch, from which salt, imported pottery (and thus probably also wine) and perhaps iron from the rich ores that are found on the south Hampshire coast were distributed inland. Certainly Hampshire was beginning to develop quite a complicated trading system before the Roman Conquest. Although Danebury was abandoned, other large sites were growing: their extent is unknown, but Silchester in the north and Winchester in the south both have histories that begin before they became Roman towns, and, beyond Hampshire, Chichester was another focal area, from which was probably controlled the whole of Portsmouth harbour.

Under the Romans, Winchester became *Venta Belgarum*; a little of its Roman wall can still be seen, but the whole of its line is important, for it is the framework within which the inner part of the city has operated ever since. By contrast, Silchester (*Calleva Atrebatum*) is now an almost empty shell; it did not revive in the Middle Ages when its urban role was taken over by Reading, so that some of the roads that served it fell out of use. The greater part of the Roman road network underlies our roads today, though not all as major routes: that from Winchester to Sarum (*Sorviodunum*) near Salisbury is only a very minor road because it was too steep and lonely for convenient use by cart traffic. The lasting effect of the Romans on the landscape can be seen in other ways, such as the creation of smaller centres like Bitterne, which can claim to be the first real port of Southampton. Tantalizing are the large, sprawling settlements such as those at Neatham near Alton and East Anton near Andover: were these places markets and were they the predecessors of the medieval towns nearby? In the countryside, it is clear that the Roman villas, such as the one which can be visited at

Rockbourne, were the centres of large estates. Hayling Island, where there was a temple, is a site on the south coast where something of Roman religion can be explored, and a little to its west is the important Saxon shore fort at Portchester, built in the third century and strengthened in the fourth, the first fortification in Portsmouth harbour. These are testimonies of the complex governmental system of the Roman period; lower in the hierarchy are the pottery industries of the New Forest, where debris from the kilns still lie under earth-covered mounds, and at Alice Holt in the north. More basic than all these were the many small farming settlements, whose occupants worked the fields as best they could in land that had already been farmed for thousands of years.

The departure of the legions and the collapse of Roman government during the fifth century did not necessarily mean that all these farms were abandoned. Although some fields fell into disuse, so that their hedge-banks can be found in woodlands today, most of the land probably went on being worked, even though the villa buildings were abandoned and the towns crumbled slowly into decay. Some new peoples moved into the area; the south-coast belt and Southampton Water were under Jutish control; the chalklands were Saxon territory. At the end of the seventh century, as paganism gave way to Christianity, the kings of the West Saxons gave us Wessex, and unified what they termed *Hamtunscire*. This is why we can call Hampshire 'Anglo-Saxon'. Under their rule, a major port flourished at Southampton, lower down the River Itchen than the site that the Romans had used. To them also we owe the first churches; the earliest of which parts survive is at Titchfield. Many of our present-day villages began life on their modern sites at this time; archaeologists have revealed settlements that were abandoned in the sixth, seventh and eighth centuries, often for locations in river and stream valleys.

During the ninth century, Viking raids disrupted the expanding economy of Wessex. Hampshire had four places at least which were defended against the enemy: Portchester, Winchester and probably Bitterne, Southampton, where Roman walls could be brought back into use, and Christchurch where a bank and ditch dug across the promontory would have had to suffice. The existing port at Southampton faded into obscurity, but the bishop and the king created a fine new town in Winchester, with churches, streets and a thriving market. In the eleventh century, Winchester perhaps more than London could claim to be the capital city of England, for the king had his treasury there, and there the great Domesday Book was compiled. From that, and from other sources, we know that Hampshire was a moderately prosperous county, though it had suffered from William's conquest, of which the new castle at Winchester was only too visible a symbol. Southampton, beginning to revive but on yet another new site, this time on the bank of the River Test, and the very small Christchurch were the only other boroughs in the county, though there were markets elsewhere, as at places like Basingstoke which were soon afterwards to be acknowledged as towns. The county was predominantly one of rural settlements, some quite large, some just single farms; the New Forest, recently created as a royal hunting preserve, had probably not supported much agriculture for two thousand years, and some small communities may have been allowed to remain in it despite forest laws, creating some of the enclaves that are there today.

The twelfth and thirteenth centuries were a time of expansion. The population grew, putting increasing pressure on resources: land that had been used for grazing was turned into ploughland, woodlands were cleared for fields. Many new towns were created, some, such as Portsmouth, by the king, others, such as Stockbridge, by private owners; four, the largest of which today is Fareham, were set up by the bishops of Winchester. Feudal landlords required the status that ownership of castles bestowed, of which the best Hampshire examples are to be seen at Portchester, where the stone keep in one corner of the

Roman walls was probably begun by William Mauduit, and Christchurch, where the stone chamber-block with its first-floor hall and its tower encased in an earthen motte survive in ruins, testimony to the de Redvers family. There are also smaller castles, ringworks and mottes, some hastily constructed in times of civil war, such as those around Bentley thrown up in King Stephen's reign and as quickly abandoned. Great country mansions at Warneford and Bishops Waltham show the large sums spent on more peaceful aristocratic living, just as deer-parks show how the nobility created preserves for themselves, both for food and for hunting, often ousting tenants to do so, a process that continued into the eighteenth century and which created parks that still survive, for instance at Highclere in the north of the county. Monasteries of this period were usually founded by the aristocracy, or even by the king—Beaulieu had King John as its grudging patron. Such houses became major landowners, often the most efficient; the results of the work of Beaulieu can be seen in the fields at the south end of the New Forest.

The fourteenth century saw great changes. Worsening climate and a run of bad harvests checked population growth, and then the Black Death made its impact, killing more than a third of the people by 1350, and making further devastations in its endemic cycles over the next 150 years. This probably saved Hampshire's remaining woodland from farmers anxious to carve out fields in the forests of Pamber, north of Basingstoke, Bere, north of Portsmouth, and others, as well as in the New Forest. Quite suddenly, there was a surplus of land, not a dearth, and villages and hamlets shrank in size, many eventually being abandoned altogether. Over 120 settlements were lost in Hampshire, mostly because it was more profitable to enclose the land and to rear sheep, and to a lesser extent cattle, than to plough it, since the demand for wool remained buoyant, and this was the key to prosperity in the Middle Ages. Hampshire's sheep do not produce best-quality wool, but Alresford had one of the busiest wool markets in

England, and Romsey had a very active industry specializing in the final stages of cloth production. Winchester, however, suffered badly, for its cloth industry dwindled, and some of the new towns failed to get established and sank back into rural obscurity. Southampton, well placed for trade with the south of France and Italy, had fluctuating fortunes: wars with France led to a catastrophic raid in 1338, and in the years that followed walls were built along the waterfront that still testify to the French threat.

One of the most interesting aspects of Hampshire's history from the fourteenth century to the present day concerns provision of facilities for warfare, both defensive and offensive. As the Crown ceased to rely on merchant ships but needed purpose-built vessels—perhaps the earliest, Henry V's *Grâce Dieu*, built in Southampton in 1416, now lies encased in the mud of the River Hamble—so naval requirements for docks and supplies grew. By the end of the fifteenth century, Portsmouth had become a royal dockyard, its first usable dry dock being built in 1495. As the reliability, accuracy and range of cannons increased, they created new needs. Southampton's fourteenth-century walls were built as a battery for small hand-guns to rake the shore if a raider landed. By the early fifteenth century, however, attacking ships would carry guns powerful enough to bombard from a distance, so that a special tower had to be built as a sturdy platform against the recoil of heavy weapons that could fire sufficiently far out into the water to prevent such ships from coming in close. Similar towers were built at Portsmouth. A hundred years later, Henry VIII felt the need to build blockhouses, sealing the entry to the Solent with Hurst Castle and to Southampton Water with Calshot, as well as with others at Netley and at the mouth of the Hamble. Outside Portsmouth he built Southsea Castle to protect the entrance to the harbour. These were part of the first nationally planned defensive scheme since King Alfred's reign.

Some of the stone for Henry VIII's forts came from the

monasteries, for the Dissolution removed from Hampshire some of its most important institutions. There were many who profited more than the king from the subsequent redistribution of land, and Thomas Wriothesley's ingenious construction of a grand house within the shell of the nave at Titchfield Abbey exemplifies the profits to be made. More modest prosperity can be seen in many timber-framed buildings; Hampshire is a county without good natural building stone, so timber continued to be used for most houses until the nineteenth century. Even brick was at first used only for chimneys, decoration, and for filling in the panels between wooden beams; later it was combined with flint to make decorative and very solid walls. There was no shortage of trees to supply the builders' needs, for natural regeneration of woodland was sufficient to keep the forests well stocked, even when the demands of the navy were at their height. Some inclosures were established in the New Forest, but felling did not lead to change in the actual amount of woodland, either there or in some other Hampshire forests; control of grazing was probably sufficient to allow the woods to recover naturally, although beech outstripped oak in these circumstances.

The sixteenth century was not one of expansion in Hampshire generally, despite developments at Portsmouth. Southampton, indeed, lost its trade almost completely to London after 1530, and declined to insignificance. The Chalk Downs continued to be grazed, but the manufacture of cloth did not revive on a large scale in the county, growth at Basingstoke, Petersfield and other towns being countered by decline at Romsey. Pottery was made in the north-east in considerable quantity, much of it for the London market, but this was never a wealth-producing industry. Experiments with new industries, for instance glass-making at Buckholt near Stockbridge, were short-lived, though iron-smelting increased along the coast, using charcoal from the New Forest and Bere, and ore from surface deposits, largely to meet the navy's needs. Salt was also produced in some quantity in this area, and the remains of the salt-works can be seen on the shore. The seventeenth century was more buoyant, except in the Civil War; the population was growing again and there was prosperity for the markets and fairs that served its needs. Demand for food rose, and the amount of arable land increased again. An important new development was the use of water-meadows: stream and river valleys were 'drowned' in early spring, to keep frosts off the early grass. Consequently more sheep could be fed, and these could then be used to manure the arable fields. The network of watercourses constructed in the meadows can be recognized in many valleys. Another industry that took advantage of Hampshire's clean and plentiful streams was paper-making, and later silk.

The Industrial Revolution had much less effect on Hampshire than on counties in the midlands and the north, and no major investments in new industries were made. The continuing development of Portsmouth dockyard provided a focus for activity, but ship-building at Bucklers Hard and elsewhere did not prove to be a long-term initiative. Roads were improved, allowing carts and coaches to travel more quickly, but canals did not have a great impact: many were planned but few were completed. Perhaps more important as a catalyst were the Napoleonic Wars, a great boost for suppliers to the navy and the army, such as the ironworks around Portsmouth, and for agriculture, whose products were distributed along the two canals that were eventually built, to Southampton and to London. The change to arable continued, and with it the long process by which small farms were enclosed and amalgated was completed. There remained, however, large areas of open heath, impervious to agriculture, although many poor people attempted to establish squatters' holdings in them.

It was because of the Napoleonic Wars that the Ordnance Survey began to produce its maps of Britain (although the Department had come into existence in 1791, following the Second Jacobite Rebellion in Scotland), with Hampshire's being among the first to be published because of the importance of Portsmouth and the defence of the coast against invasion. The first edition therefore does not show the product of the Industrial Revolution that most affected the county, the railway. By it, north Hampshire could be reached in a couple of hours from the capital, and one result was that large areas of its heathland were used for military training, served from Aldershot, Hampshire's first new town since the Middle Ages. The age of steam transformed Southampton, for steamships could get up the Water whatever the wind and tide, and from there it was a relatively quick journey for passengers and mail to London. The docks were already being improved when the railway arrived in 1840, making overland transport of bulk goods economical. Southampton's attractions as a seaside resort declined, but resorts developed at Southsea and Hayling Island, Lymington and Christchurch to cater for the new demand for cheap, short holidays. The New Forest began to become a leisure facility, with a station at Brockenhurst and a branch line to Lymington. Most towns and villages saw expansion, with buildings of brick made from Hampshire's prolific clay deposits, now easily transported on railways that were themselves major customers because of viaducts, tunnels and bridges. Some of the clay and other poor soils could be used profitably at last, for dairying, pig-rearing and market gardening, particularly between Southampton and Portsmouth with their growing populations. There were disadvantages in the new transport systems for the large-scale farmers established on the better ground, however, as grain from the Baltic, and later the United States, could be sold more cheaply. Increasingly they turned to sheep again, but even grazing was hardly profitable by the end of the century.

Hampshire's only 'railway town' is Eastleigh, to which the London and South Western Railways carriage works were moved in 1890. Its streets of terraced houses testify to rapid growth, as further engineering works were added. The other heavy industry in the county was ship-building at Southampton. Portsmouth's dockyard remained, hugely expanded, and protected by the forts on Portsdown Hill and out in Spithead Water which were built in the 1860s. There were ironworks near Andover, and similar ventures in other towns, but they were relatively small-scale, and agricultural depression sent many into decline. Winchester remained genteel, social life revolving round the cathedral.

A new transport system began to develop in Hampshire in 1892, when the army established a balloon factory at Aldershot. Military needs led to airfields at Gosport and Beaulieu, and sea-planes were manufactured along Southampton Water. The First World War increased these requirements. Eastleigh opened in 1918, but did not become a municipal field until 1932; Hurn is a product of the Second World War, as are many others either still used by the military, like Middle Wallop, or used by private light planes, like Blackbushe, or which remain unused, their buildings removed, like Stoney Cross in the New Forest. Aeroplane manufacture was an industry around Southampton until the 1950s, and components are still made. But the main impact of air transport on the county now is caused by Heathrow, and to a lesser extent by Gatwick, which have been the cause of housing and other growth around Yateley in the north. A small oil refinery was built in Southampton Water in 1920, and in the 1950s was hugely expanded. There have been failures: the hovercraft must represent a lost opportunity. And there are ironies: in the 1960s, Portsmouth already feared the loss of its dockyard and tried hard to attract new industries. It was a bitter blow when its biggest site failed to tempt a nylon textile factory that went elsewhere—and has now closed. Disappointed Portsmouth had to make do with a little-known second-best: IBM.

Hampshire now thrives on its microchips and its electronics. Some of its largest towns have been hugely expanded, and its fields are under increasing pressure for development. Agricultural changes have created vast open fields on the chalkland, its intensively ploughed soil maintained in fertility by artificial fertilizers, not by sheep manure. Yet underneath the prairies, the motorways, the housing estates and the shopping centres, much can still be recognized of the framework that has shaped Hampshire's history over thousands of years. The study of maps is one of the paths into exploration of that framework.

Winchester Road, Wickham, in 1908, typical of artisan and other housing in a small country town. In this area of Hampshire, the primary building materials are bricks. tiles and chimney-pots, all made from the local clay (see page 100).

Isle of Wight

The Bulton family outside their cottage in Luccombe in about 1890. The village was abandoned in 1910 because of land movement.

N TERMS OF THE VAST AEONS of geological history, the Isle of Wight is a very recent development. In the last Ice Age sea level was so low that there was no Solent and no English Channel. When the great ice-sheets that had covered much of the northern continents began to melt about 10,000 years ago, sea level began to rise. The sea gradually inundated the English Channel and then the Solent, but the Isle of Wight remained attached to the mainland by a ridge of Chalk downs extending westwards to what is now the Dorset coast. About 8000 years ago the sea severed this last connection. The island that was formed was much larger than the one we see today. Continuous coastal erosion over the intervening centuries has produced this, and the process continues so that the island is gradually disappearing into the sea.

Man reached the area long before the island became separated from the mainland. These early visitors were nomadic palaeolithic hunter-gatherers following migrating herds of big game animals, and apart from the occasional flint implement, they left no evidence of their passing.

About 3500 BC the first neolithic farmers arrived on the island. They used polished stone axes to clear some of the primeval woodland, and in the cleared areas they planted their crops and herded domesticated animals. They left behind three earthen long barrows at Tennyson Down, Afton Down and Mottistone. These communal tombs are the oldest field monuments left by man on the island. Woodland clearance was continued by the Bronze Age people who arrived about 2000 BC. Like their neolithic predecessors, they settled largely on the Chalk, although later they appear to have spread over much of the southern and north-eastern areas of the island. The early Bronze Age communities buried their dead in round barrows but from about 1400 BC simple pit burials were used. The island is especially rich in round barrows and over 200 sites have been identified, although many of these have been damaged or lost. The neolithic and

Bronze Age people probably laid down a network of trackways which became the basis of the Island's road system.

Iron began to replace bronze in the economy from about 550 BC. On the mainland this change led to a population expansion, times became unsettled and hill tops began to be fortified. The Isle of Wight appears to have escaped the unrest. The so-called hill-fort on Chillerton Down was never completed and was probably intended to be a cattle enclosure rather than a defensive structure. During the first century BC southern England began to be affected by the expansion of the Roman Empire across Gaul. The most immediate effect was the migration of the Belgic tribes from the Continent, and by about 50 BC one of these, the Atrebates, had occupied central southern England, including the Isle of Wight.

The Sicilian writer Diodorus Siculus, writing in about 25 BC, stated that Cornish tin was carried to a certain island off Britain called Ictis before being shipped to France and the Mediterranean. It is often suggested that this island of Ictis was the Isle of Wight, whose Roman name was Vectis. However, Diodorus mentions that there was a causeway exposed at low tide between the mainland and the island, which eliminates any possible identification of Ictis with the Isle of Wight since there is no evidence for a causeway across the Solent. It appears unlikely that tin traders would have brought the tin ore overland all the way from Cornwall at a time when marine transport directly across the English Channel to the Continent would have been more efficient.

In AD 43 or early 44 the Isle of Wight surrendered to the Roman Second Legion commanded by Vespasian, probably without military occupation. Subsequently at least seven, and possibly eight, villas were built on the island. These were typical Roman estate farms practising a mixture of sheep-farming, cattle-raising and cereal-growing. Whether the villas were occupied by retired Roman army officers or by Romanized Britons is not known, but the extensive mosaic pavements in the Brading villa imply that it was owned by someone of importance. Little is known of the native settlements during this period but finds of coins, pottery and other artefacts suggest that the island was well populated.

For some 200 years the island was apparently peaceful and prosperous, but then in the latter half of the third century the southern and eastern coasts of the Roman province of Britannia were threatened by raiding parties of Saxon pirates. As a defensive measure a series of coastal forts and watchtowers was built along the so-called Saxon Shore. The remains of a rectangular stone fort are visible beneath the later medieval walls of Carisbrooke Castle. There is a strong presumption that this is a Roman structure which might be related to other Saxon Shore forts.

The history of the Anglo-Saxon conquest of the island is unclear. Documentary and archaeological evidence indicates that the earliest settlers in Kent and the Isle of Wight were distinct from those of other parts of south-east England. Bede recorded that these people were Jutes, and not Angles or Saxons. The initial phase of settlement took place in the late fifth or early sixth century. The island appears to have remained independent of the other Anglo-Saxon kingdoms until the middle of the seventh century when it was captured by Wulfhere, King of Mercia. Wulfhere promptly gave it to one of his vassals, Aethelwalh, King of the South Saxons. It has been suggested that several villages, such as Arreton, Brading, Carisbrooke and Freshwater, were founded during the reign of Aethelwalh. In 686 Aelthelwalh was killed on the mainland by the West Saxon Caedwalla. Caedwalla then invaded the Isle of Wight, exterminated the inhabitants and settled it with his own followers from the mainland. From that time the island became an integral part of the kingdom of Wessex.

After Caedwalla's conquest, peace returned until the beginning of the Danish raids from 897 onwards. In the first phase of attacks raids took place all along the south coast. The island was repeatedly threatened and several landings are recorded. Surprisingly, during King Alfred's organization of the defences of southern England it was not considered necessary to construct a stronghold on the island. One incident recorded in the *Anglo-Saxon Chronicle* is often associated with it. In 896 a fleet of six Danish ships raided along the south coast including the Isle of Wight. Alfred's fleet trapped them in an estuary where they went aground and a battle was fought, from which some of the Danish ships escaped as the tide rose but were captured later. One possible location for this incident is Brading Haven, which in Saxon times extended from St Helens southwards to Sandown Bay.

During and after Alfred's reign, the Danes were gradually brought under control and the number of attacks decreased. The respite lasted for about eighty years before a second and more violent wave of raids began in 980. Initially these were simple hit-and-run attacks but later large-scale organized plundering expeditions were mounted. Not only was the Isle of Wight constantly harried but the fleet overwintered on the island on three occasions and used it as a base for raiding the mainland. This second wave of Danish attacks ceased when Cnut gained the throne of England in 1016.

After the Norman Conquest the Isle of Wight achieved an unusual status. William the Conqueror gave the lordship of the island with absolute authority to his relative William Fitz Osborn. The Isle of Wight thus became effectively a separate state. Fitz Osborn established himself at Carisbrooke, where he began to build a fortified keep and bailey, a structure of earthworks and wooden palisades. All the Saxon estates were given to Fitz Osborn's friends. On Fitz Osborn's death in 1071, the lordship of the island passed fairly rapidly through several hands until 1100 when it was granted to the de Redvers family, who held it for nearly 200 years.

The Domesday Book provides a snapshot of the economy and

landscape of the island as it was in 1086, shortly after the Norman takeover. The population was surprisingly small, at just over 1000, and these people lived in small manorial settlements and isolated farmsteads. Settlement was much denser in the central and southern parts of the island than in the north, which reflects the poorer quality of the land in the latter area. Many of the places mentioned in the Domesday Book were to be sites of village and hamlet development in later times. A passing mention is given to a 'Park of the King' at Watchingwell. Later manuscripts make it clear that this was an extensive royal chase governed by the severe Norman forest laws. It appears to have stretched from the Medina to the Newtown River, and Parkhurst Forest is the last vestige of this royal park where the island lords once went hunting.

In 1107 Baldwin de Redvers inherited the lordship and rebuilt the original fort at Carisbrooke with a stone-built keep and curtain wall. He also founded Quarr Abbey. The stone for these buildings was quarried at Quarr, and stone was also exported from here to the mainland where it was used in the construction of many churches, including Chichester Cathedral, Winchester Cathedral and Romsey Abbey. Surprisingly, although Baldwin chose to support the wrong side in the civil war between Stephen and Matilda, he was not deproved of the lordship. The family retained it until 1293 when Edward I persuaded, or perhaps forced, the dying Isabella de Fortibus, the Lady of Wight, to sell him the island for 6000 marks, a ludicrously low sum. From that time the island lost its independence and the Crown appointed the Lords. The title Lord was changed to 'captain' in 1509, and then, in 1583, to 'governor', the term which is still used today.

Throughout medieval times the Isle of Wight was a relatively isolated rural area and for the most part not very prosperous. Very little development took place down the years. In the twelfth century the de Redvers built towns at Newport and Yarmouth, which these were followed in the thirteenth century by the foundation of Newtown by the Bishop of Winchester. That none of these planned towns prospered is probably a reflection of the problems which affected the island at the time. In the later Middle Ages it is clear that the island suffered from depopulation, with some villages becoming totally or partly deserted, as at East Ashey, near Ryde. Several reasons have been advanced to explain this, but the most important appear to have been a change from arable to sheep farming and the recurrent threat of French attacks throughout the fourteenth, fifteenth and sixteenth centuries.

The geographical position of the Isle of Wight at the entrance to Southampton Water gave it some military importance. During the intermittent wars with France, several landings took place when towns and villages on the island were pillaged and burnt. Until the sixteenth century surprisingly few precautions were taken to guard against such raids, although it would have provided an ideal base for the enemy. In the fourteenth century a local militia was established and a chain of beacons set up, but little else was done. By the sixteenth century the emergence of Portsmouth as a naval base had increased the strategic importance of the island. Accordingly Henry VIII constructed coastal artillery forts at Yarmouth, East and West Cowes, and Sandown as part of an overall defensive scheme for the region. These forts were precursors for the more comprehensive defences for the Solent which were constructed in the middle of the nineteenth century.

The island escaped unscathed from the ravages of the Civil War and as a result prospered to some extent. It was, however, touched by one event. In 1647 Charles I sought refuge there but was imprisoned by the Parliamentarians in Carisbrooke Castle. Various attempts were made, to free him, but none of them was successful. Later in the year the King was moved to the King James's Grammar School in Newport for a short period before being conveyed across the Solent to his trial and eventual execution in London.

After these events the island once again became a rural backwater, although there were signs of prosperity in some areas. In the seventeenth century West Cowes grew into a thriving port with considerable trading links with the American colonies. At the same time a shipbuilding industry developed, initially at East Cowes, and later spreading to include West Cowes.

In the early nineteenth century a series of factors began radically to influence the island's economy and landscape. Firstly, visiting writers, such as Keats, began to extol the picturesque beauties of the island, which coincided with the growth of the middle classes with time and money to spend on leisure activities. Another factor was the growth of yachting as a hobby for the rich, with the choice of Cowes as the headquarters of the Royal Yacht Squadron. And at the same time a number of publications by eminent physicians pronounced on the medical benefits of the island's climate. Finally, a major impetus was given when, in 1844, Queen Victoria and Prince Albert purchased Osborne House at East Cowes as a summer retreat. The original house was too small and so, between 1846 and 1848, the present structure was built to Prince Albert's own designs. All this contributed to the transformation of the island into a fashionable summer resort, and the rapid expansion of many of the coastal towns can be dated to the years between 1850 and 1880. Urban growth was particularly rapid after the construction of the railway system, with much of the development consisting of lodging houses for the accommodation of visitors and private villas, many of which were modelled on Osborne House.

The prosperity of the island was also boosted by a large military presence. It had been little affected by the Napoleonic Wars, but in the mid nineteenth century there was a renewed threat of invasion by the French under Napoleon III which stimulated a major review of the coastal defences of the United Kingdom. As a result of this review, the Isle of Wight was seen as an integral part of the defensive ring around the Royal Navy base at Portsmouth. A number of forts, gun emplacements and barracks were built on the island, and these works, plus the increased number of soldiers, stimulated the expansion of several local industries, such as milling and brewing.

In this century the island economy has in general fluctuated in concert with that of the United Kingdom as a whole. The overall trend has been one of increasing prosperity. Tourism continued to grow in importance, although the clientele changed as the population as a whole became more affluent, with more and more working-class families able to take holidays. This and the changing fashions in leisure activities led to the construction of holiday camps, chalet sites and caravan parks, as well as the conversion of many of the large Victorian and Edwardian villas into self-catering flats. Industries remained reasonably prosperous until the late 1950s when a local industrial decline set in. Paradoxically, the population continues to expand because of the recent trend for people retiring to the island. With the working population having to move away to seek employment and the elderly migrating to the island, the balance of the community has altered considerably. If these trends continue, they will inevitably change the character of the Isle of Wight.

Map Section

The chain-pulled floating bridge between Gosport and Old Portsmouth began to operate in 1840. Only a flat-bottomed boat could be relied upon in the strong current that runs past the Point. It was closed in 1959. The wooden ship on the right is not H.M.S. Victory, *but the* St Vincent, *which was used as a boys' training ship. She is saluting the Royal Yacht*, Victoria and Albert.

KEY TO ONE INCH MAPS

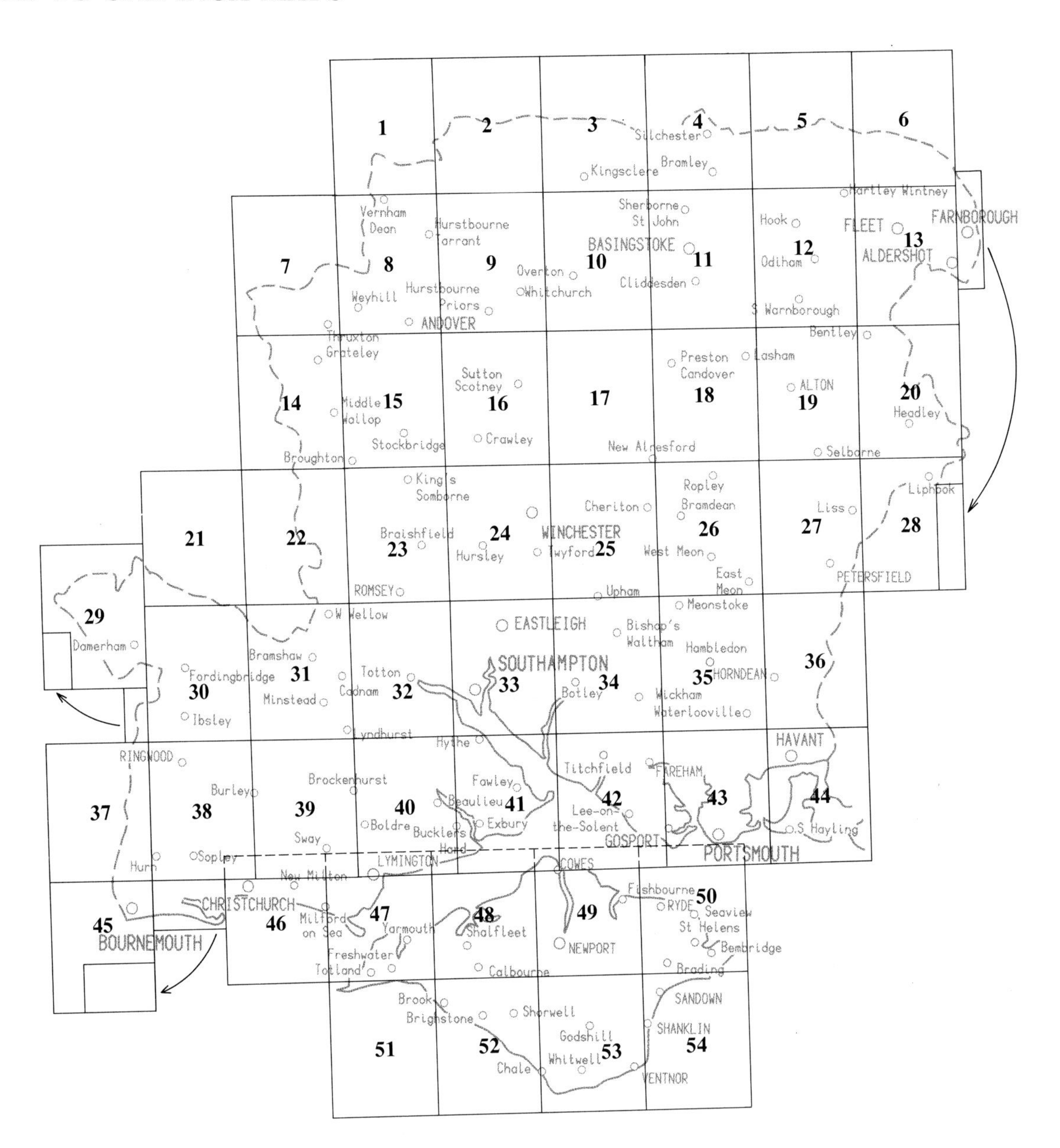

The unusual alignment of the one-inch coverage of the county is due to the projection used in the construction of this mapping. Unlike today where all Ordnance Survey maps are based on one national survey projection, early Ordnance Survey one-inch mapping was plotted on more than one projection. Six in all were used for the first edition one-inch map coverage of the country. This is particularly noticeable in the gazetteer key map (page 154) where the modern Landranger sheet lines are also shown.

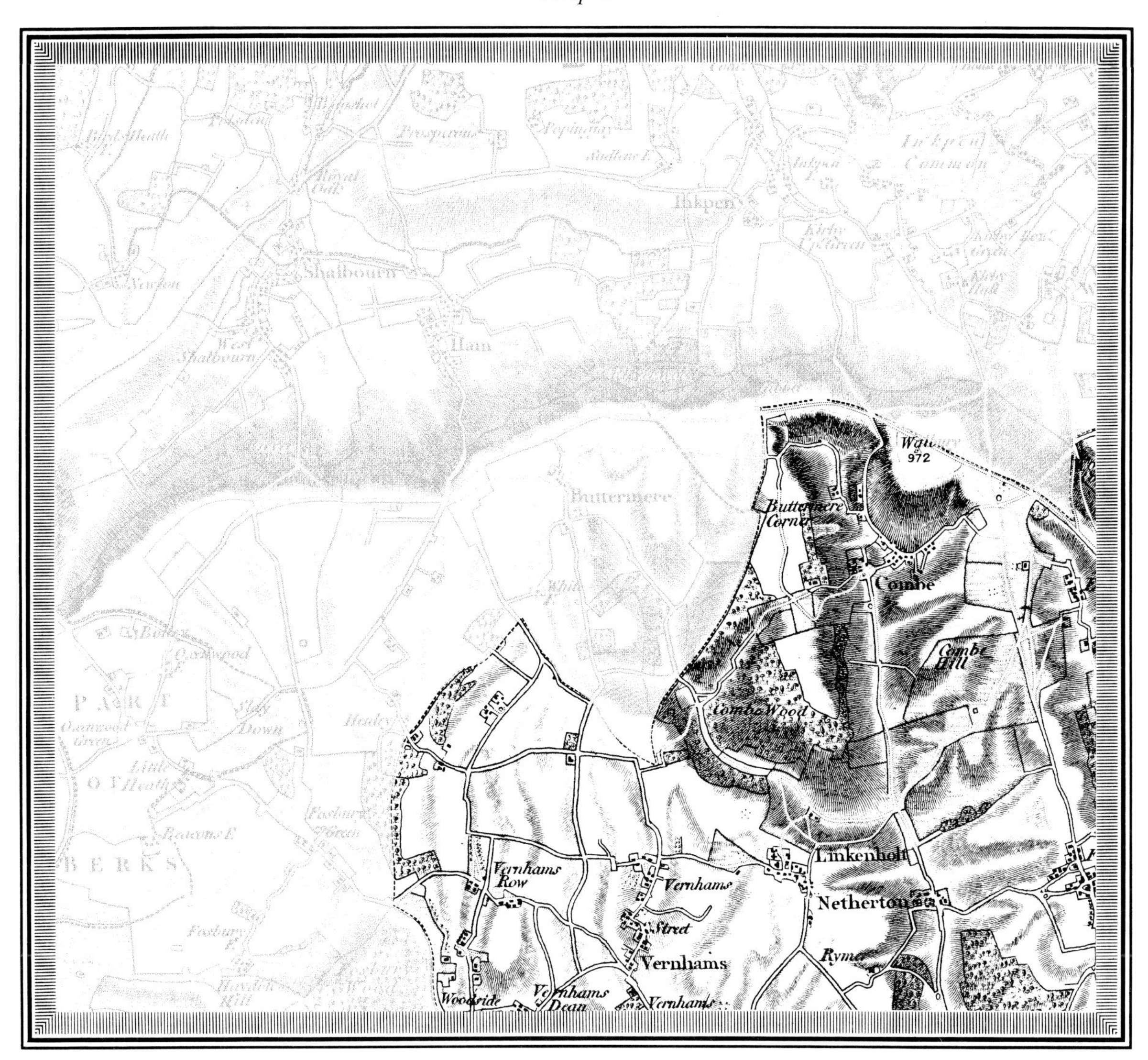

Map 1 The north-west corner of Hampshire is a country of steep slopes and narrow valleys. The Iron Age hill-fort of Walbury was the highest point in the county; although now entirely in Berkshire, it used to be bisected by the county boundary. Modern farming methods have not had much impact here, and the area still has many of the same woods; nor has there been any significant change in the size of the hamlets. The geology is chalk with clay cappings in places. The north-facing slope gives a very good view over the Kennet Valley—hence presumably the siting of Walbury. The county boundary briefly follows the scarp-line, and then plunges down the slope, off the high chalk and into the clay and gravel vale below.

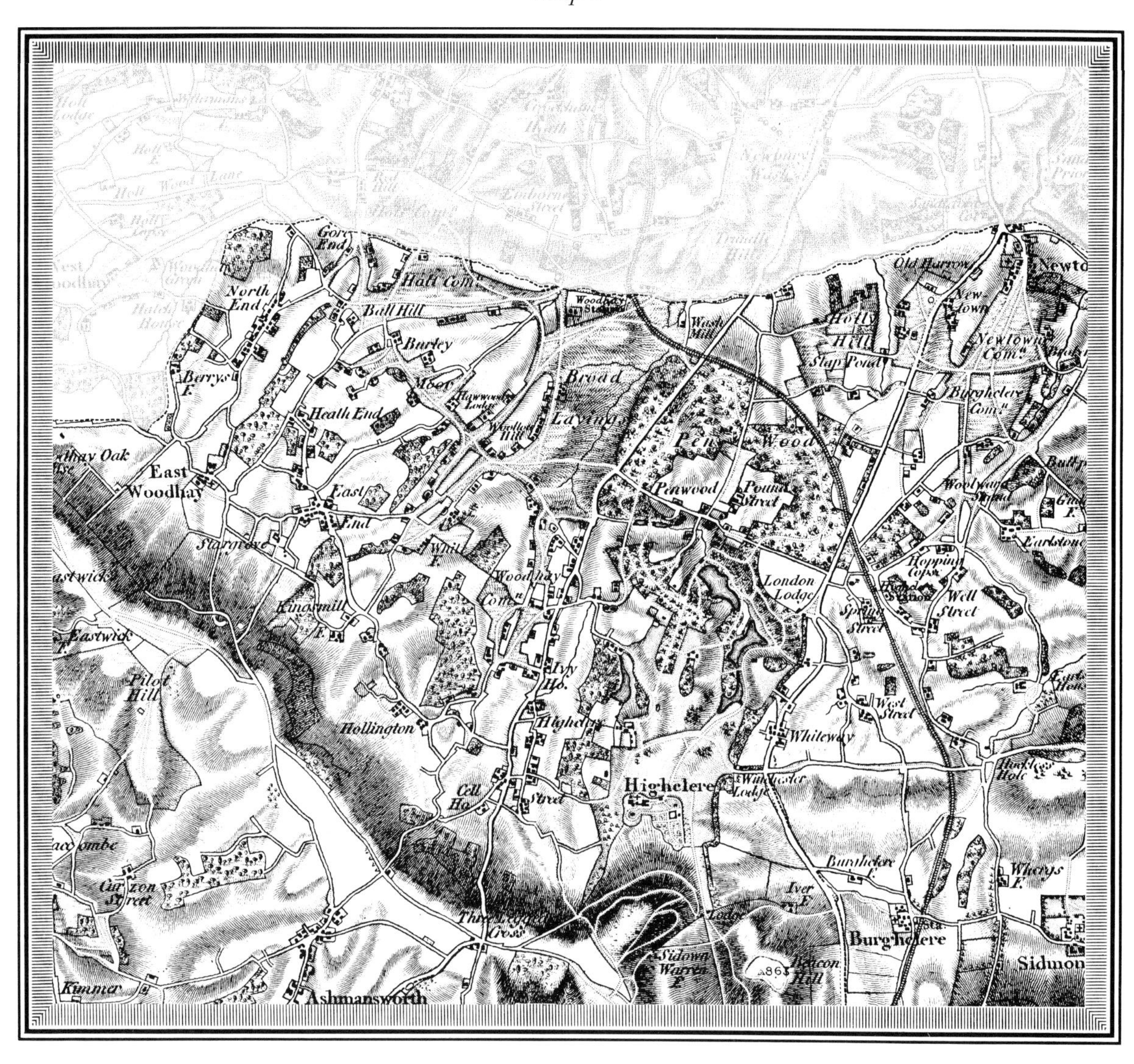

Map 2 The county boundary follows a small river, now called the Enborne, but perhaps once called the Cleare, accounting for names like Burghclere and Highclere. Off the chalk hills, it encompasses an area of broken woodland. Highclere 'Castle' is actually a fairly recent name for the mansion there, and is not the site of a medieval castle. Newtown represents an attempt in the thirteenth century by the bishops of Winchester to establish a market town on their Burghclere estate. For a time this was a success, with fifty-two burgesses being recorded in the new borough; but by the end of the sixteenth century little remained, perhaps because of competition from nearby Newbury. The site was landscaped in the eighteenth century for Newton House park, so that almost nothing of it can now be seen, its name the only trace of it on the map. Another transient was the Newbury–Southampton railway line, opened in 1885 (as far as Winchester), and now dismantled.

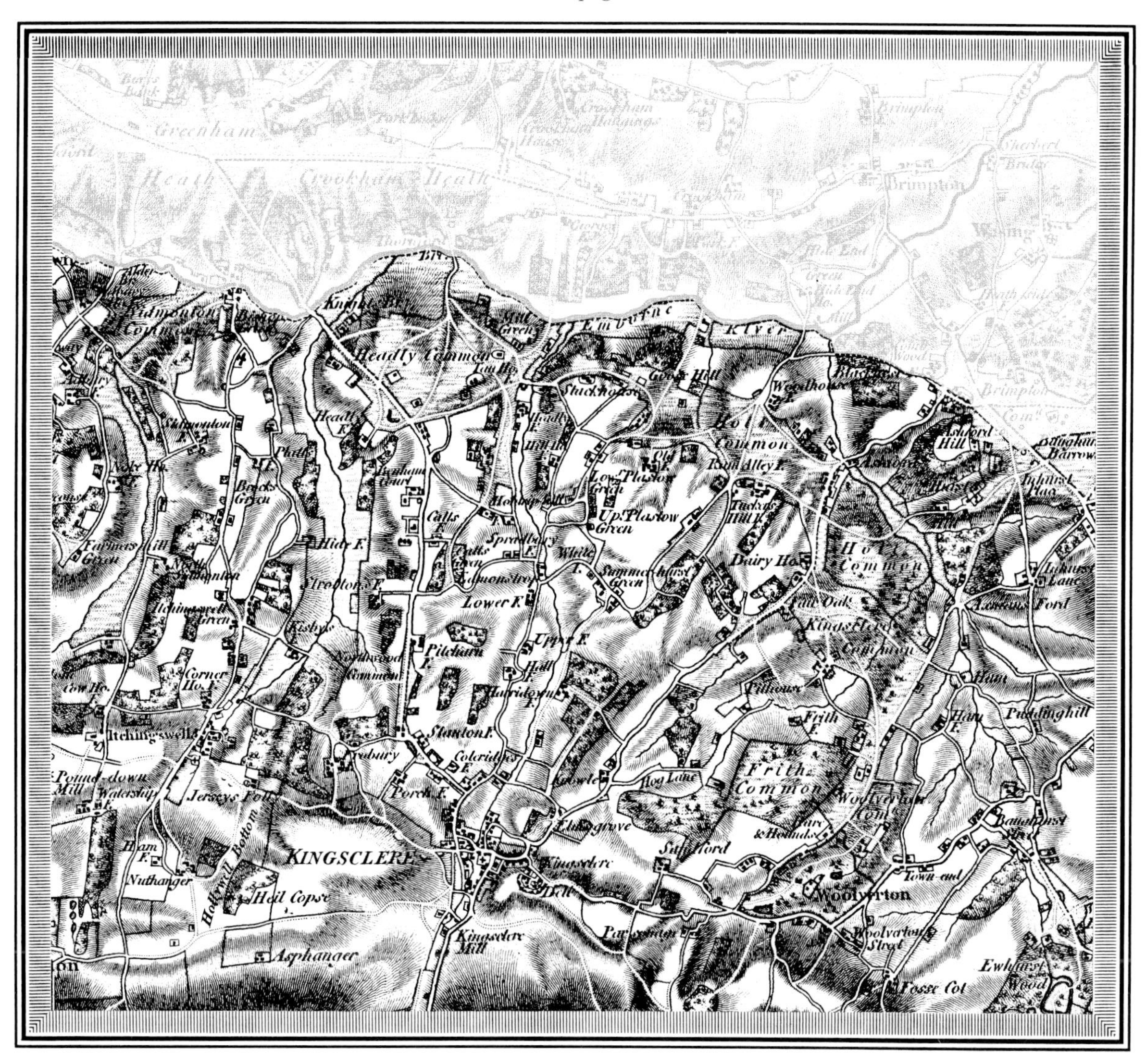

Map 3 Along much of the southern edge of this part of the map can be seen the steep north-facing scarp of the chalk hills, while most of the area is made up of a scatter of farms interspersed with the commons from which many of them had originally acquired their land, a pattern typical of low-lying sandy and clay soils. The largest settlement is Kingsclere, classically sited at the foot of the hills and an important road centre, with its market-place alongside the churchyard. The main road from Reading to Basingstoke now bypasses the town, but otherwise most of the early nineteenth-century tracks have become the metalled roads of today. Much of the common land has been enclosed, however, with Frith Common, for example, now known as Sandford Woods. The park for Wolverton House shows the location of the only 'big house', for the heavy, damp soils did not make this a fashionable area.

Map 4 The Roman town of Calleva Atrebatum (Silchester) is shown as an enclosure empty but for the small church and hamlet in one corner. It is little different today. Some of Silchester and Tadley Commons survive, but much has disappeared under Tadley, whose housing estates serve Aldermaston on the other side of the county boundary. Part of Pamber Forest remains: this was a great tract of medieval royal forest, some nine miles by six, which covered the whole of this part of the map. The many 'green' names indicate clearings made within it, as royal control relaxed after the middle of the thirteenth century. Although it is not obvious from the map, many of the farms, e.g. Wyeford, are built within moats, another sign of the establishment of new farms from cleared, or 'assarted', land.

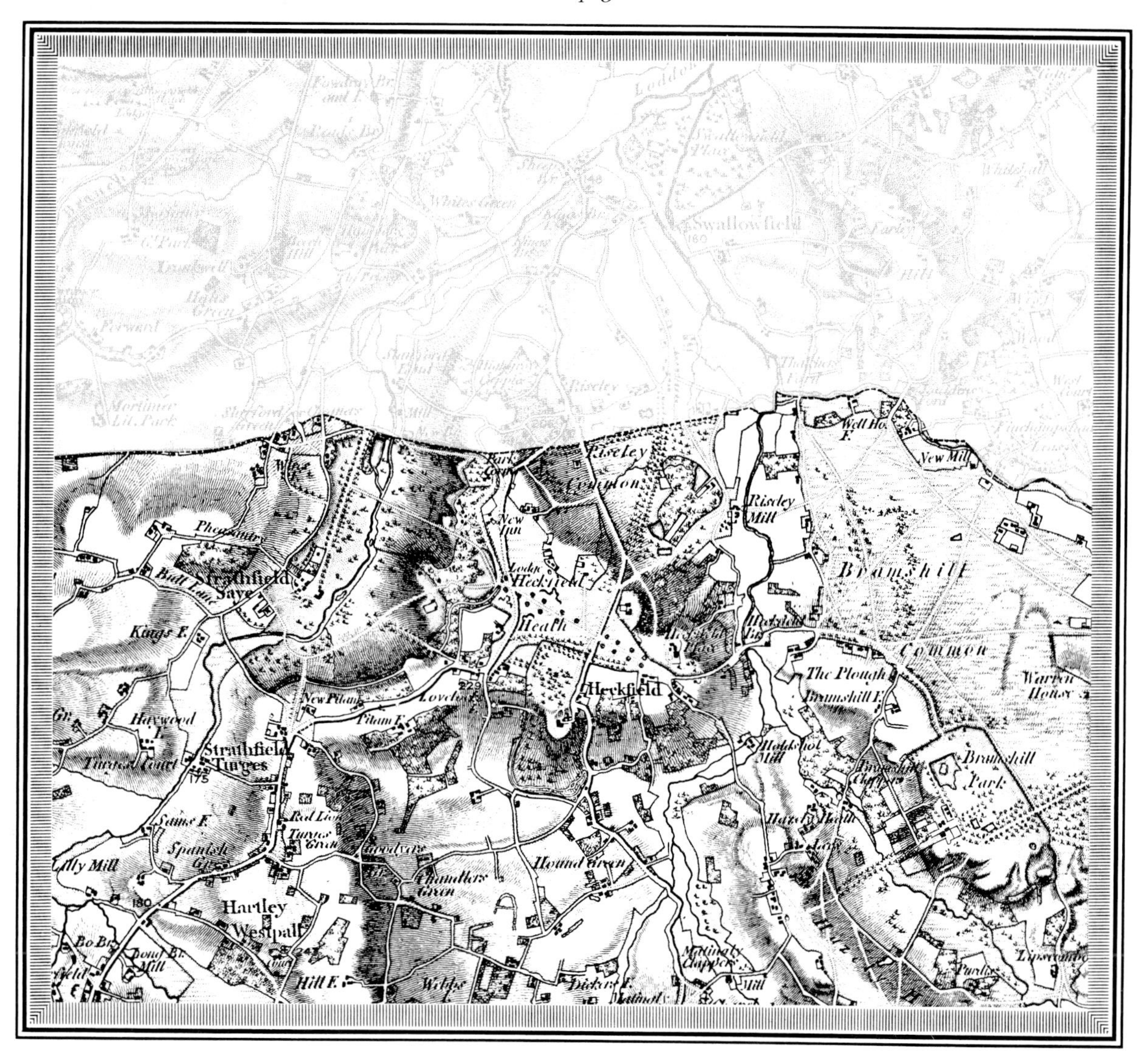

Map 5 Three great houses dominate this part of Hampshire: Stratfield Saye, acquired by the nation for the Duke of Wellington in 1817; Heckfield; and Bramshill, now a police college. Avenues of trees are an important feature of their parks – which often had their origins much earlier, as medieval deer-parks. These great houses took advantage of the slightly better-drained land provided by the rivers Loddon and Whitewater. Bramshill Common, however, is a vast heathland which shows just how poor the soils, here clays and plateau gravels, are in the north-east of the county. Most of it is now enclosed and used for conifer plantation.

No Entry
For Vehicles Over 30 cwt.
Height Restriction 7ft 6ins
Commercial Vehicle Entrance
Via Heckfield
AHEAD
Barrier - 25 Yards
Ramp - 50 Yards
10
POLICE STAFF COLLEGE
NO ENTRY
UNLESS AUTHORISED

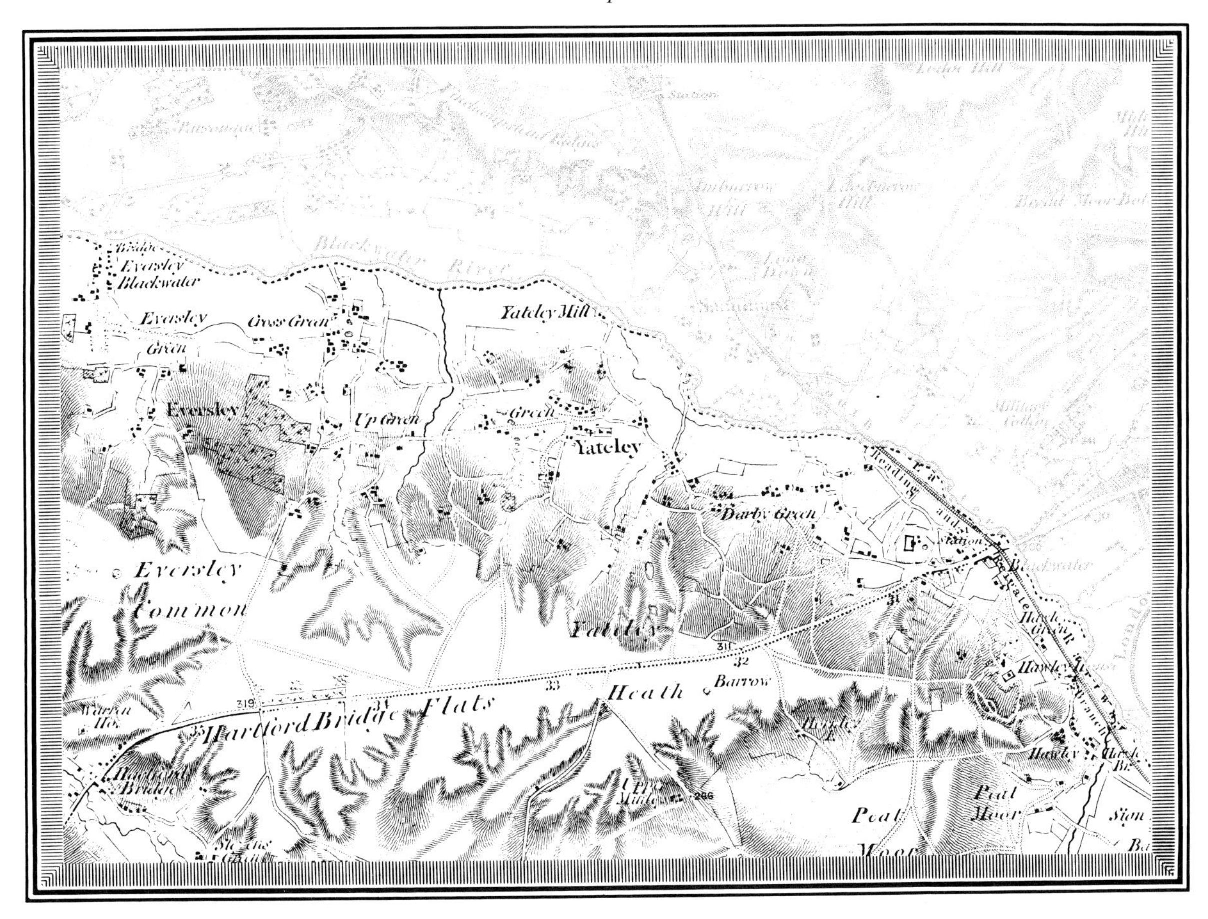

The grand entrance lodge to Bramshill Park from the Hartley Wintney road before the First World War (opposite above), when a great country house could be run on cheap labour. The avenue of trees provided an impressive vista through the extensive park that surrounded the early seventeenth-century house. The gatehouse is of brick with stone dressings and matches the house architecturally. The lodge is virtually unchanged but the enclave that it separates from the outside world now has a very different function, as a police training college (opposite below). The house's new, public role is emphasized by the royal coat of arms and police badges that have replaced the escutcheons for the private owners' arms over the three entrance arches.

Map 6 The Blackwater River is the country boundary here, and names like Peat Moor and Yateley Heath show how barren is much of the soil. Blackbushe Aerodrome has submerged part of the latter, and the area now is a confusing mixture of vast housing estates, gravel pits and conifer woods, yet with some vestiges of the earlier pattern of greens surviving. The 'Barrow' is a witness to Bronze Age activity in the area.

Detail map 6 (overleaf) Until a few years ago, Yateley must have seemed a classic English village, centred upon a church facing onto a small triangular green. Nearby are the manor

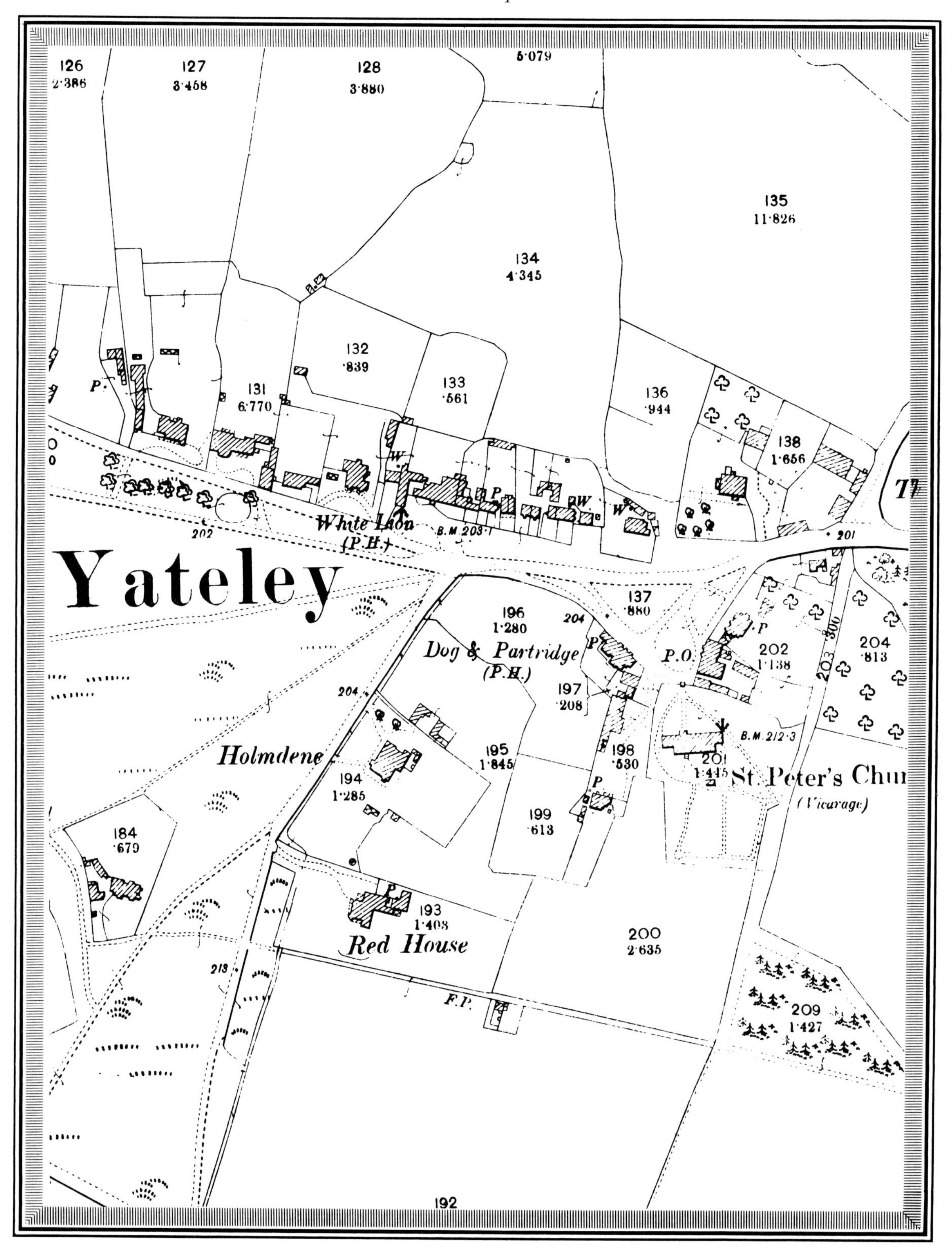

126
2·386
127
3·458
128
3·880
5·079
135
11·826
134
4·345
132
·839
131
6·770
133
·561
136
·944
138
1·656
White Lion
(P.H.)
B.M. 203·1
202
201
Yateley
137
·880
196
1·280
204
Dog & Partridge
(P.H.)
P.O
202
1·138
204
·813
197
·208
Holmdene
195
1·845
198
·530
B.M. 212·3
201
1·445
St. Peter's Chu
(Vicarage)
194
1·285
199
·613
184
·679
193
1·403
Red House
200
2·635
213
F.P.
209
1·427
192

Detail map 6 cont.

house, the biggest house in the area, the Dog and Partridge Inn, and a line of houses straggling along the main road. Not all is quite as antique as it seems, however; even the church did not become an independent 'Vicarage' until as late as the sixteenth century, until then being a chaplaincy of Crondall, part of a big estate owned for a long time by the Bishops of Winchester, who would have been responsible for the building of the Anglo Saxon church. The manor house (at the extreme east of this map section) was merely called Hall Place until modern times, and may not have had manorial pretensions. Nor can it be assumed that the village green is an 'original' feature of the village, for greens can result from changes made to a settlement long after its foundation.

In the eighteenth century, the village stocks and whipping-post stood on the green. The Dog and Partridge seems to have been the Church House, partly owned by the Church Wardens, and used for social functions. Ale may have been brewed there for church festivals and to keep the bell-ringers at their work. Only in the nineteenth century did the inn become officially divorced from the life of the church.

Yateley church before the First World War, from the south. The wall of the nave to the left of the porch is Anglo-Saxon; the fifteenth-century timber-framed west tower is typical of many in Hampshire. There has been a lych gate since at least 1625. Yateley was still small enough for its population to use a church virtually unchanged in size since the sixteenth century (see page 50).

Visitors to Yateley today will find church, green, inn and big house, and they will recognise one or two of the smaller houses too. But they will not find a village. 'The Croft' has been swallowed up by a housing estate, and everywhere there are new buildings. There is still a field behind the church, however, and the little bit of open heathland on the left of the map still comes up to the road. Despite huge social changes, something of the older skeleton remains.

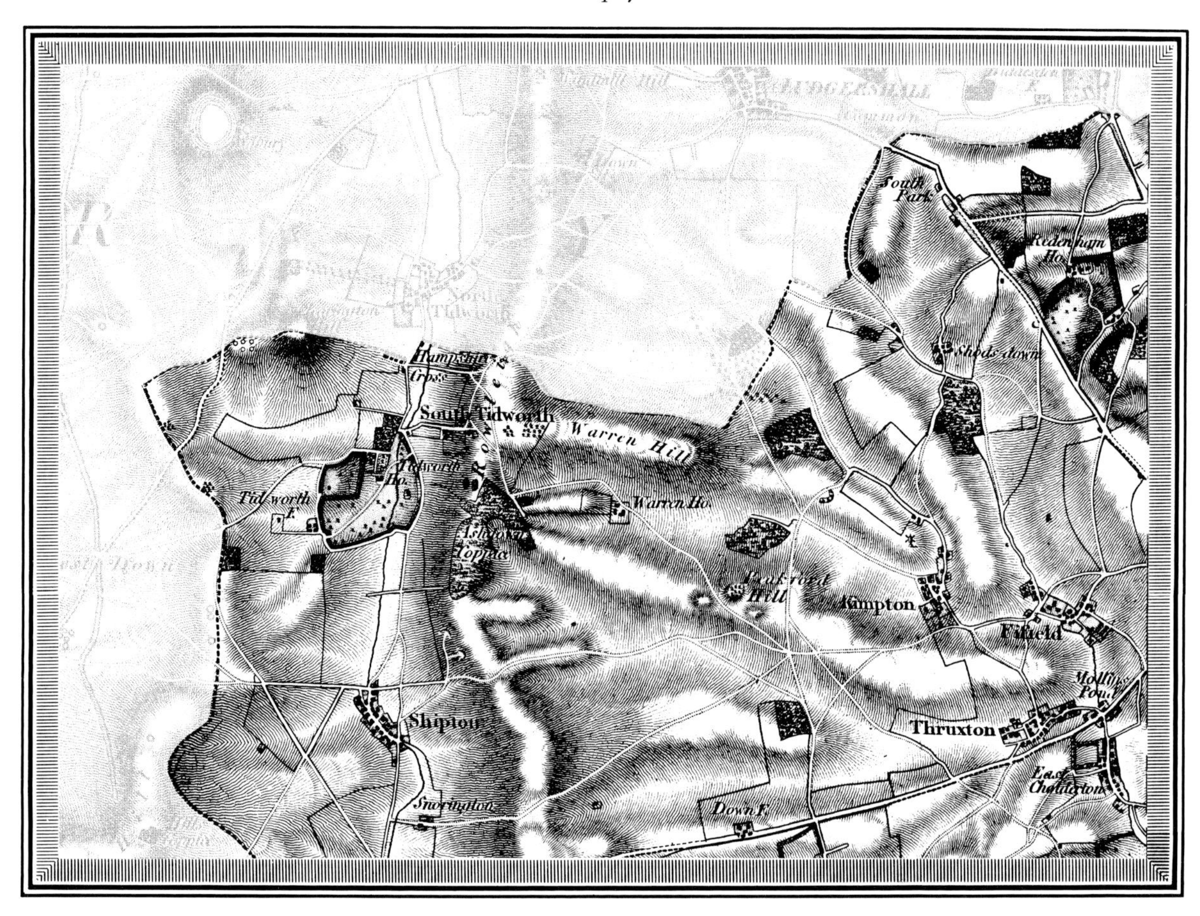

Map 7 (above) This part of western Hampshire is really the edge of Salisbury Plain: South Tidworth is now a garrison town, with Tidworth House an Officer's Mess, preserving the surrounding parkland. 'Rowleigh' is the name of a chalk ridge. One of the county's major roads, the A303 through Tidworth, was well established, having been created by a Turnpike Trust in 1754. The windmill symbol north of Tidworth shows that this was cereal country; when the Napoleonic Wars increased the demand for home-produced grain, large swathes of the chalk downland were ploughed up for arable, fertility being dependent on the manure of grazing sheep.

Map 8 (opposite) Andover was a typical country town in the early nineteenth century; the importance of its market-place is clearly shown. It has always been a favoured crossing-place of the River Ann, and its inns had a high reputation. Weyhill was the site of an ancient fair, which by the seventeenth century attracted buyers and sellers of sheep from a wide area, the animals being brought along drove-roads from as far away as the Welsh mountains. The railways arrived in dribs and drabs: the London line in 1854 (continued to Salisbury in 1857), the Southampton line in 1865, and the Swindon line in 1882; only the first survives. The town has of course now hugely expanded, to engulf Charlton, Foxcotte and East Anton. Yet travel a little to the north, and there have been surprisingly few

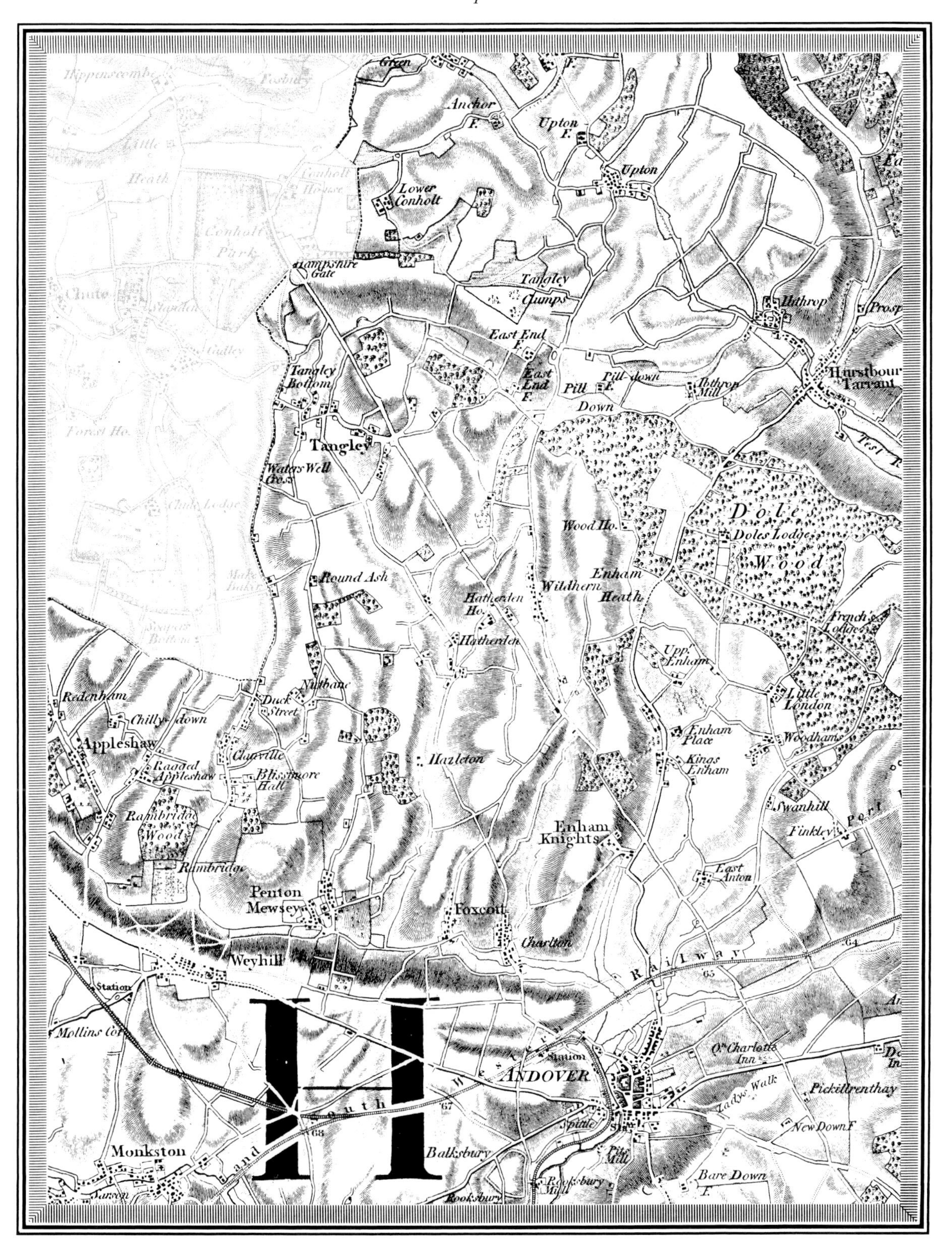
Anchor F.
Upton F.
Upton
Lower Conholt
Hampshire Gate
Tangley Clumps
Hathrop
East End F.
East End F.
Pill Down
Pill-down F.
Ibthrop Mill
Hurstbourne Tarrant
Tangley Bottom
Tangley
Waters Well Cro.s
Doles Wood
Doles Lodge
Wood Ho.
Round Ash
Wildhern
Enham Heath
Hatherden Ho.
Hatherden
French's Lodge
Upp.r Enham
Nutbane
Redenham
Duck Street
Chilly down
Little London
Appleshaw
Enham Place
Woodhams
Clanville
Ragged Appleshaw
Blissmore Hall
Hazleton
Kings Enham
Swanhill
Rambridge Wood
Finkley
Enham Knights
Rambridge
East Anton
Penton Mewsey
Foxcott
Charlton
Weyhill
Railway
Station
Mollins Cor.
Station
ANDOVER
Q.n Charlotte Inn
Ladys Walk
Pickillrenthay
New Down F.
Spittle
Monkston
Balksbury
Pits Mill
Rooksbury Mill
Bare Down F.
Rooksbury
H

Andover in 1880 was a market town with prominent railway facilities, ironworks (marked by the tall chimney in the background), farms and water meadows along the River Anton. The dominating building is the 1836 workhouse, with the cottage hospital of 1877 in front of it. Cricklade House in the middle distance on the right is now the site of the Technical College (see page 67). The houses in the foreground on the left with the long, narrow gardens fronted on to Chantry Street.

Map 8 cont.

changes, though much of Dole Wood (mainly planted over a large patch of clay overlying the chalk) and others have been enclosed for farming. Near East Anton, two almost straight roads cross: the road to the north-west is the line of the Winchester to Mildenhall and Cirencester Roman road; the 'Port Way' is the Silchester to Sarum (Salisbury) road, and is probably pre-Roman in origin. A Roman market underlies East Anton, taking advantage of the road junction.

Map 9 This is a classic area of chalk downland, cut through by the rivers Bourne and Test. Hampshire's clear chalk streams were ideal for paper-making; mills that can be seen on the Test here were established in the early eighteenth century. One of their products was banknotes. Several prehistoric earthworks are shown: Devil's Ditch is probably late Bronze or Iron Age, perhaps intended to act as a frontier between those living in the Andover area, and the dwellers in the Bourne valley and beyond. To the north, Beacon Hill and Ladle Hill are both sited on the steep scarp of the chalk to oversee the valley below—Ladle Hill was never completed. The 'Seven Barrows' (there are really more than seven) are Bronze Age, and have narrowly been preserved from road-widening for the A34, which was created by a Turnpike Trust in 1762. Its line was unfenced across those parts of the downs that were still unenclosed in the early nineteenth century. Whitchurch could have become an important railway junction, but the Winchester–Didcot line was never a great success, and has closed.

Map 9

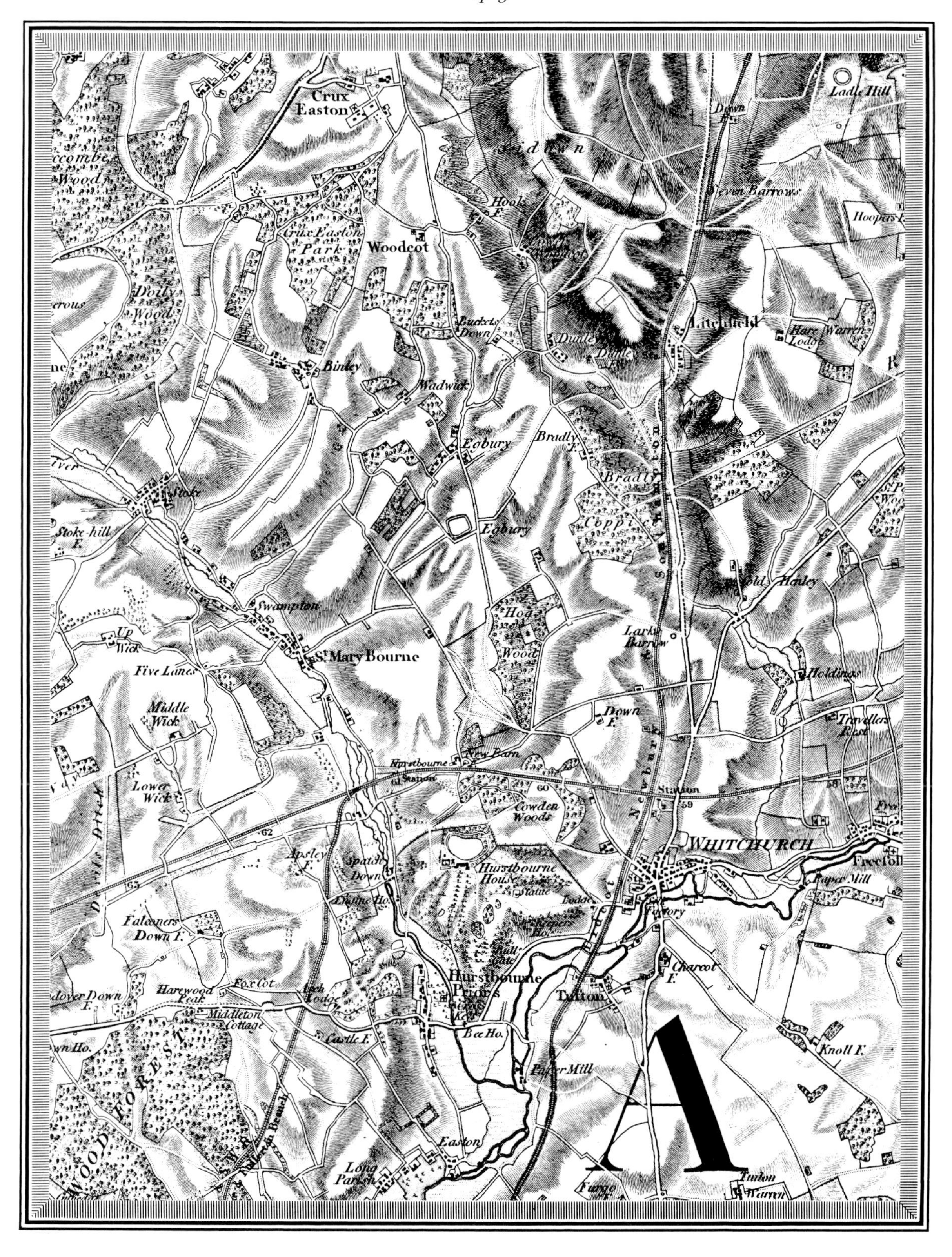
Crux Easton
Ladle Hill
Down
Seven Barrows
Hook F.
Crux Easton Park
Woodcot
Doily Wood
Buckets Down
Litchfield
Hare Warren Lodge
Binley
Wadwick
Egbury
Bradly F.
Bradly
Stoke
Stoke hill F.
Egbury
Coppice
Old Henley
Swampton
Up Wick
S.t Mary Bourne
Hod Wood
Larks Barrow
Holdings
Five Lanes
Middle Wick
Down F.
Travellers Rest
Hurstbourne
New Barn
Station
Lower Wick
Cowden Woods
Station
WHITCHURCH
Apsley F.
Spatch Down
Hurstbourne House
Paper Mill
Falconers Down F.
Factory
Charcot F.
Hurstbourne Priors
Harewood Peak
Fox Cot
Middleton Cottage
Castle F.
Bee Ho.
Tufton
Knoll F.
Paper Mill
WOOD FOREST
Easton
Long Parish
A
Tinton Warren

Map 10

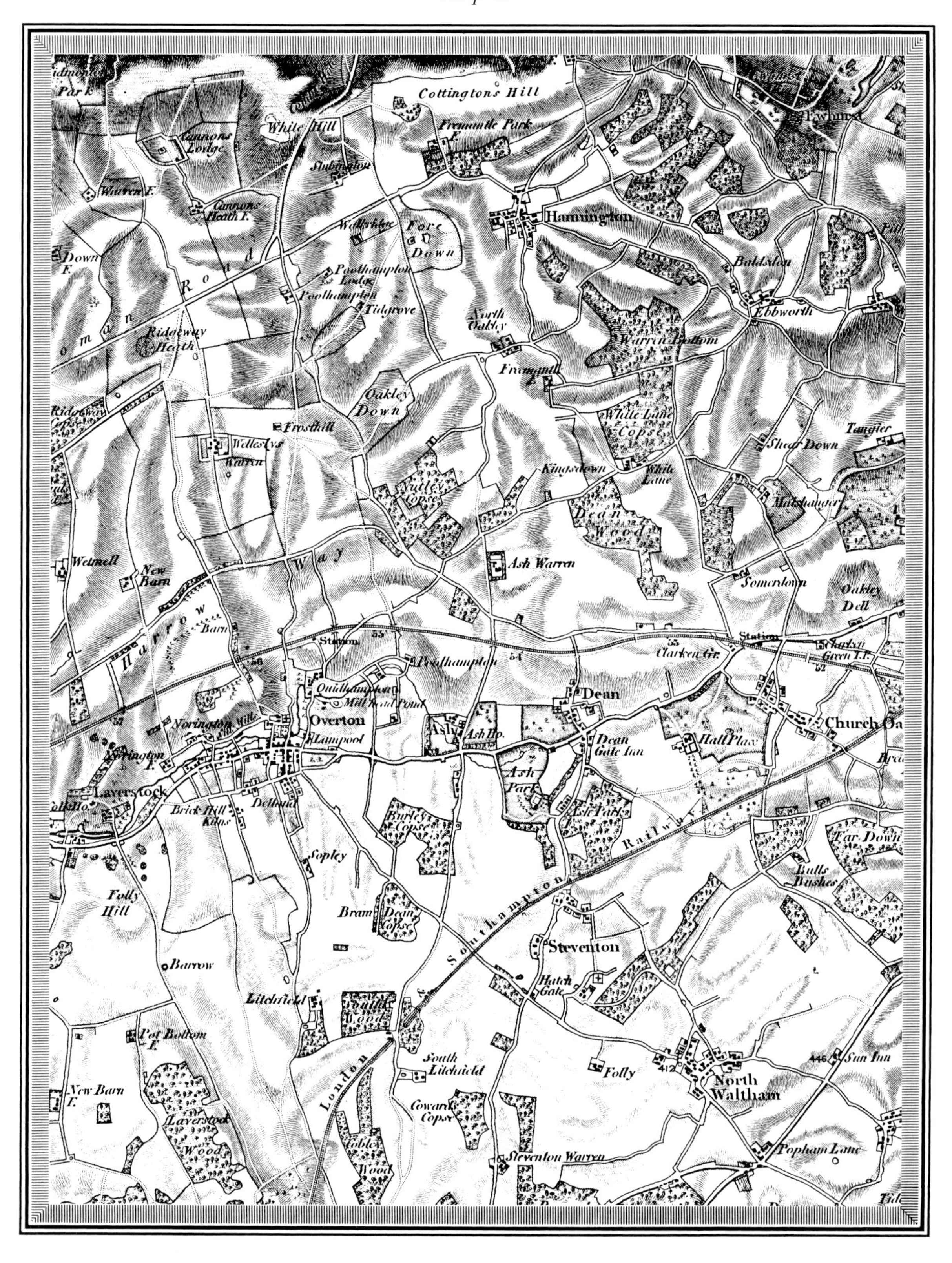
Cottingtons Hill
White Hill
Cannons Lodge
Fremantle Park F.
Stubbington
Warren F.
Cannons Heath F.
Hannington
Fore Down
Down F.
Poolhampton Lodge
Poolhampton
Tidgrove
Baldslen
Ebbworth
Roman Road
Ridgeway Heath
North Oakley
Warren Bottom
Fremantl
Ridgeway Copse
Oakley Down
Frosthill
Wellesly's Warren
White Lane Copse
Tangier
Shear Down
Kingsdown
White Lane
Yutley Copse
Dean Wood
Malshanger
Wetmell
New Barn
Ash Warren
Way
Somerlown
Oakley Dell
Harrow
Barn
Station
55
53
Clarken Gr.
Station
54
Poolhampton
56
52
Quidhampton
Mill Road Pond
Dean
57
Norington
Overton
Lampool
Ash
Ash Ho.
Dean Gate Inn
Hall Place
Church Oa
Norington F.
Ash Park
Laverstock
Brick Hill Kilns
Dellond
Burley Copse
Ash Park
Railway
Far Down
Sopley
Bulls Bushes
Folly Hill
Bram
Dean Copse
Southampton
Steventon
Barrow
Hatch Gate
Litchfield
South Wood
Pot Bottom F.
South Litchfield
Folly
412
446
Sun Inn
North Waltham
New Barn F.
London
Cowards Copse
Laverstock Wood
Table Wood
Steventon Warren
Popham Lane

Map 10 The silk mill marked at Overton testifies to the best-known feature in this part of Hampshire; the industry was established in the area in the eighteenth century, using raw silk imported from India. Most of the women in Overton were employed in the industry in the 1840s, and over a hundred people worked in it in Whitchurch, where the 'Victoria Mill' is still in production—there was a bigger centre at Winchester, which did not outlast the nineteenth century. On the downs were a few nucleated and widely spaced villages such as Hannington, and isolated farms, some founded since the Middle Ages as a result of enclosures. This is shown by farm names such as 'Tangier' (after part of Charles II's wife's dowry), and others named after military and naval actions. They are a contrast to the older English names such as Ebbworth and Hannington. The brick kilns south of Overton seem to have had only a brief history; both the north-east and the south of the county had better clays, closer to the main sources of demand, the rapidly growing towns. Central Hampshire was not an expanding area.

Map 11 (overleaf) Basingstoke was a market town, with no function other than to supply its local region and to attract buyers of the region's cattle, sheep, corn and cheese. To facilitate the transport of this local produce to London, and also to carry chalk for marling farmland in the Wey valley, the canal running east to connect to the River Wey was opened in 1794. Basingstoke is close to the edge of the chalk, with typical downland to the south, and clays and gravels to the north. Both these districts have great houses, but it is interesting that The Vine had very little parkland attached to it because of the difference in the soils, the clays needing a great deal of drainage if they are to grow fine trees and swards of grass. Winklebury is an Iron Age hill-fort, sited close to the chalk scarp and controlling access westwards up the stream valley into the central chalklands. Old Basing was the Saxon predecessor of Basingstoke, and the circle to its south marks Basing House, a medieval castle converted into a Renaissance mansion, whose owner paid the price for defending it for the Royalists in the Civil War. Much of the downland south and west of Basingstoke had only been enclosed for twenty-five years when the Ordnance Survey map was drawn up, the roads having been turnpiked a generation earlier.

Modern map 11 (page 49) The effect of the decision to make Basingstoke a London overspill town can be seen dramatically: from a 1931 population of less than 14,000 and 17,000 in 1951, numbers rose to 52,500 in 1971 and *c*68,000 in 1981. Roads predominate for communication, as is shown by the M3 motorway and the bypass ring with its labyrinth of roundabouts. The inadequacy of the early nineteenth-century map is shown by the number of monuments which it did not notice, such as the medieval motte and bailey north of Basing House. South of the M3, the degree of change is very much less. Villages like Cliddesden and Farleigh Wallop are hardly any bigger; Hackwood and Herriard have lost bits of their parks, but the woods are remarkably unscathed, and the settlement and road pattern is fundamentally the same. The worst casualty is the canal, come and all but gone in 150 years.

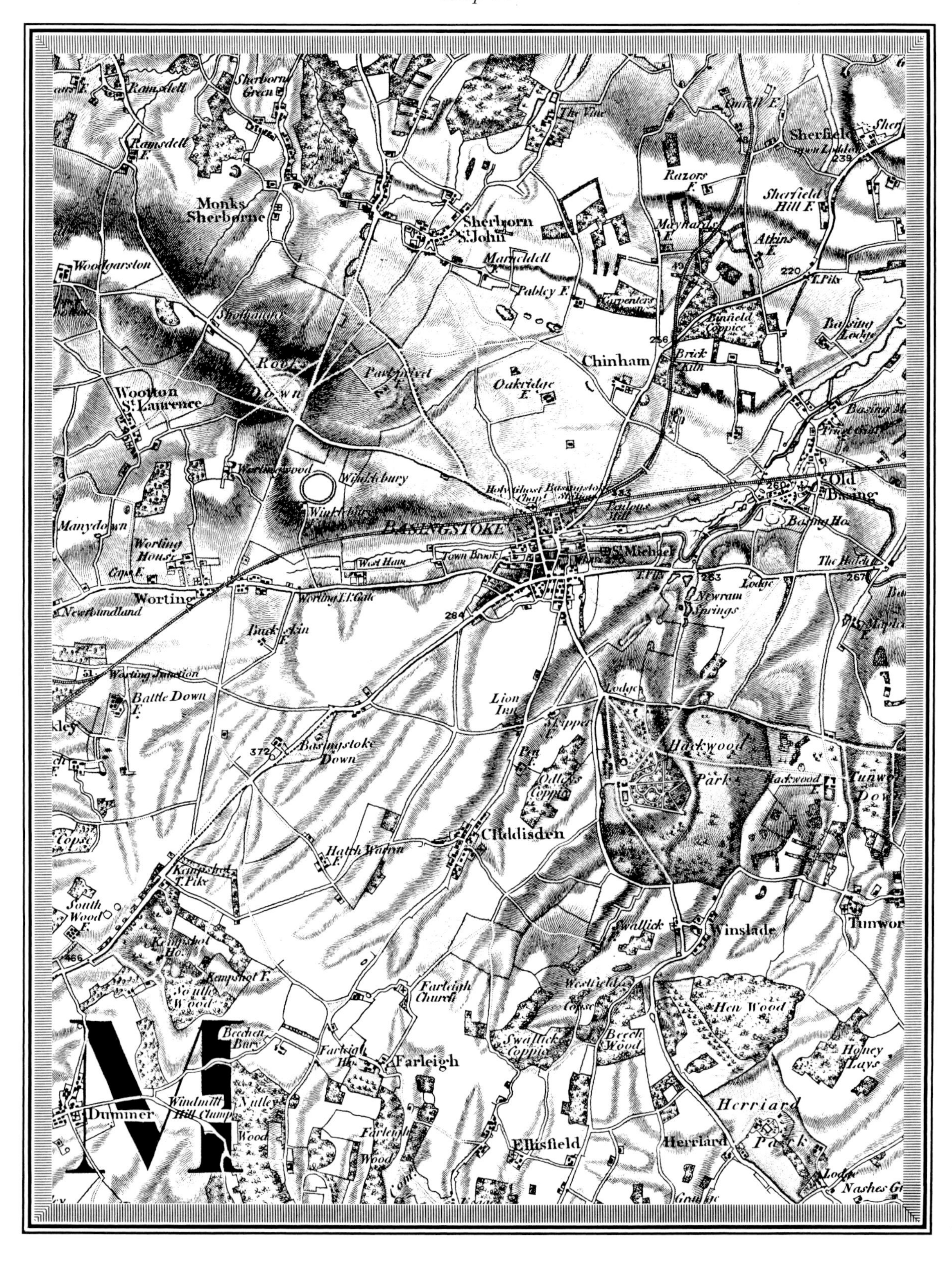
Ramsdell
Sherborne Green
The Vine
Sherfield
Ramsdell F.
Razors F.
Sherfield Hill F.
Monks Sherborne
Sherborn St. John
Maynards
Atkins F.
Woodgarston
Pabley F.
Carpenters Down
Binfield Coppice
Basing Lodge
Chinham
Brick Kiln
Rooks Down
Oakridge F.
Wootton St. Laurence
Winklebury
Old Basing
BASINGSTOKE
St. Michael
Basing Ho.
Manydown
Worting House
Town Brook
West Ham
The Hatch
Worting
Newfoundland
Worting T.P. Gate
Lodge
Newram Springs
Worting Junction
Battle Down F.
Lion Inn
Hackwood
Basingstoke Down
Park
Hackwood F.
Cliddisden
Hatch Warren F.
Kempshot T. Pike
South Wood F.
Swallick
Winslade
Tunworth
Kempshot Ho.
Kempshot F.
South Wood
Farleigh Church
Westfield Copse
Hen Wood
Beechen Bury
Swallick Coppice
Beech Wood
Honey Lays
Farleigh Ho.
Farleigh
Windmill Hill Clump
Dummer
Nutley Wood
Farleigh Wood
Herriard
Ellisfield
Herriard Park
Lodge
Nashes Gr
260
283
267
284
372
220
239
256
466

Moat
Wyeford Fm
Bramley
Pamber End
Pamber Fm
ROMAN ROAD (course of)
Floods Fm
Sluice
West Heath
Stony Heath
Bow Brook
Fort
Beaurepaire Ho
Priory Fm
The Firs
Hill End Fm
Sherfield on Loddon
Charter Alley
Salters Heath
Beaurepaire Fm
Vyne Lodge Fm
Cufaude
Ramsdell
Rawlins Fm
Cranes Copse
Lancs
North Foreland Lodge
Skyer's Fm
Morgastor Wood
The Vyne
Sherfield Court
Skyer's Wood
Privett Copse
Vyne Park
Church End
Kiln Green
Monk Sherborne
Lower Fm
Sch
Razor's Fm
Sherfield Hall
Wildmoor
Sherborne St John
Ellis Fm
Manor Fm
Spier's Copse
Carpenter's Down Wood
Crockford's Fm
Moulshay Fm
Field Barn Fm
Motte
Woodgarston Fm
Chy
Sewage Works
Upper Wootton
Marnel Dell
Popley Fields Ho
Four Lanes End
Blackland's Fm
Resr
Elm Bottom Cross
Popley
Chineham
Park Pale
Lodge Fm
R Loddon
Whitedown
CH
Hospls
Hotel
Sch
Pyott's Hill
Poors Fm
Wootton St Lawrence
A 339(T)
Oakridge
Gold's Fm
Schs
Daneshill
Oliver's Battery
Motte & Bailey
Tangier
Hodd's Fm
Worting Wood Fm
Fort
Sch
Houndmills
South View
Old Basing
Cemy
Basing Ho
Priory Fm
BASINGSTOKE
Winklebury
Worting
Worting Ho
West Ham
B 3400
Mus
Eastrop
Sch
A 30
Hatch
Newfound
Coll
Cemy
Buckskin
South Ham
King's Furlong
Black Dam
New Park
Huish Ho
Mapledurwell
White Barrow
Sch
Sch
Coll
Moorhams Fm
Dicken's Lane Plantation
Sch
Battle Down Fm
Cranbourne
Home Fm
Well's Copse
Long Barrow
Down Grange
Sch
Tumuli
Polecat Corner
Breach Fm
Kempshott
Brighton Hill
Audleys Wood
Hackwood
East Oakley
Hackwood Ho
Roundtown
Tunworth Ho
Down Fm
Hackwood Park
Cliddesden
Hatch Warren Fm
Manor Fm
Bushes
M3
B 3046
A 339
dismtd rly
Tunworth
Winslade
South Wood
Farleigh Hill
White Hill
Swallick Fm
The Dower Ho
Hen Wood
Broadmere
Kennel Fm
Farleigh Wallop
Weston Corbett
Allwood Copse
Manor Fm
Northgate Fm
Inn (PH)
Farleigh House Sch
Herriard Park
Inwood Copse
Bedlam Bottom
Herriard Ho
Park Fm
Clump Fm
Cemy
Dummer
Dummer Clump
Great Wood
Ellisfield
Manor Fm
Ellisfield Manor
Merritts Fm
Herriard Grange
Herriard
Wayfarer's Walk
Nutley Wood
Gobley Hole
Norton's Wood
Earthwork
Wr Twr
Upper Common
Nashes Green
Lee Fm
Little Wood
Dummer Down Fm
Tidley Hill
Dummer Grange
Lower Common
College Fm
High Wood
Bagmore
Southrope
Hale Fm
High Wood
Dummer Grange Fm
Nutley
Windmill Hill
Nutley Down
Great Matt's Copse
Herriard Common
Holt
Flockmoor Cott
Berrydown Fm
Preston Oak Hills

(Top) At first glance Yateley church seems unaltered in the colour picture above, but in fact a fire gutted it in 1979, and it has been completely rebuilt and extended. This wider view of its surroundings shows how modern building has changed Yateley into suburbia; in so far as it has a core, the Health Centre provides it more appositely than the church. The churchyard and its yew tree, flag-pole, lych gate and rustic fence are almost as they were eighty years ago (see page 41).

The lower picture was taken in about 1904 and shows the Basingstoke–River Wey canal west of Basing House. For many years it was more picturesque than profitable.

In contrast with the modest but rather drab prosperity of the nineteenth-century town (page 7), Basingstoke today (top) is brash, thriving and full of new buildings. Few of these have architectural merit, and scenes like this can be found in most towns—with the same banks, building societies and chain stores.

(Above) Most of the canal around Basingstoke has now been filled in, and nothing is left of the scene of 1904 (opposite below). Further east, determined attempts are being made to restore it for leisure purposes.

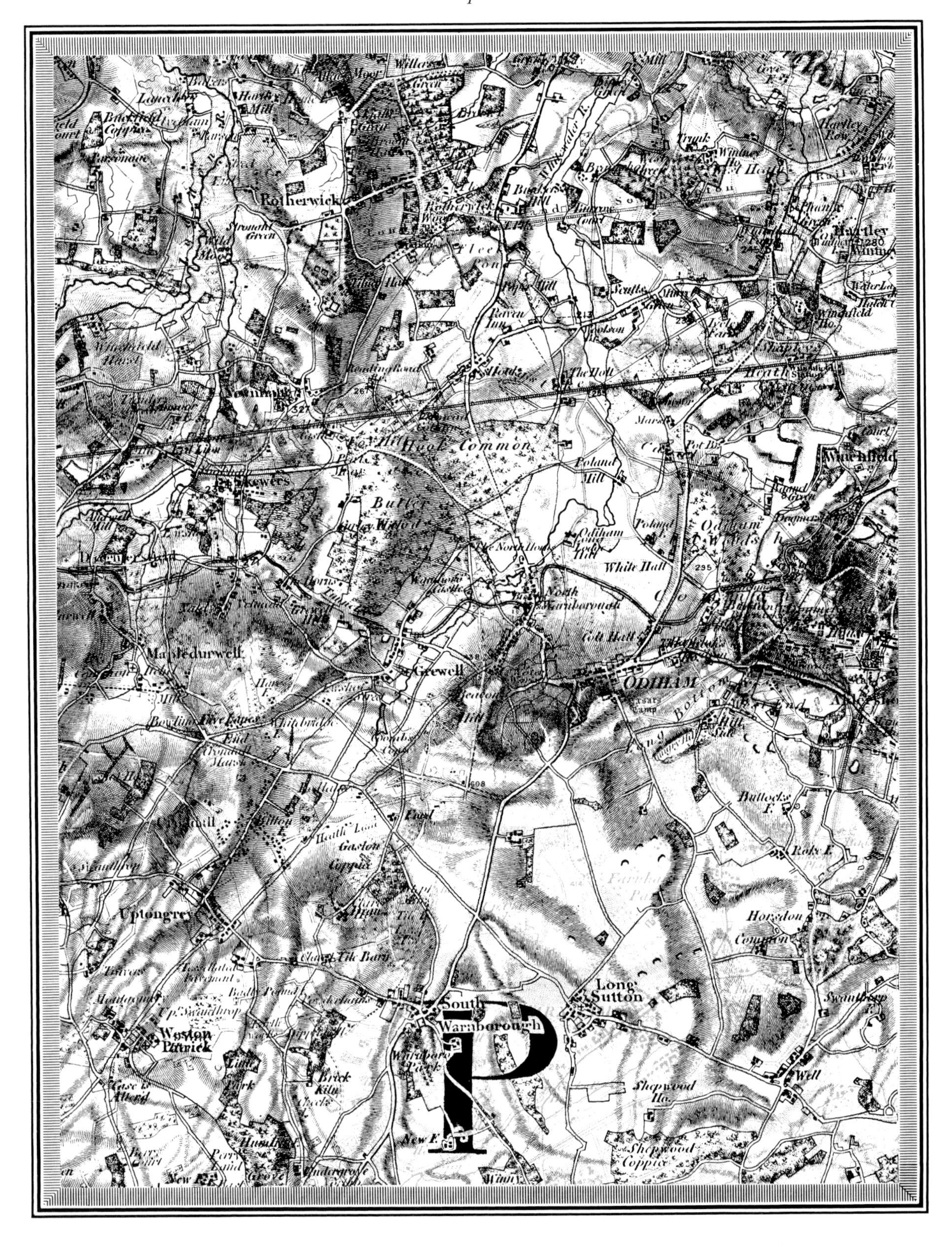
Rotherwick
Hartley
Winchfield
Hook Common
Poland Hill
Odiham
White Hall
North Warnborough
Mapledurwell
Grewell
ODIHAM
Hill Side
Bullocks F.
Horsdon Common
Uplongrey
Gaston Coppice
Long Sutton
South Warnborough
Weston Patrick
Brick Kiln
Shepwood Ho.
Shepwood Coppice
Swanthorp
Well
P

Odiham High Street in about 1914 (see also page 68) was a thriving shopping street dominated by the hotel which shows the town's former importance on a coaching road. Public street lighting had arrived—it was not yet provided in Basingstoke in 1866 (page 7).

Map 12 Odiham is no longer the most important place in this part of the map: the railway line has seen to that, creating commuter settlements in what were previously obscure hamlets like Hook. Hook Common and Shapley Heath show how the soils change just north of Odiham, the northern clays having barren expanses, the southern chalkland nucleated villages and wide tracts of downland. Proximity to London partly accounts for the increasing number of big houses, such as Dogmersfield, an eighteenth-century mansion that is now a college. The Basingstoke–Wey canal runs across the centre of the map; much of this section survives, although it was closed in 1906. The tunnel under Greywell Hill was a major expense for its backers, and it had to take a very circuitous route round Dogmersfield, in an effort to keep as close as possible to a horizontal line. The ponds shown in that area still exist.

In about 1904, Station Road in Winchfield (above) was half-way between country lane and a road in a dormitory town, with the woodland carefully fenced off, and a line of newly erected telegraph poles. Few cars were yet to be seen; the pony and trap was a common sight.

Amazingly, Station Road, Winchfield, today is still as rural as at the turn of the century—but not for long. Buildings are now going up behind the trees on the left, and the contractor's lorry is a harbinger of what is to come. The north-east of Hampshire is under great pressure from developers, for houses are extremely expensive in the area.

Map 13 As well as adding railway lines to their map in 1885, the Ordnance Survey also added the military camps which the railways had helped to make possible by the speed with which men and supplies could be brought from London. Aldershot Common had been all but empty heathland, ideal for training large battalions of infantry and cavalry, and for artillery ranges. The barracks were a product of the Crimean War: Aldershot's population grew from 875 in 1851 to 16,720 in 1861! An older military interest is suggested by the name of Caesar's Camp, although this is in fact an Iron Age hill-fort with nothing whatever to do with the Roman general. In the Middle Ages, its defences were partly reused to create a section of the boundary of one of the Bishop of Winchester's deer-parks. Fleet has swallowed up most of the centre of the map, although Fleet Pond remains. The area east of Aldershot, including Farnborough is inset on the map on page 85.

Map 13

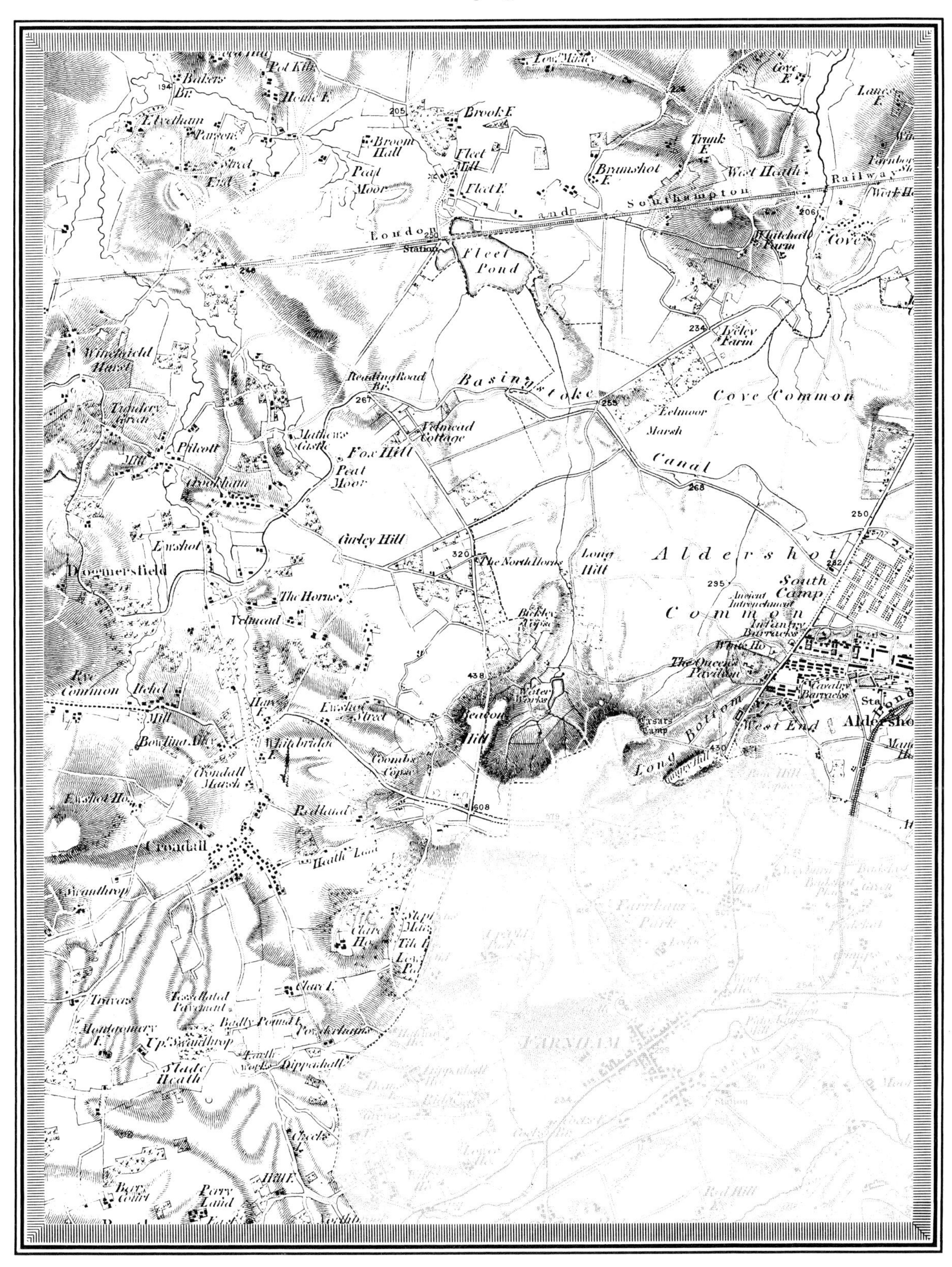

Pot Kiln
Bakers Br.
Home F.
Brook F.
Broom Hall
Fleet Mill
Peat Moor
Fleet F.
Brunshot F.
Trunk F.
West Heath
Cove F.
Lanes F.
Railway
Southampton
and
London
Station
Fleet Pond
Whitehall Farm
Cove
Ively Farm
Winchfield Hurst
Reading Road Br.
Basingstoke
Cove Common
Eelmoor Marsh
Velmead Cottage
Mathews Castle
Fox Hill
Peat Moor
Canal
Philcott
Mill
Crookham
Ewshot
Dogmersfield
Curley Hill
The North Horns
Long Hill
Aldershot
South Camp
Ancient Intrenchment
Common
Infantry Barracks
The Horns
Velmead
Bickley Copse
White Ho.
The Queens Pavilion
Cavalry Barracks
Rye Common
Itchel Mill
Ewshot Street
Water Works
Beacon Hill
Caesars Camp
West End
Long Bottom
Aldershot
Bowling Alley
Whitebridge F.
Coombs Copse
Crondall Marsh
Ewshot Ho.
Redland
Crondall
Heath Lane
Swanthrop
Clare F.
Travas
Tessellated Pavement
Badly Pound F.
Powderham
Montgomery F.
Up. Swanthrop
Earth Work
Dippenhall
Slade Heath
Check
Hill F.
Barn Court
Perry Land
Farnham

Map 14

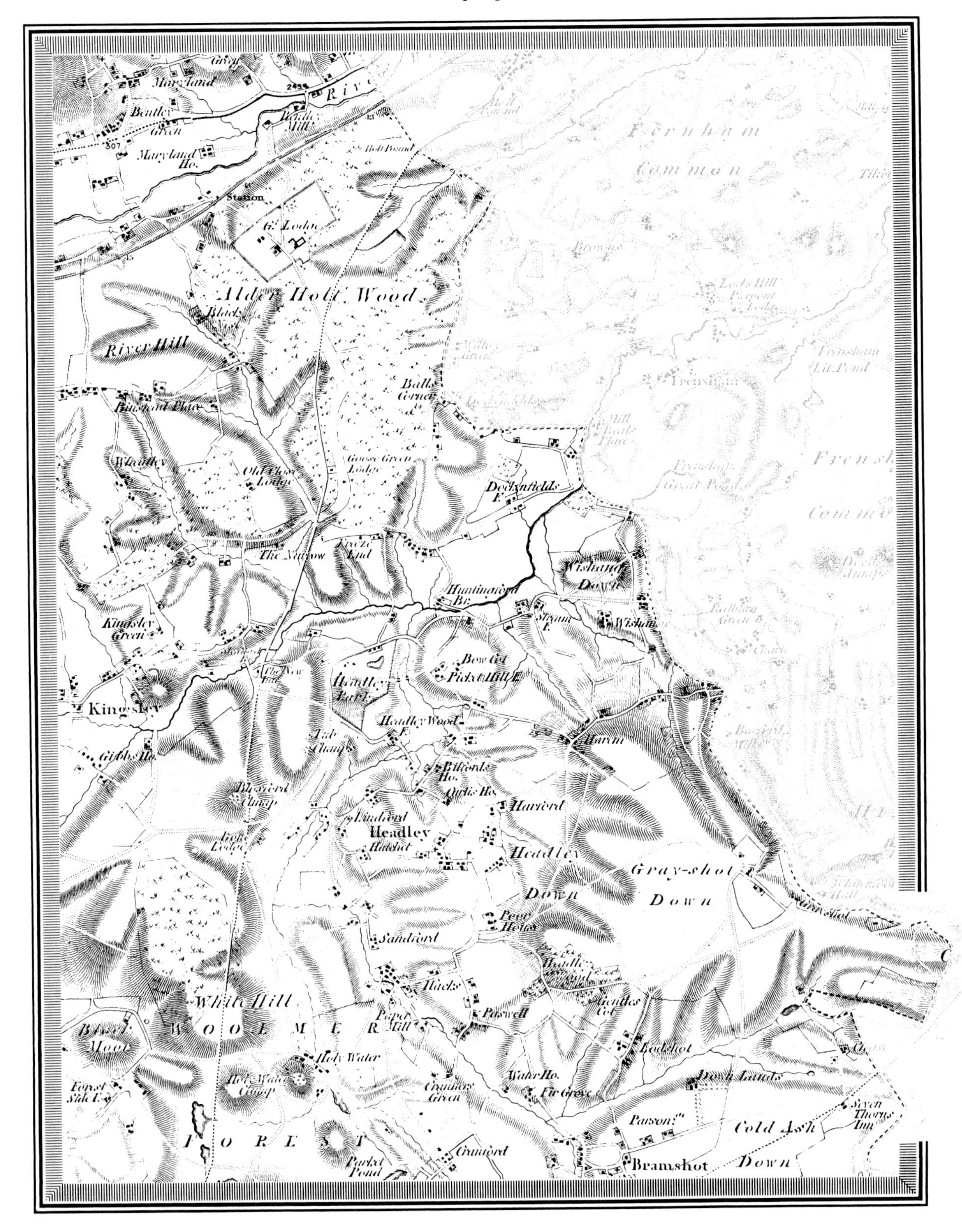

Maryland
Bentley Green
Maryland Ho.
Station
Alder Holt Wood
River Hill
Binstead Place
Old Close Lodge
Goose Green Lodge
Balls Corner
Dockenfields F.
The Narrow
Huntingford Br.
Wishanger
Kingsley Green
Kingsley
Headley Park
Bow Cot
Headley Wood F.
Gibbs Ho.
Harrow
Headley
Headley Down
Gray-shot
Down
Sandford
White Hill
W O O L M E R
F O R E S T
Black Moor
Holy Water
Holy Water Clump
Paper Mill
Passwell
Ludshot
Water Ho.
Fir Grove
Down Lands
Cold Ash
Seven Thorns Inn
Bramshot
Down
Cranford
Common

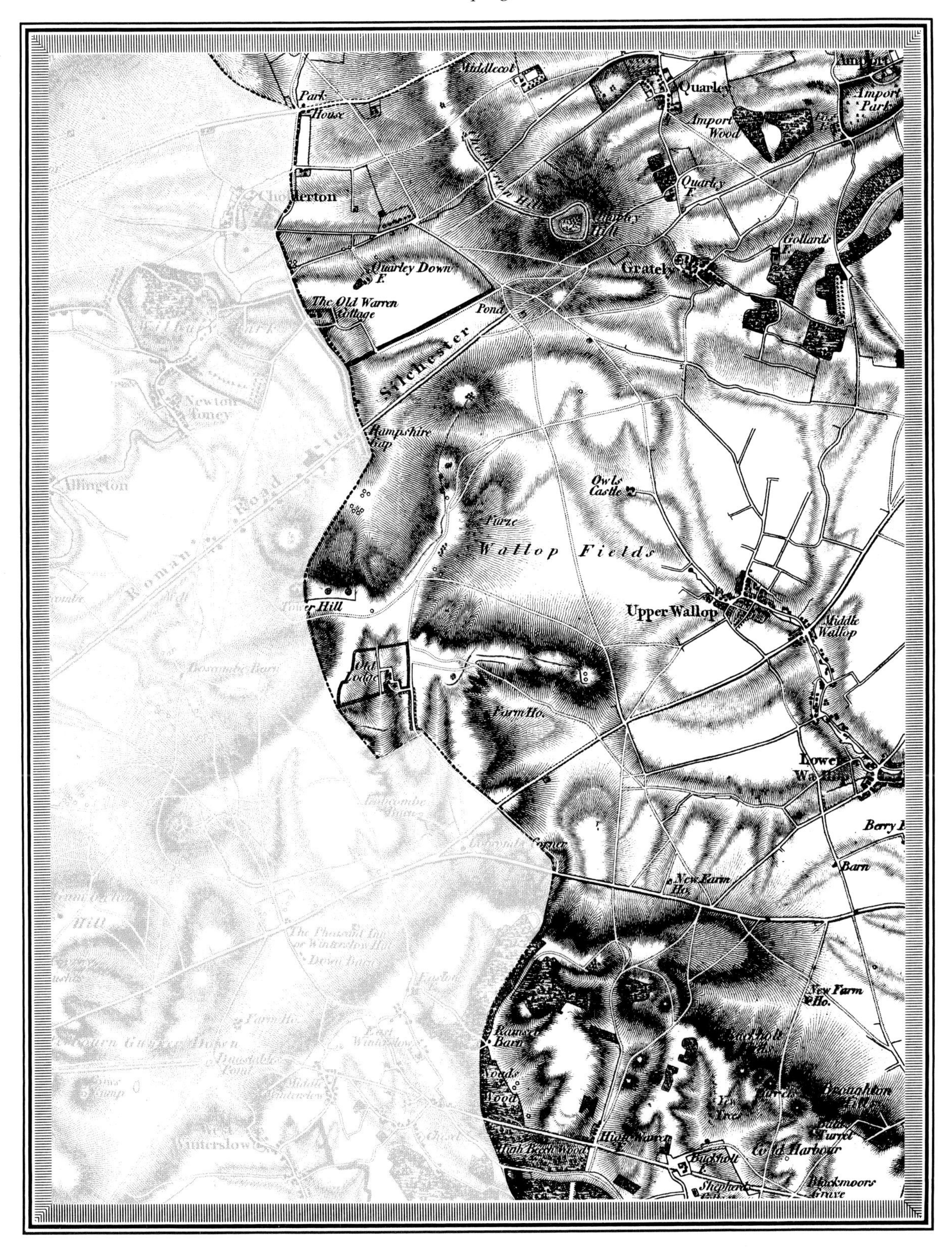
Middlecot
Park House
Quarley
Amport Wood
Amport Park
Cholderton
Quarley F.
Quarley Hill
Gollards F.
Quarley Down F.
Grately
The Old Warren Cottage
Pond
Silchester
Newton Toney
Allington
Roman Road
Hampshire Gap
Owls Castle
Furze
Wallop Fields
Tower Hill
Upper Wallop
Middle Wallop
Old Lodge
Farm Ho.
Barn
New Farm Ho.
New Farm Ho.
Ramsey Barn
Noads Wood
Broughton
Yew Trees
High Beech Wood
Buckholt F.
Cold Harbour
Blackmoors Grove

Map 14 (page 56) South of the River Wey, Alder Holt Wood is more usually known as Alice Holt, an area of clay exploited both in Roman and medieval times for pot-making, with many of the products going to the London market. Further south again is Woolmer Forest, one of the areas subject to medieval Forest Law. Villages like Headley and Bramshott probably owe their origins to clearings in this woodland.

Map 15 (previous page) Wallop Fields were enclosed in 1786, 'Fields' preserving the memory of their recent, open-common status. The Wallop villages line the stream that gives them their name, a British rather than an Old English name; it is from the English rather than the British (or Celtic) language that most names in Hampshire derive, except those of many rivers and streams. Quarley is an Iron Age hill-fort, but Owls Castle is not an antiquity: it is a 'joke' name for an isolated spot. Buckholt is interesting as the site of a late sixteenth-century experimental glass-works. Buckholt Warren was wood converted to rabbit warrens in 1660, an experiment abandoned in 1714.

Map 16 (overleaf) The pre-Roman importance of this part of Hampshire is suggested by the four Iron Age hill-forts that are its most prominent features: Balksbury and Bury Hill where the Pillhill Brook meets the River Anton, 'Worlbury' (now usually spelt Woolbury) and greatest of all 'Deanbury' (a better spelling than Danebury, since it has nothing to do with Vikings, though the older 'Dunbury' is even better, *dun* being the Old English 'hill'). South of it, the Race Ground is still used by a racing stable. The main crosssing of the River Test is at Stockbridge, where a causeway was

laid probably in the twelfth century, replacing a Roman crossing to the south. There are deep deposits of peat along the lower Test, and there were many peat pits like that marked by Marsh Court. The railway was built in 1865, much of it over the canal which it replaced. The canal had been partly responsible for the development at Clatford of an iron and engineering works, founded there just after the First Edition of the Ordnance Survey map was printed.

Map 17 (overleaf) There are two very straight roads on this portion of the map, but only the one that runs north-west from Winchester to Cirencester is Roman; the road that crosses it at Barton Down is a mid eighteenth-century turnpike, its straight line possible because it

The Salisbury–Andover road, looking north-west across the junction with the Nether Wallop road at Middle Wallop, just before the First World War (above). Although cars were no longer a novelty, pedestrians could still linger nonchalantly in the road.

was constructed through what was still unenclosed chalk downland. The settlements for the most part kept off the higher, drier ground and clustered along the stream lines. Three of the four railway lines have gone, as has Worthy Down race course, whose presence on the map is another sign that much of the land was still open down. Two wayside inns are marked as 'huts', isolated landmarks on the roads north-east and south of Crawley; Deluge Hut is still a public house, as is Leckford Hut.

A rare traffic-free moment on what is now the A343 (above), which has been widened at the junction by the demolition of the inn, its site now partly a petrol station. The thatched cottages on the left are almost unchanged, and have the same low brick wall separating them from the road. On the opposite side, hedging has become more fashionable than timber paling.

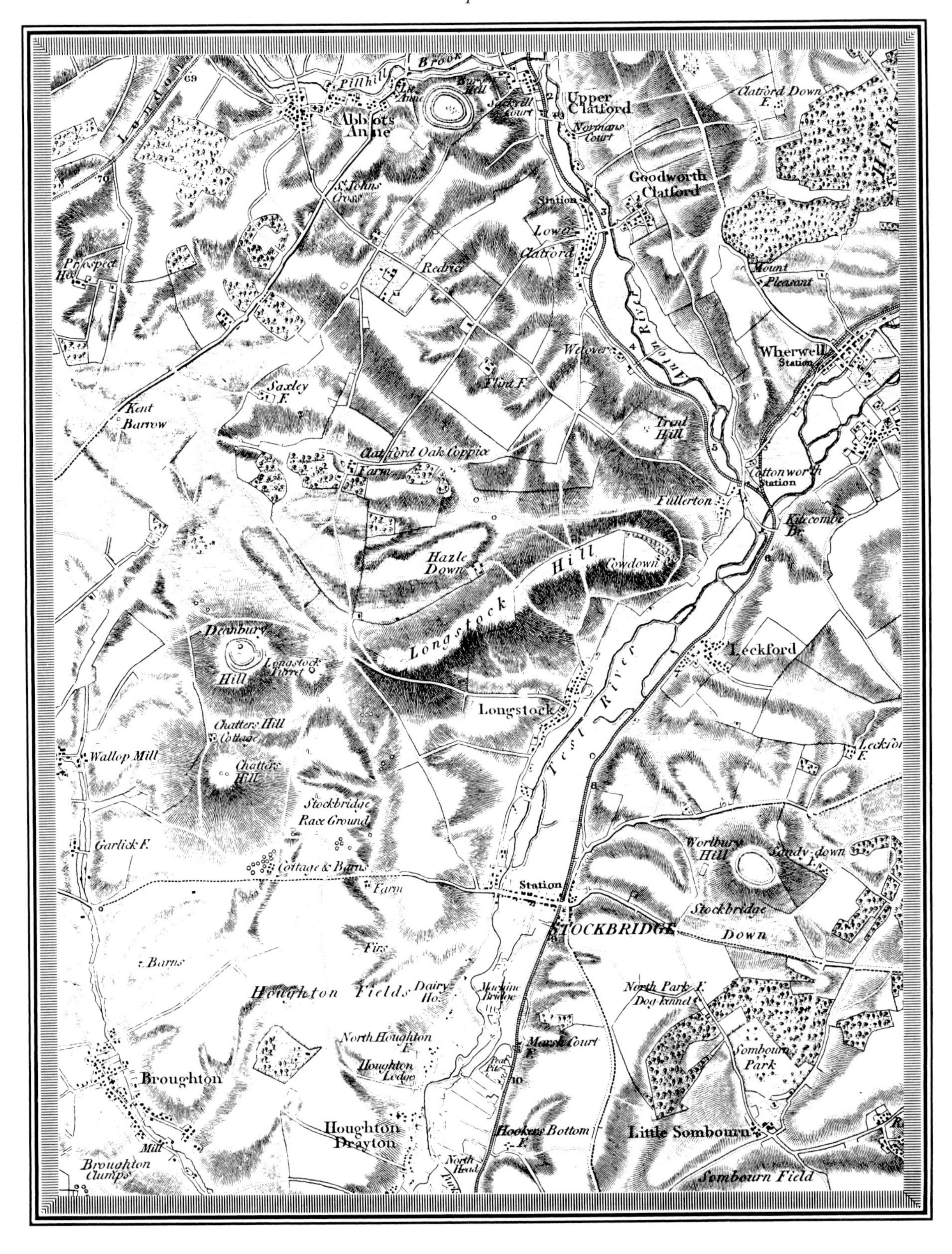
Abbots Anne
Pillhill
Brook
Upper Clatford
Normans Court
Goodworth Clatford
Clatford Down F.
Station
Lower Clatford
St. Johns Cross
Prospect Ho.
Redrice
Mount Pleasant
Wherwell
Station
Wetover
Anton River
Saxley F.
Flint F.
Kent Barrow
Trent Hill
Clatford Oak Coppice
Farm
Cottonworth Station
Fullerton
Kitcombe Br.
Hazle Down
Longstock Hill
Cowdown
Danbury Hill
Longstock Turret
Leckford
Longstock
Chatters Hill Cottage
Chatters Hill
Wallop Mill
Test River
Stockbridge Race Ground
Garlick F.
Worlbury Hill
Sandy-down F.
Cottage & Barns
Farm
Station
STOCKBRIDGE
Stockbridge Down
Firs
Barns
Houghton Fields
Dairy Ho.
North Park F.
Dog-kennel
North Houghton F.
Houghton Lodge
Marsh Court
Sombourn Park
Broughton
Houghton Drayton
Hookers Bottom F.
Little Sombourn
Mill
Broughton Clumps
North Head
Sombourn Field

Map 17

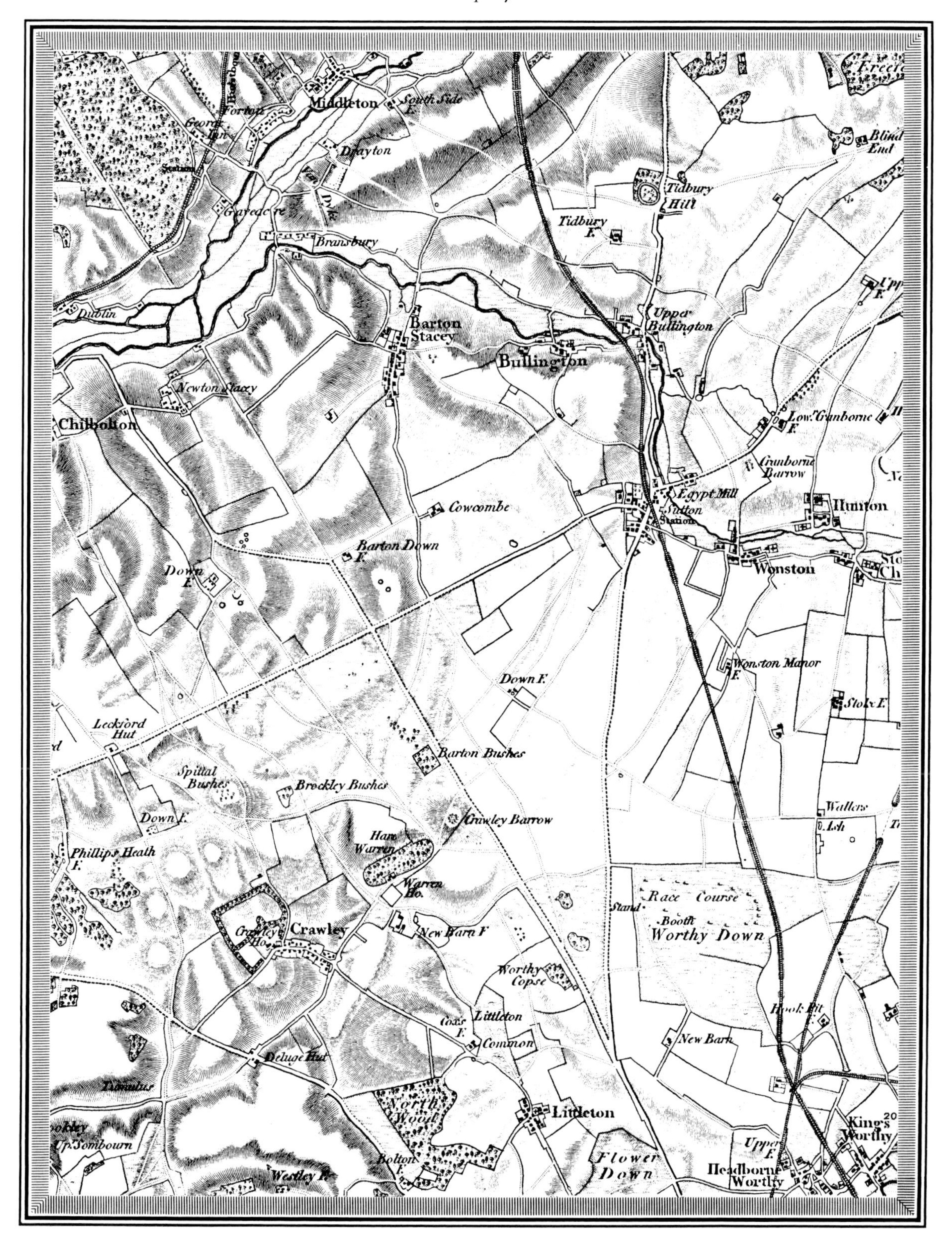
Middleton
South Side F.
Drayton
Bransbury
Dublin
Barton Stacey
Bullington
Upper Bullington
Tidbury Hill
Tidbury F.
Blind End
Newton Stacey
Chilbolton
Low. Cranborne F.
Cranborne Barrow
Egypt Mill
Sutton
Station
Hunton
Wonston
Cowcombe
Barton Down F.
Down F.
Wonston Manor F.
Stoke F.
Leckford Hut
Barton Bushes
Spittal Bushes
Brockley Bushes
Crawley Barrow
Down F.
Wallers Ash
Phillips Heath F.
Ham Warren
Warren Ho.
Stand
Race Course
Booth
Worthy Down
Crawley Ho.
Crawley
New Barn F.
Worthy Copse
Hook Pit
Littleton Common
Cox's F.
New Barn
Deluge Hut
Tumulus
North Wood
Littleton
Up. Sombourn
Bolton F.
Westley F.
Flower Down
Upper F.
Headborne Worthy
King's Worthy

Map 18

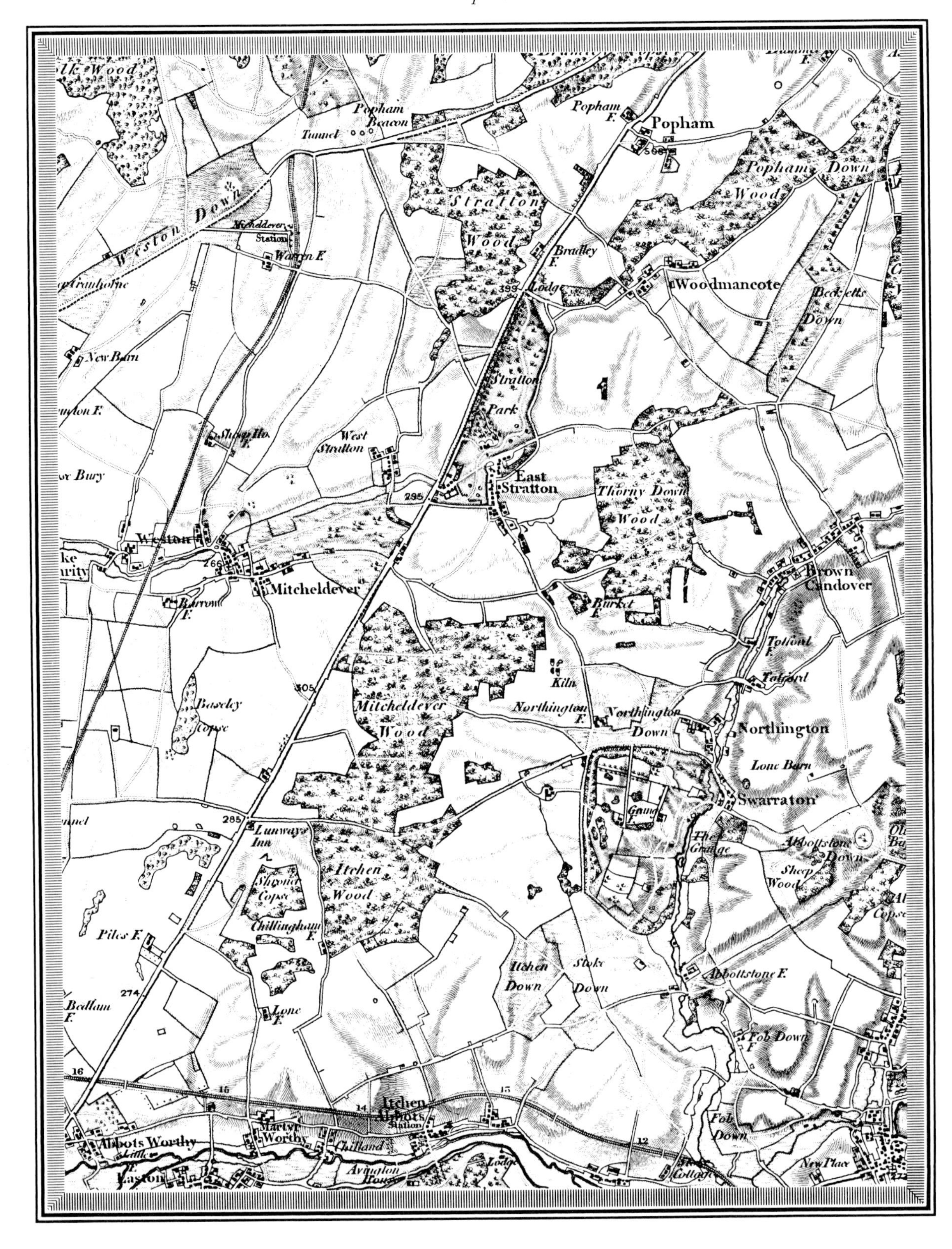

Popham Beacon
Tunnel
Popham F.
Popham
Popham Down
Popham Wood
Stratton Wood
Weston Down
Micheldever Station
Warren F.
Bradley F.
Lodge
Woodmancote
Becketts Down
New Barn
Stratton Park
West Stratton
East Stratton
Thorny Down Wood
Weston
Mitcheldever
Brown Candover
Burket F.
Totford F.
Totford
Kiln
Baseley Copse
Mitcheldever Wood
Northington F.
Northington Down
Northington
Lone Barn
Swarraton
Grange F.
The Grange
Lunways Inn
Itchen Wood
Abbottstone Down
Sheep Wood
Chillingham F.
Piles F.
Itchen Down
Stoke Down
Abbottstone F.
Bedlam F.
Lone F.
Fob Down F.
Fob Down
Itchen Abbots Station
Martyr Worthy
Abbots Worthy
Chilland
Avington House
Lodge
New Place

Map 19

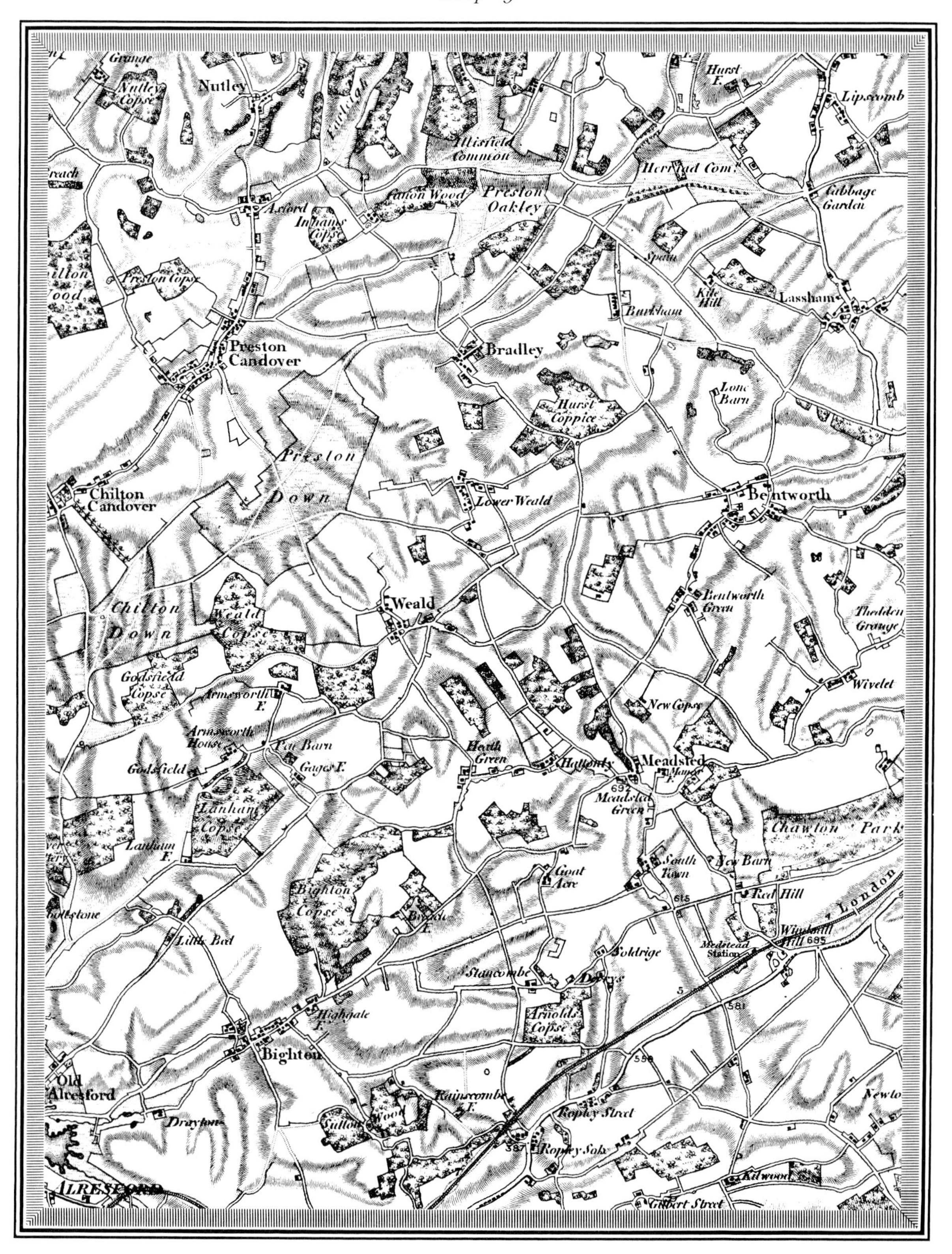
Nutley
Nutley Copse
Illisfield Common
Hurst F.
Lipscomb
Herriad Com.
Preston Oakley
Cabbage Garden
Axford
Preston Copse
Lassham
Burkham
Bradley
Preston Candover
Lone Barn
Hurst Coppice
Preston Down
Chilton Candover
Lower Weald
Bentworth
Bentworth Green
Weald
Chilton Down
Weald Copse
Thedden Grange
Godsfield Copse
Armsworth F.
Wivelet
New Copse
Armsworth House
Heath Green
Meadsted
Godsfield
Gages F.
Manor F.
Meadsted Green
Lanham Copse
Chawton Park
Lanham F.
Goat Acre
South Town
New Barn
Bighton Copse
Red Hill
Little Bal
Soldrige
Medstead Station
Stancombe
Highgate F.
Arnolds Copse
Bighton
Old Alresford
Rainscombe F.
Ropley Street
Drayton
Ropley Soke
Kitwood
Gilbert Street
ALRESFORD
London
692
615
685
581
550
387

Map 18 (page 62) The Roman road north-east from Winchester to Silchester gave its line to the A3, now supplanted by the motorway. Stratton is the *tun* (farm) on the *straet*, the usual Old English word for a paved or metalled road. In the south-east corner, Alresford and Old Alresford mark where the Bishop of Winchester created a new town adjacent to his existing manor—which thus became 'Old' (see map opposite). The pond was a vast fishery retained by a weir over which the main route from Southampton and Winchester to London crossed. In the late Middle Ages, Alresford had a flourishing wool market, and the stream from its pond turned several mills, at least one of which was for fulling, the process of cleansing, shrinking and thickening, cloth. The area is otherwise distinguished for its great houses, most notably The Grange, a vast early nineteenth-century enlargement of a seventeenth-century core, now a roofless if picturesque ruin.

Map 19 (previous page) This part of the map was completely rural in the early nineteenth century; not even the most insignificant market town intruded upon it. It is an area of mixed soils, broken up into small parcels of land producing a large number of small settlement units, and with none of the great houses that occur to its west and north—even Chawton Park is a park and no more. The area is not all that different today, except that the A31 has spawned a settlement at Four Marks where nothing existed in the early nineteenth century. This is also where the soils change from chalk in the west to clays in the east; consequently the land was less valuable and less protected from housing. The railway is the 'Watercress Line', closed by British Railways, but now maintained by private enthusiasts.

Map 20 (overleaf) Alton is the medieval successor to a Roman market centre at Neatham, on the Christchurch–Silchester road, a route that has left no trace of itself on the map as the abandonment of Silchester made it redundant. The road to London may have considerable antiquity, however, and was a major reason for the market. In the seventeenth century, Alton's fair specialized in cattle, for most of the area was pasture less suited to sheep and corn than the downland. Nevertheless, enough barley and hops were produced for Alton to become a brewing centre, intially mainly for local consumption, but later for London, as London's own rivers became increasingly foul and unusable, and railway transport became cheaper. To the south is Selborne, famous because of Gilbert White's detailed study over many years of its natural history; it is an area in which different types of soil produce varied habitats.

(Opposite) The London brewery of Courage had bought out Halls of Alton seven years before this picture was taken in about 1910. The London and South-Western Region Railway wagon emphasizes the importance for the Alton brewers of being able to get their product quickly to London, but horses were still used for more local deliveries, and one reason for the number of small houses close to the brewery was so that the stable-hands would not be far from their charges.

Bass is now bottled where Hall and Courage brewed in Alton and the railway siding has been converted into a car park (above). The building with loading doors in the gable end is still there, as is the range alongside. Housing has spread up the slopes in the background, but not yet right over the hill.

Map 20

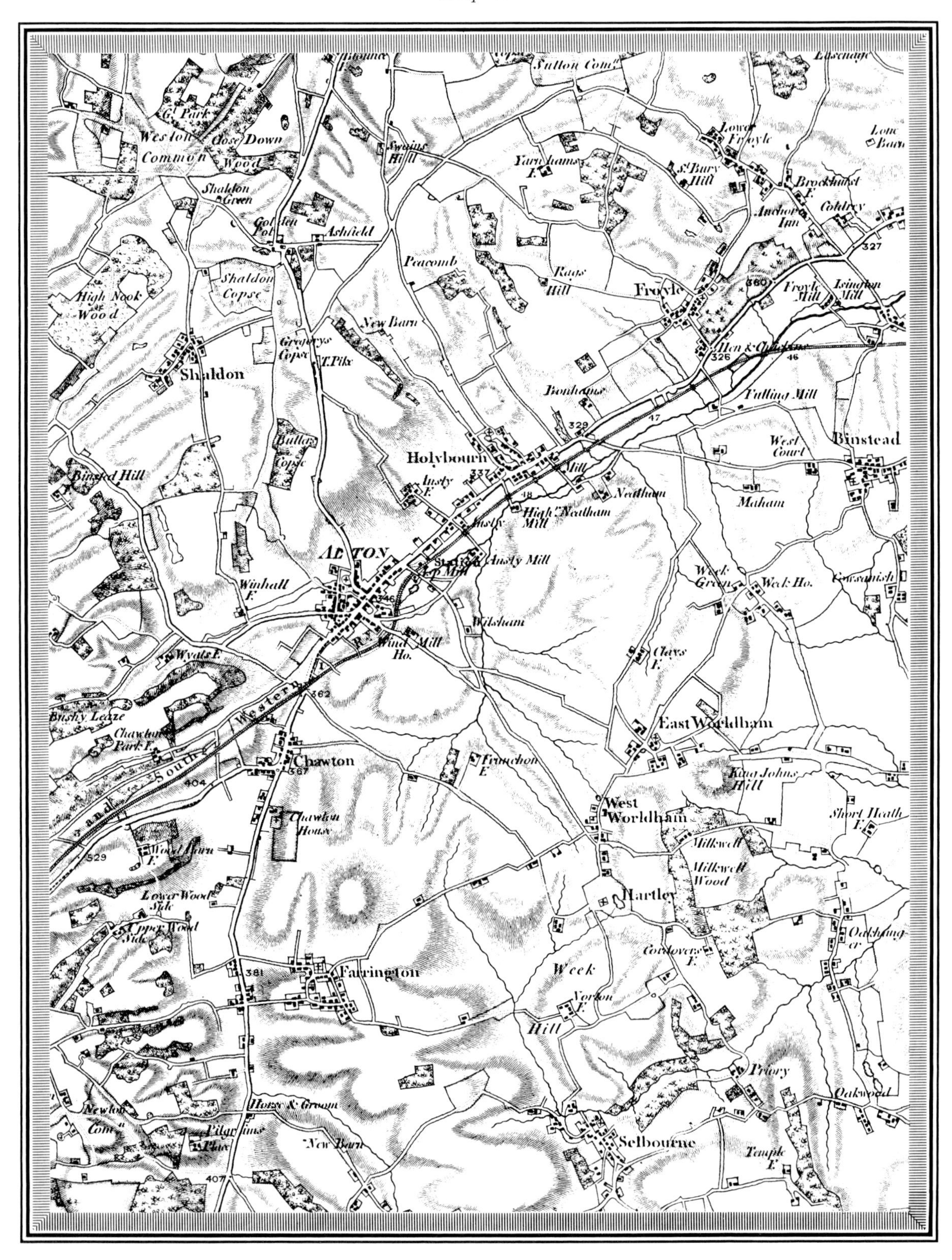
Sutton Com.
Weston Common
Close Down Wood
Swains Hill
Lower Froyle
Lone Barn
Yarnhams F.
St. Bury Hill
Brockhurst F.
Shaldon Green
Golden Pot
Ashfield
Anchor Inn
Coldrey
327
Peacomb
Rags Hill
Shaldon Copse
High Nook Wood
Froyle
360
Froyle Mill
Isington Mill
New Barn
Gregorys Copse
T. Pike
Hen & Chickens
326
46
Shaldon
Bonhams
Fulling Mill
329
47
Binstead
West Court
Holybourn
Binsted Hill
Insty F.
Mill
Neatham
48
High Neatham Mill
Maham
ALTON
Ansty Mill
Week Green
Week Ho.
Cowsanish
Winhall F.
346
Wilsham
Wind Mill
Wind Ho.
Wyats F.
Clays F.
362
Bushy Leaze
Chawton Park F.
East Worldham
Chawton
367
Truncheon F.
404
King Johns Hill
West Worldham
Short Heath F.
Chawton House
Wood Barn F.
Milkwell
Milkwell Wood
329
Lower Wood Side
Hartley
Upper Wood Side
Oakhanger
Coldovers F.
Week
381
Farrington
Norton F.
Hill
Priory
Oakwood
Newton Com.
Horse & Groom
Pilgrims Place
New Barn
Selbourne
Temple F.
407
South Western

The view of Andover on the previous page is different to that of 1880 on page 44, but is also taken from the church tower, and emphasizes that roads now matter more to Andover than railways. Some attempt has been made to keep a core of old buildings, such as the Georgian houses in the foreground, but post-Second World War housing of varying quality is what makes the most impression. Although still surrounded by countryside, many fields have been completely submerged.

Latter-day Odiham (above) has been bypassed by through traffic, which increases its appeal for shoppers. Nevertheless, pedestrians need protection to cross the road safely—the traffic light and the widening of the pavement are the most obvious signs from the picture on page 53, for the George Hotel still flourishes. The contrast to the centre of nearby modern Basingstoke (page 50) could hardly be greater.

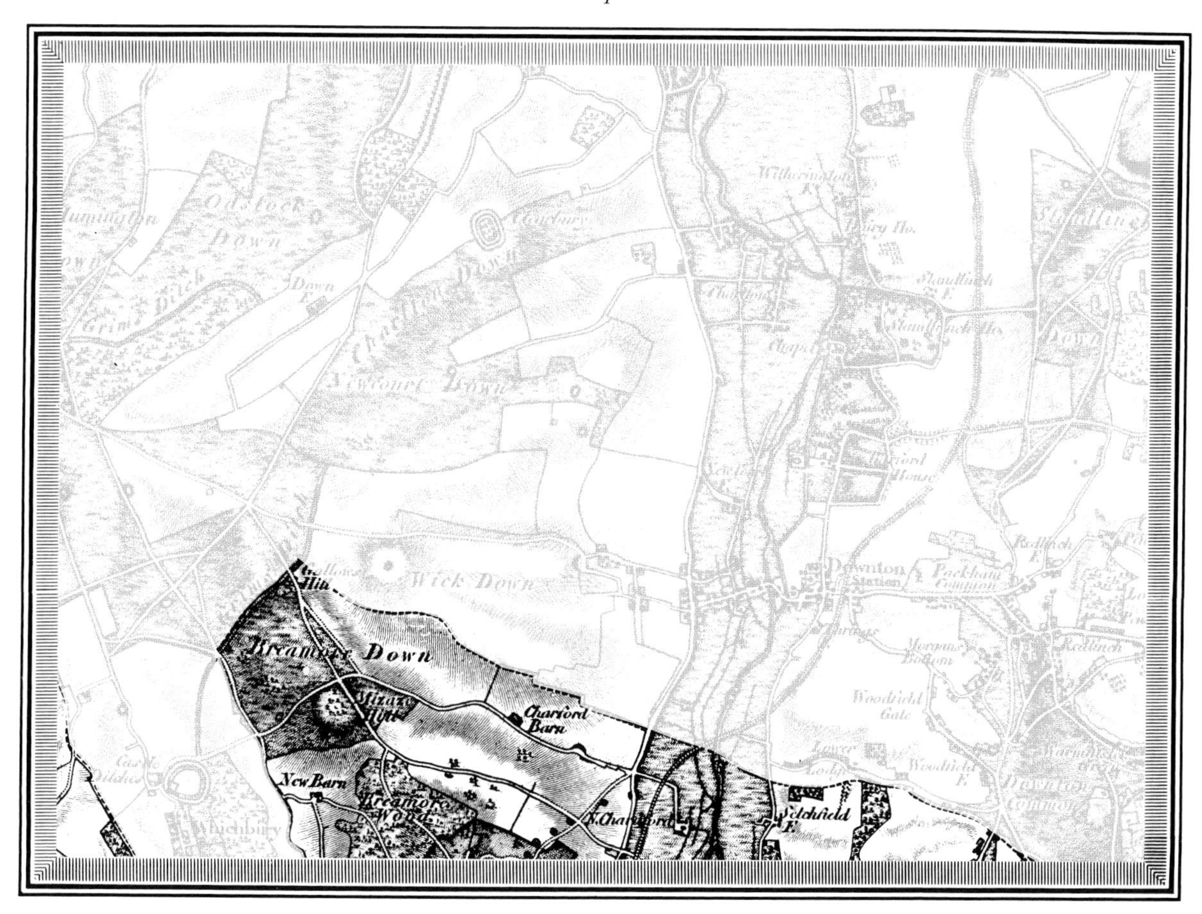

Map 21 This small area contains one feature of considerable interest, misleadingly called Mizaze Hill, but really Mizmaze, for on its summit is a maze cut out of the turf. A tortuous path leads eventually to the centre of the circle, an idea that is originally an image or symbol of the pilgrim's difficult path to Jerusalem, and the soul's to heaven. It may have been laid out by the canons of Breamore whose priory was in the valley below, but it could also be associated with fanciful garden fashions of the sixteenth and seventeenth centuries, and with Breamore House.

Map 22

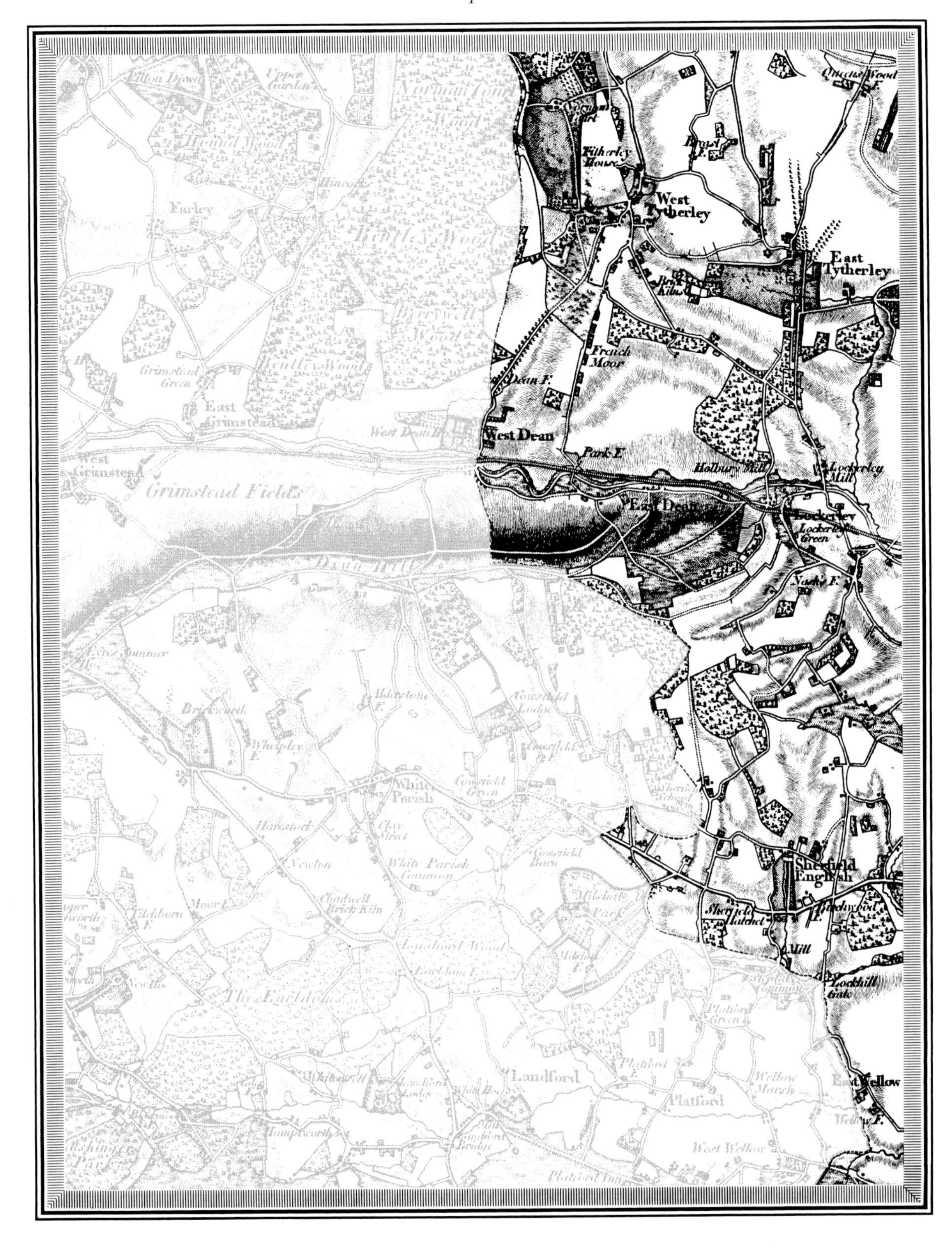

West Tytherley
East Tytherley
Tytherley House
Brick Kilns
French Moor
Dean F.
West Dean
Park F.
Holbury Mill
Lockerley Mill
East Dean
Lockerley
Lockerley Green
Nash's F.
Sherfield English
Sherfield Hatchet
Mill
Lockhill Gate
East Wellow
Farley
Grimstead Green
East Grimstead
West Grimstead
Grimstead Fields
Brickworth
Whepley F.
White Parish
Clay Street
Newton
White Parish Common
Chadwell Brick Kiln
Moor F.
Cowsfield Green
Cowsfield Barn
Landford Wood
The Earldom
Landford
Platford
Platford Green
Wellow Marsh
West Wellow
Hampworth

Romsey Abbey from the River Test near Burn House Mill at the turn of the century, with meadows between the river and the church school. Trees have grown and now obscure this view, and the timber bridge has been replaced by steel and concrete (page 80).

Map 22 Vestiges of Wiltshire's great Clarendon Forest here creep over the border into Hampshire. The houses in the northern part look impressive, but they were not owned by great magnates, although some of the owners had played a prominent part in the Civil War. The railway line replaced a canal which branched from the Andover–Redbridge (Southampton) canal, and was never completed as far as Salisbury as had been intended. The steep scarp of Dean Hill, a tongue of chalk, dies away into the valley, whose sands and clays make it an area of many small farms recently taken in from heathland.

The road to the south of Sherfield English was an eighteenth-century turnpike, which bypassed the old church and the original road; between the old church and the new road, the straight lines presumably mark watercress beds, still there today.

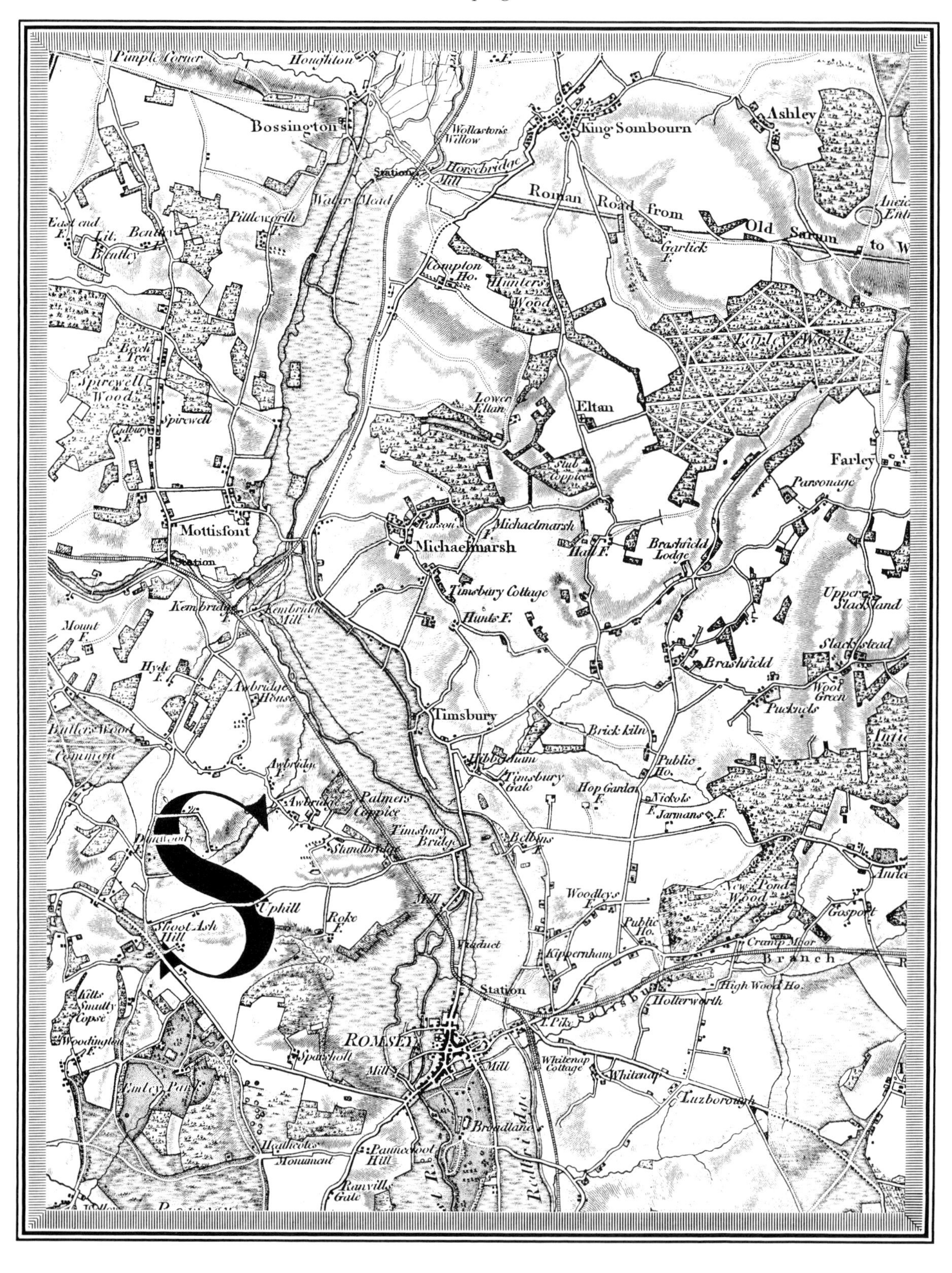
Houghton
Bossington
Wollaston's Willow
King Sombourn
Ashley
Horsebridge
Station
Mill
Water Mead
Roman Road from Old Sarum to W
Garlick F.
Pittleworth F.
East end F.
Lit. Bentley
Compton Ho.
Hunters Wood
Beech Tree
Spirewell Wood
Spirewell
Cadbury F.
Lower Eltan
Eltan
Stub Coppice
Farley
Parsonage
Mottisfont
Station
Parson
Michaelmarsh F.
Michaelmarsh
Hall F.
Brashfield Lodge
Timsbury Cottage
Hunts F.
Upper Slackstead
Kembridge F.
Kembridge Mill
Mount F.
Hyde F.
Slackstead
Brashfield
Wool Green
Pucknels
Timsbury
Brick kiln
Public Ho.
Hop Garden F.
Nickols F.
Jarmans F.
Timsbury Gate
Ambridge
Palmers Coppice
Timsbury Bridge
Stanbridge
Belbins F.
New Pond Wood
Woodleys F.
Uphill
Roke F.
Mill
Gospor
Shoot Ash Hill
Viaduct
Public Ho.
Kippernham
Cramp Moor
Branch
Station
High Wood Ho.
Hollerworth
Kills Smutty Copse
T. Pike
ROMSEY
Sparsholt
Mill
Mill
Whitenap Cottage
Whitenap
Luzborough
Broadland
Heathcotes Monument
Pauncefoot Hill
Ranvills Gate

This scene in Winchester has hardly changed in eighty years (see page 78), although there are now no gas lamps, and the signpost shows how many thousands of visitors come to the city every year. Some stay in the old mill, which the National Trust has turned into a youth hostel. Even the new timber rails along the river are almost exactly the same as the old ones.

Map 23 The steep-sided valley created by the River Test was used in the late eighteenth century by the Andover–Redbridge (Southampton) canal, and after 1865 for the railway line that is now just a footpath north of Mottisfont. The old path of the Roman road from Winchester to Sarum (Salisbury) was not a major east-west highway, and only part of it survives as a public route. Romsey was a prosperous market town with paper and grain mills and a thriving wool industry, but the basic pattern was of scattered farms, with few larger clusters of houses. There were fewer farms in the south where clays and sands were less attractive for agriculture. Particularly noticeable is the large unenclosed heathland east of Luzborough: much of this has been built up since the 1930s by the North Baddesley housing estates, but some parts of it remain as protected, undrained marsh and scrub. The woods further north are the

The River Itchen in the water meadows outside Winchester, in 1912 (above). In the background is St Catherine's Hill, an Iron Age hill-fort. Its lower slope is scarred by a chalk-pit such as could be found everywhere on the chalklands at that time, when planning controls scarcely existed.

Even the trees on the top of St Catherine's Hill look as though they have hardly altered this century (opposite). Appearances deceive in this picture, however, for between the river and the hill is now the 1930s bypass, soon itself to be bypassed by an extension of the M3.

remains of the former forests of Buckholt, west of the Test, and of West Bere, to the east, both extensively encroached upon for farmland. The next hundred years were to see the building of more large country houses, but some already existed, such as Broadlands, around which the A27 has been routed from Luzborough. The 'ancient enclosure' in the north-east is a Roman camp; the medieval castle earthworks at Ashley are not shown.

Map 24 (overleaf) Winchester's focal position is emphasized by the roads leading to it, some but not all of Roman origin. The 'Itching' (Itchen) River has more than one stream because parts of it were deepened and straightened for inland navigation and use by barge traffic after an Act of 1665. There were stretches of open chalk downland west and

south of Winchester, much of it unenclosed, then to the south of Hursley and Otterbourne the soil changes to the less productive clays and sands. Cromwell's Battery is that unusual thing, a site named after Oliver Cromwell which was actually used by him (though he did not construct it in the first place). St Catherine's Hill is an Iron Age hill-fort, Marden (usually Merdon) Castle is Norman or slightly later. At Otterbourne, the map does not make it clear that the church was then near the river, not with most of the houses on the main road, where a new church was built in 1839. Of Winchester itself, the map shows strikingly the street layout within the Roman walls. The main east-west street and part of the main north-south streets overlie the Roman ones, but the others have changed and have been shown to be Saxon in origin.

Modern map 24 (overleaf) Winchester has grown in all directions, but its basic core can still be recognized. Much of the downland survives, though now enclosed and with parts of Crab Wood turned into conifer plantation. Most of the big houses—Hursley, Brambridge and Lainston—are still with us although no longer family homes. The biggest change is in the south-west; Chandler's Ford has grown from nothing, over heath and wood. Some of the old names survive—Friers Hill as the more arcane Fryern. New developments here have so far left unscathed the cluster of houses and fields near the old church at North Baddesley.

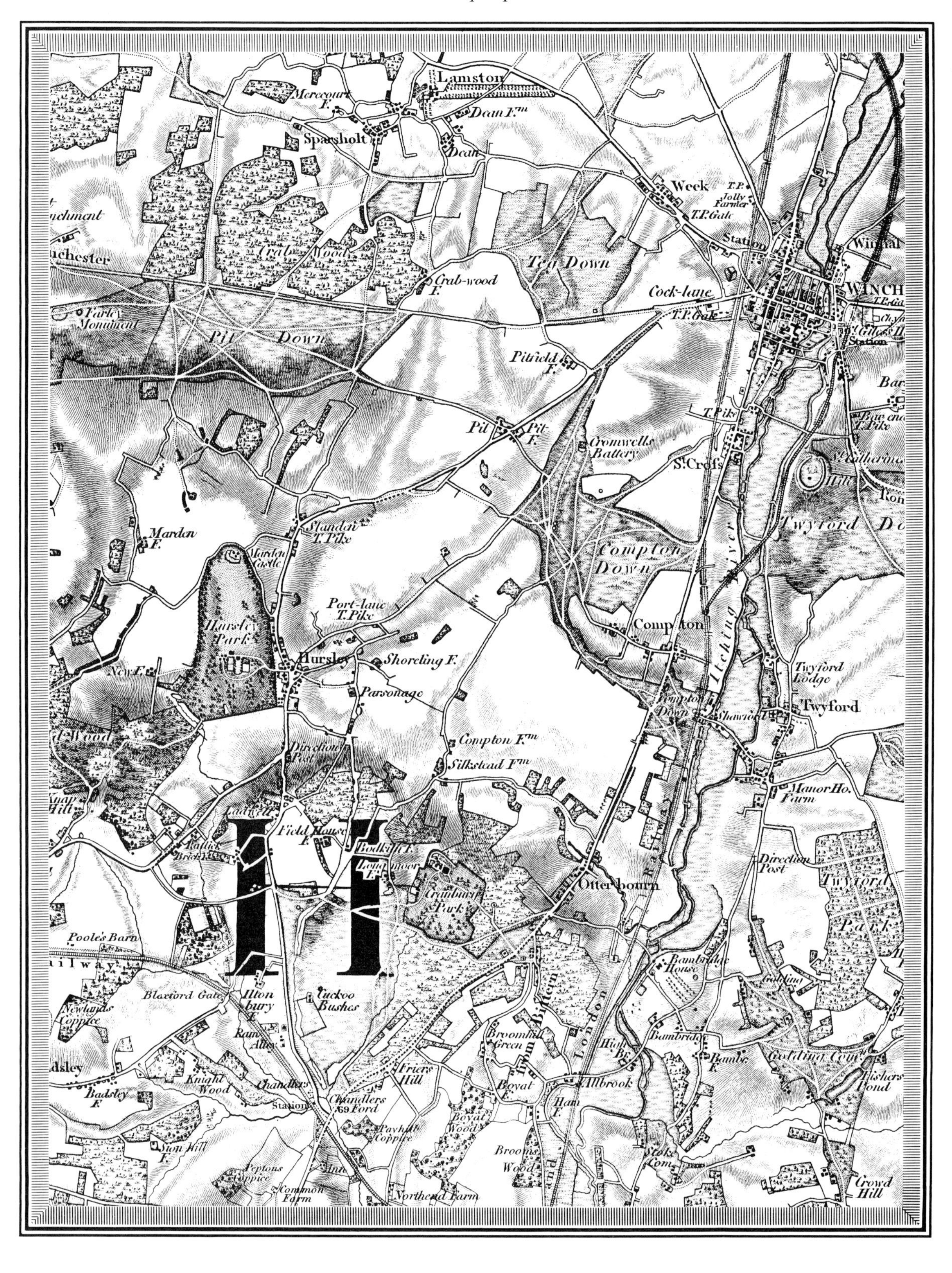
Lamston
Mercecourt F.
Dean F.m
Sparsholt
Dean
Week
T.P. Jolly Farmer
T.P. Gate
Station
Crab Wood
Crab-wood F.
Teg Down
Cock-lane
T.P. Gate
Farley Monument
Pit Down
Pitfield F.
Pit
Pit F.
Cromwells Battery
St. Cross
Twyford
Marden F.
Standen T. Pike
Marden Castle
Compton Down
Port-lane T. Pike
Hursley Park
Compton
Hursley
Shoreling F.
New F.
Parsonage
Twyford Lodge
Twyford
Compton F.m
Direction Post
Silkstead F.m
Manor Ho. Farm
Field House F.
Bodkin F.
Longmoor
Cranbury Park
Otterbourn
Direction Post
Twyford Park
Poole's Barn
Bambridge House
Blaxford Gate
Ilton bury
Cuckoo Bushes
Newlands Coppice
Broomhill Green
Bambridge
Badsley F.
Knight Wood
Chandlers
Station
Chandlers Ford
Friers Hill
Boyat
Allbrook
Ham F.
Golding Court
Fishers Pond
Boyat Wood
Payhill Coppice
Sion Hill F.
Brooms Wood
Stoke Com.
Peptons Coppice
Common Farm
Northend Farm
Crowd Hill
Itching River
H

Up Somborne
College of Agriculture
Moor Court Fm
Sparsholt
Northwood Park
Lainston Ho
Dean
Ham Green
Littleton
Flowerdown Barrows
Harestock
Headbourne Worthy
Abbots Worthy
Hinton Ho
Barton Fm
Abbotts Barton Ho
Abbott's Barton
WINCHE
Lone Barn
Great Up Somborne Wood
Tumulus
Well Copse
West Wood
Crab Wood
Crabwood Farm Ho
Teg Down
Weeke
Fulflood
HM Prison
Winnall
Winnall Down Fm
St Giles's Hill
Magdalen Down
Forest of Bere Fm
Beacon Hill
Farley Mount Country Park
Mount Down
Pitt Down
Enmill Fm
Sleepers Hill
Stanmore
Bar End
Farley Fm
Berrydown Fm
Grovelands Cops
South Lynch
Violet Hill
Pitt
Oliver's Battery
Oliver Cromwell's Battery
St Cross
St Catherine's Hill
ROMAN ROAD
Twyford Down
Deacon Hill
Southlynch Plantn
Standon
Nan Trodds Hill
Compton Down
Gudge Copse
Merdon Manor Fm
Merdon Castle
Upper Slackstead
Yew Hill
Compton End
Morestead Down
Morestead Fm
Lower Slackstead
Home Fm
Hursley Park
Hursley
Shawlands Fm
Compton
New Barn Fm
Twyford Lodge
Northfields
Twyford
Hazeley Down
Bunstead
Silkstead
Four Dell Fm
Shawford Ho
Shawford
South Down
Hazeley Fm
Field Wood
Knapp
Ladwell
Freemantles Copse
Knighton
Gabriel's Copse
Ampfield
The Potter's Heron (Motel)
Ratlake
Hawstead Fm
Field Ho
Home Fm
Cranbury Ho
Cranbury Park
Hocombe
Otterbourne
Twyford Moors
River Itchen
Gosport
Broadgate
Hiltingbury
Otterbourne Hill
Manor Ho
Brambridge Ho
Colden Common
Hensting Fm
Hensting
Leigh Ho
Flexford
Bucket Corner
Broom Hill
Allbrook
Brambridge
Nob's Crook
Swifts Fm
Marwell Hall
Zoological Pa
Knightwood Fm
Highbridge
Fisher's Pond
Marwell Manor
Chandler's Ford
Fryern Hill
Boyatt Wood
Zionshill Fm
Sand Pit
Stoke Common
Stoke Park Fm
Crowdhill
Low Hill Fm
Nutburn
Great Covert
Park Hills Wood
Stoke Park Wood
North Baddesley
Velmore Fm
ROMAN ROAD (course of)
Fleming Park
Bishopstoke
Pylehill
Hall Lands Ho

The City Bridge in Winchester (previous page) has been the main route out of the town since Bishop Swithun built the first stone bridge in the 850s. This picture was taken in 1910, when the streets were gaslit.

Romsey Abbey (above) from slightly further south than the view on page 71. There are rather more houses in the meadows now, and although there are paths along bits of the river, children can no longer play in it with the freedom that they could in the old days.

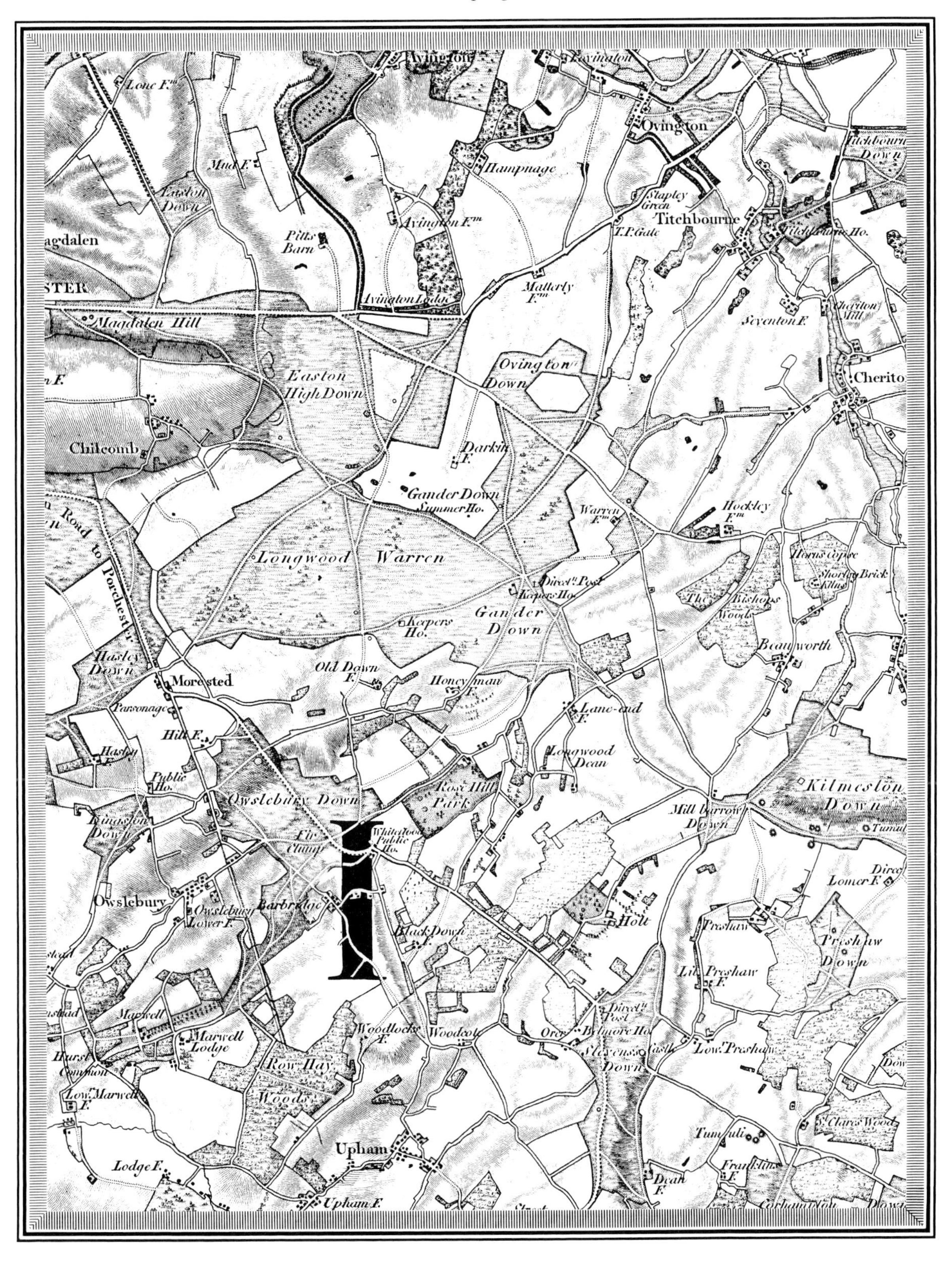
Avington
Lone Fm
Ovington
Titchbourne Down
Hampnage
Mud F.
Easton Down
Stapley Green
Titchbourne
Avington Fm
Pitts Barn
T.P. Gate
agdalen
STER
Mallerly Fm
Avington Lodge
Cheriton Mill
Seventon F.
Magdalen Hill
Ovington Down
Cherito
Easton High Down
Chilcomb
Darkin F.
Gander Down Summer Ho.
Hockley Fm
Warren Fm
Road to Porchester
Longwood Warren
Horns Copse
Shorley Brick Kilns
Direct Post
Keepers Ho.
The Bishops Woods
Gander Down
Keepers Ho.
Beauworth
Hasley Down
Old Down F.
Morested
Honeyman F.
Lane-end F.
Parsonage
Hill F.
Longwood Dean
Hasley F.
Public Ho.
Kilmeston Down
Owslebury Down
Rose Hill Park
Mill barrow Down
Fir Clump
Public Ho.
I
Lomer F.
Owslebury
Owslebury Lower F.
Barbridge
Holt
Preshaw
Black Down F.
Preshaw Down
Lit. Preshaw F.
Marwell
Marwell Lodge
Woodlocks F.
Woodcot
Direct Post
Belmore Ho.
Stevens's Down
Low. Preshaw
Hurst Common
Row Hay Woods
Low. Marwell F.
St. Clairs Wood
Tumuli
Upham
Lodge F.
Franklins F.
Dean F.
Upham F.
Corhampton

Map 26

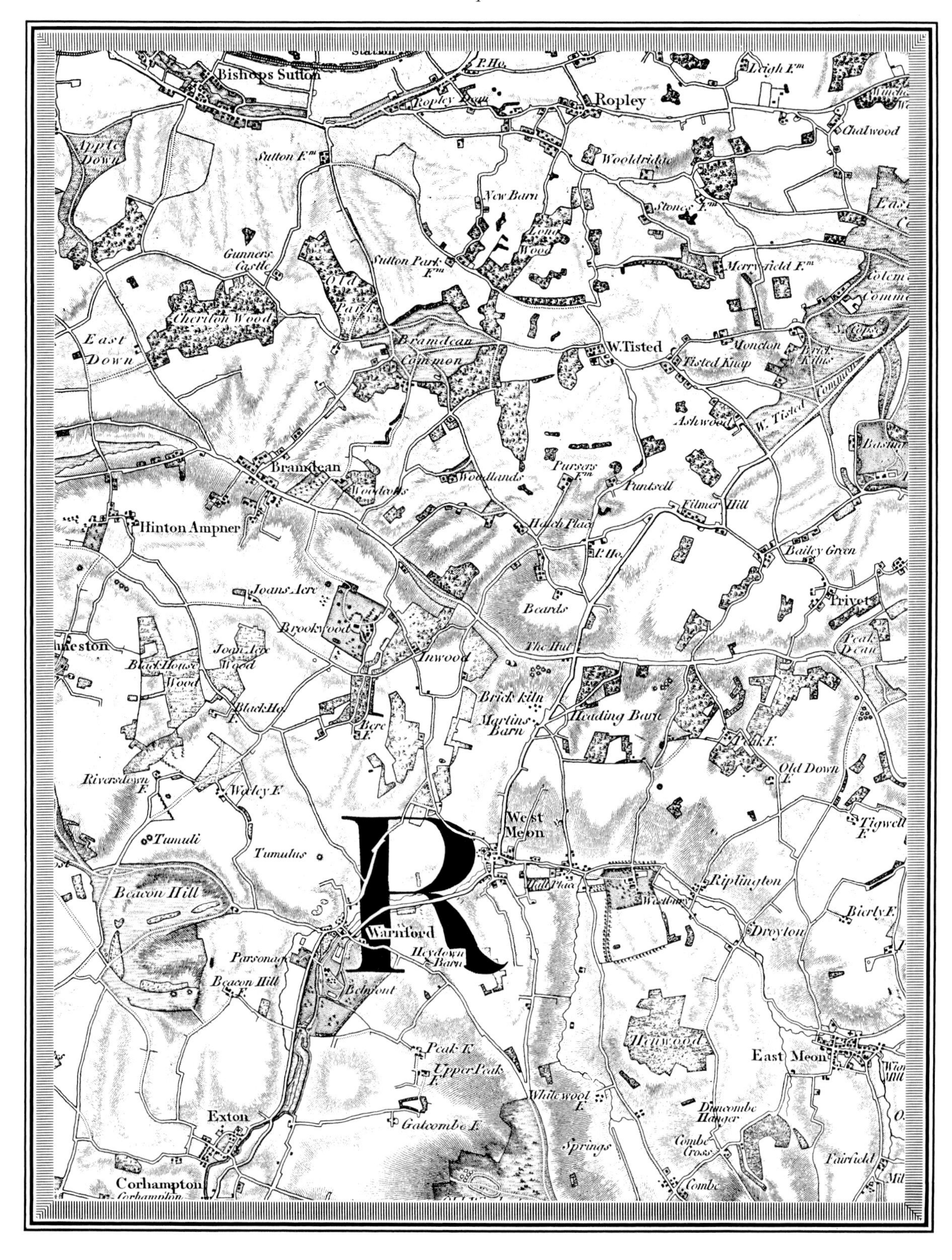

Bishops Sutton
Ropley
Leigh Fm
Chalwood
Sutton Fm
New Barn
Long Wood
Gunners Castle
Sutton Park Fm
Merryfield Fm
Old Park
Cheriton Wood
East Down
Bramdean Common
W.Tisted
Tisted Knap
Brick Kilns
Ashwood
W. Tisted Common
Bramdean
Woodlands
Pursers Fm
Puntsell
Filmer Hill
Hinton Ampner
Hatch Place
P. Ho.
Bailey Green
Joans Acre
Beards
Privet
Brookwood
The Hut
Peak Dean
Black House Wood
Joans Acre Wood
Inwood
Brick kiln
Martins Barn
Heading Barn
Black Ho F.
Bere F.
Peak F.
Old Down F.
Riversdown F.
Worley F.
West Meon
Tigwell F.
Tumuli
Tumulus
Beacon Hill
Hall Place
Riplington
Westbury
Bierly F.
Warnford
Droyton
Parsonage
Heydown Barn
Beacon Hill F.
Belmont
Henwood
East Meon
Peak F.
Upper Peak F.
Whitewool F.
Exton
Duncombe Hanger
Gatcombe F.
Springs
Combe Cross
Fairfield
Corhampton
Combe
R

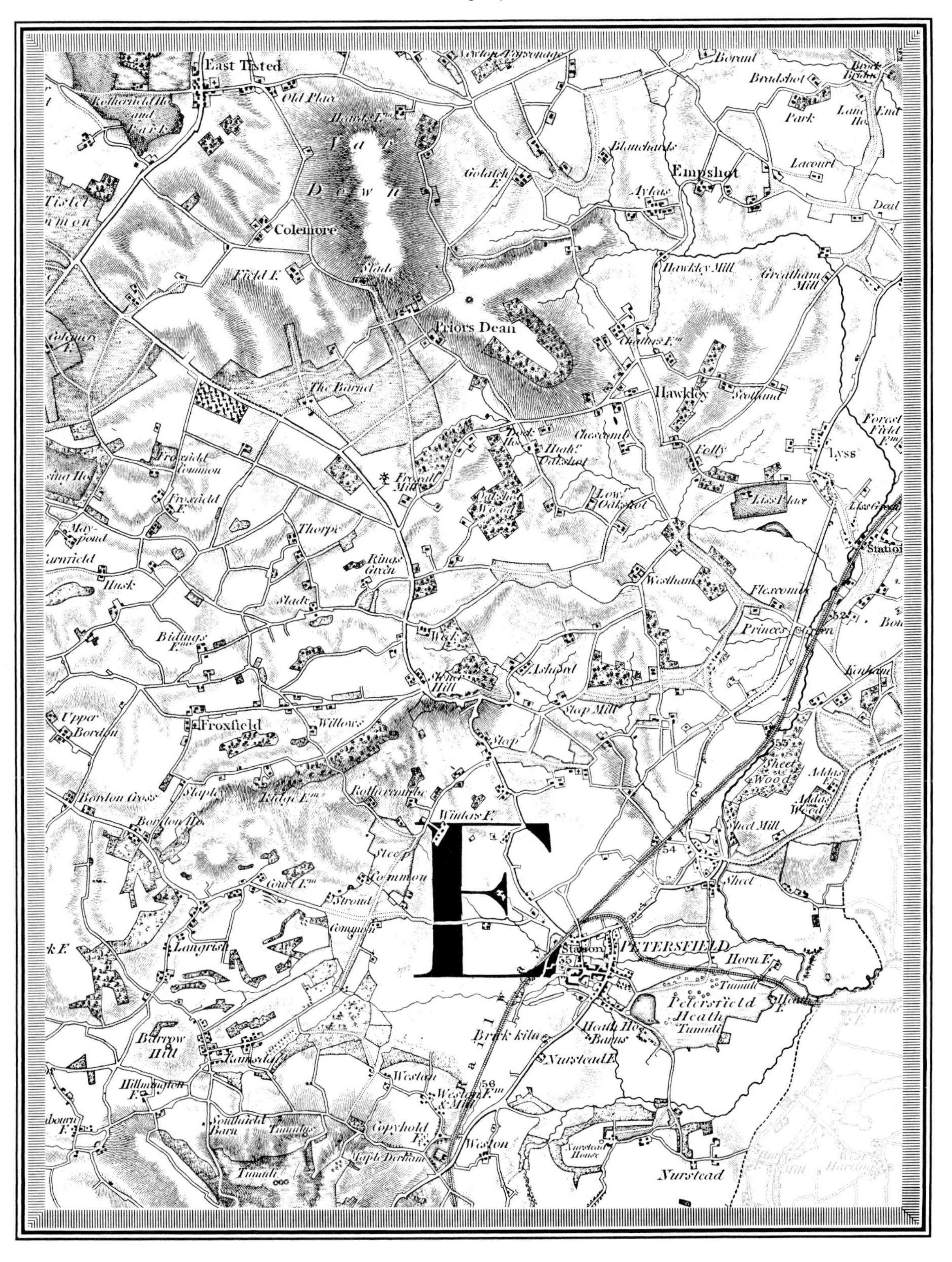
East Tisted
Colemore
Priors Dean
Empshot
Hawkley
Lyss
Froxfield
Langrish
PETERSFIELD
Station
Nurstead
Petersfield Heath
Barrow Hill
Weston
Steep
Sheet
Hawkley Mill
Greatham Mill
Liss Place
Froxfield Common
Bordon Cross
Nurstead House
Copyhold F.

Map 25 (page 81) There is fine downland countryside in this part of the map, although the great open stretches at Easton High Down and Longwood Warren are now enclosed. Unusually, there are villages high on the hills—Owlesbury and the aptly named Upham. Tichborne and Ovington keep more conformably to stream valleys. An oddity is 'Stevens's Castle' in the southern part; this is probably not a medieval castle site, although there are earthworks which local tradition ascribes to King Stephen's civil war. Some of the 'tumulus' symbols are neolithic long barrows, others are Bronze Age round barrows, showing prehistoric use of the chalk, which is attested also by many occupation sites, known from aerial photographs and excavations, but too insignificant on the ground to be mapped. Similarly ignored is Hampshire's best-known example of a deserted medieval village, south-east of Lomer Farm. It was probably abandoned in the fourteenth and fifteenth centuries as the population declined after the Black Death, and fields were converted from arable to sheep pastures.

Map 26 (page 82) West and East Meon take their names from the river that meanders through this bit of downland. In the early Saxon period the area was presumably part of the territory of the *Meonware*, a people with Jutish connections. Old Winchester Hill is a fine Iron Age hill-fort; it seems to be one of a roughly spaced line of big hill-forts that includes Danebury, St Catherine's, and the Trundle in Sussex, each perhaps dominating a block of territory down to the coast. The plan of East Meon village is interesting, its regularity suggesting that it was formally laid out south of the church, with space allowed for a small market area, perhaps as early as the twelfth century. The church is itself a fine, mainly Norman building.

Map 27 (previous page) Petersfield is on the River Rother, at a point where stream valleys give access into the high ground around it. It was founded as a market town in the late twelfth century. There was a large cattle market in the sixteenth century, with a leather industry resulting from it. Sheep were sold in Sheep Street, horses in the Spain. These interests reflect the mixed pattern of farming on the local soils, which are predominantly clays in this part of the county. There are several Bronze Age barrows on the unenclosed heath west of the town, and many others on the edge of Butser Hill, to the south-west. The railway is the main Portsmouth–London line, finally opened in 1859, with a branch opened in 1864 going east to Midhurst.

Map 28 (opposite) The army has encroached on to Hampshire's eastern border, with Longmoor Camp and rifle ranges taking up what in the early nineteenth century was heathland and the remains of Woolmer Forest. The eastern fringe is more like part of the heavily wooded West Sussex downs than the rest of Hampshire. Inset is a small area east of Aldershot, which includes Farnborough, unrecognizable as a small village now that the railway and the army have turned it into a town.

Map 28

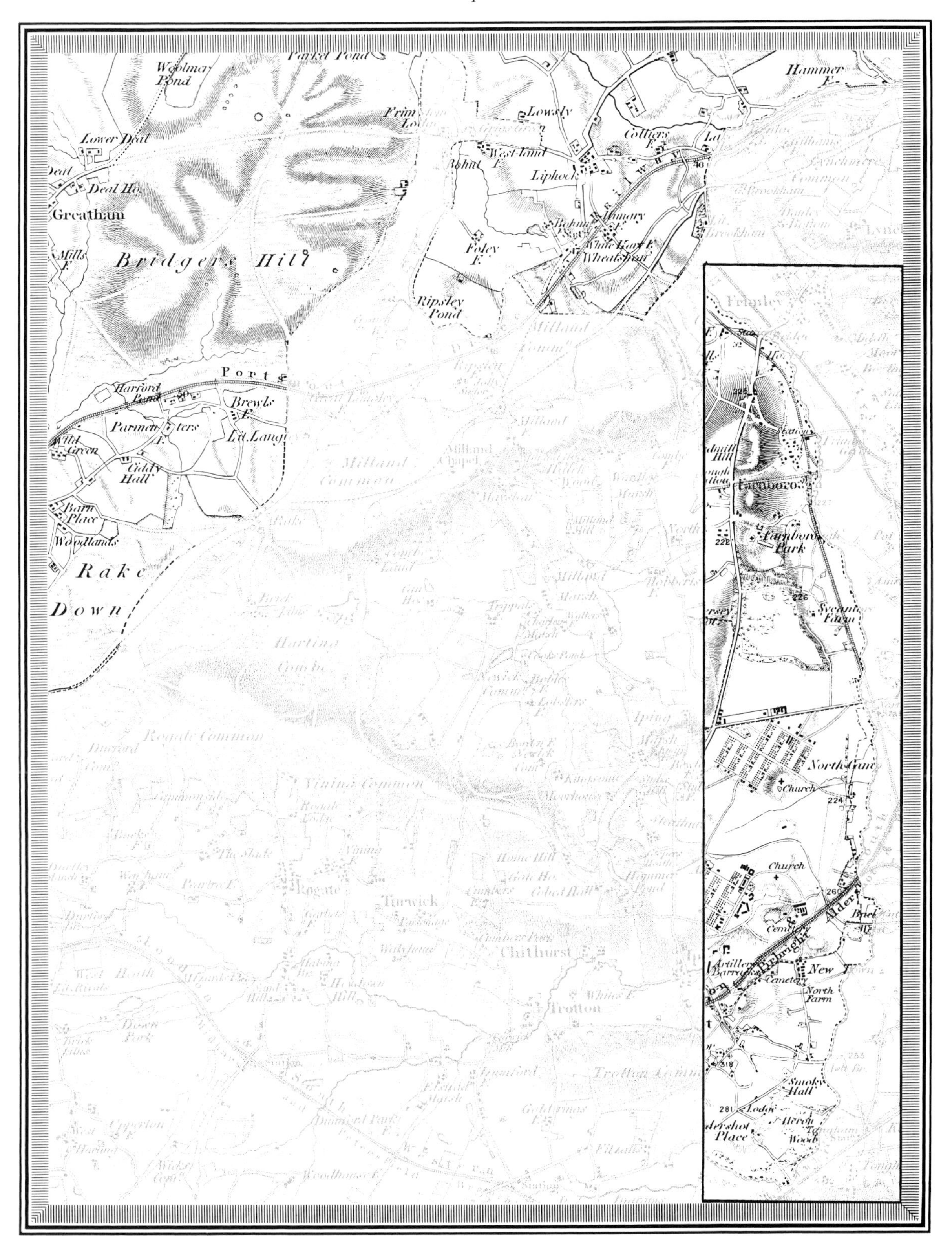

Woolmer Pond
Lower Deal
Deal Ho.
Greatham
Bridgers Hill
Frimstone Lodge
Lowsly
Colliers F.
West-land F.
Liphook
Foley F.
Ripsley Pond
Wheatsheaf
Hammer F.
Harford Pond
Brewls F.
Parmenters F.
Lit. Langley
Wild Green
Giddy Hall
Barn Place
Woodlands
Rake Down
Milland Common
Rogate Common
Rogate
Turwick
Chithurst
Trotton
Frimley
Farnboro'
Farnboro' Park
North Camp
Church
Cemetery
Artillery Barracks
New
North Farm
Smoky Hall
Lodge
Heron Wood
Aldershot Place

Headley Road, Liphook in about 1912 (left), with semi-detached respectability by a speculative builder cramming as many pattern-book houses into as rigid a line as he could manage. This scene could be repeated all over the county, but particularly on the east side because of the presence of the railways and the army bases.

There are changes to front doors and window glazing, but the houses in Headley Road, Liphook, are otherwise the same as when they were built (below). Unfortunately, no allowance was made for car ownership in 1912. Electricity and parking restrictions are the only significant innovations.

Map 29 The parish of Martin was only taken from Wiltshire and added to Hampshire in 1895, but the transfer has given the county some extremely interesting archaeological features, such as Bokerley Dyke. Martin Down, on the eastern edge of Cranborne Chase, is happily still unenclosed, open chalk downland, now preserved by the County Council, and one of the best places in Hampshire in which to see the landscape much as it was in the eighteenth century. Inset is a small area of plantation woodland that lies to the west of Ibsley (opposite).

Map 30 (page 88) Until Martin and Damerham were added to Hampshire in 1894, Rockbourne formed an isolated projection into Wiltshire. The River Avon here divides the chalk downs on the west from the clays and sands of the New Forest, and its pastures provided for a line of villages and a larger market centre at Fordingbridge. Between Breamore and Hale, the network of lines in the valley shows where a water-meadow system had been created, with a tissue of artificial watercourses controlled by sluices so that the land could be flooded ('drowned') in late

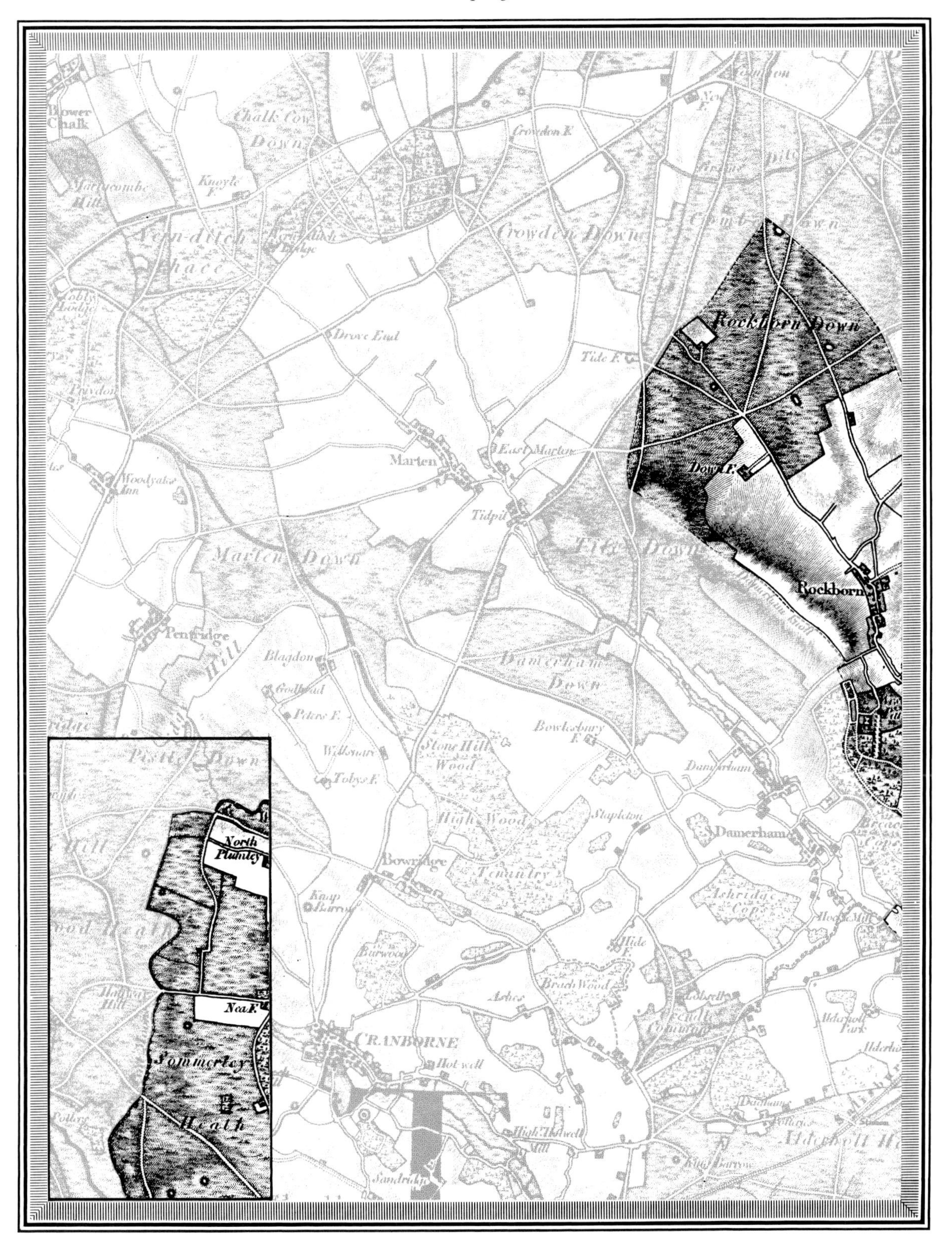
Bower Chalk
Chalk Cow Down
Crowdon F.
Knoyle F.
Crowden Down
Rockborn Down
Drove End
Tide F.
Marten
East Marten
Woodyates Inn
Down F.
Tidpit
Marten Down
Rockborn
Pentridge
Hill
Blagdon
Damerham Down
Bowlesbury F.
Tobys F.
Stone Hill Wood
Damerham
Stapleton
High Wood
Damerham
Bowridge
Tenantry
Knap Barrow
North Plumley
Burwood
Hide F.
Brach Wood
Alderholt Park
CRANBORNE
Hot well
Sommerley
Heath
Sandridge

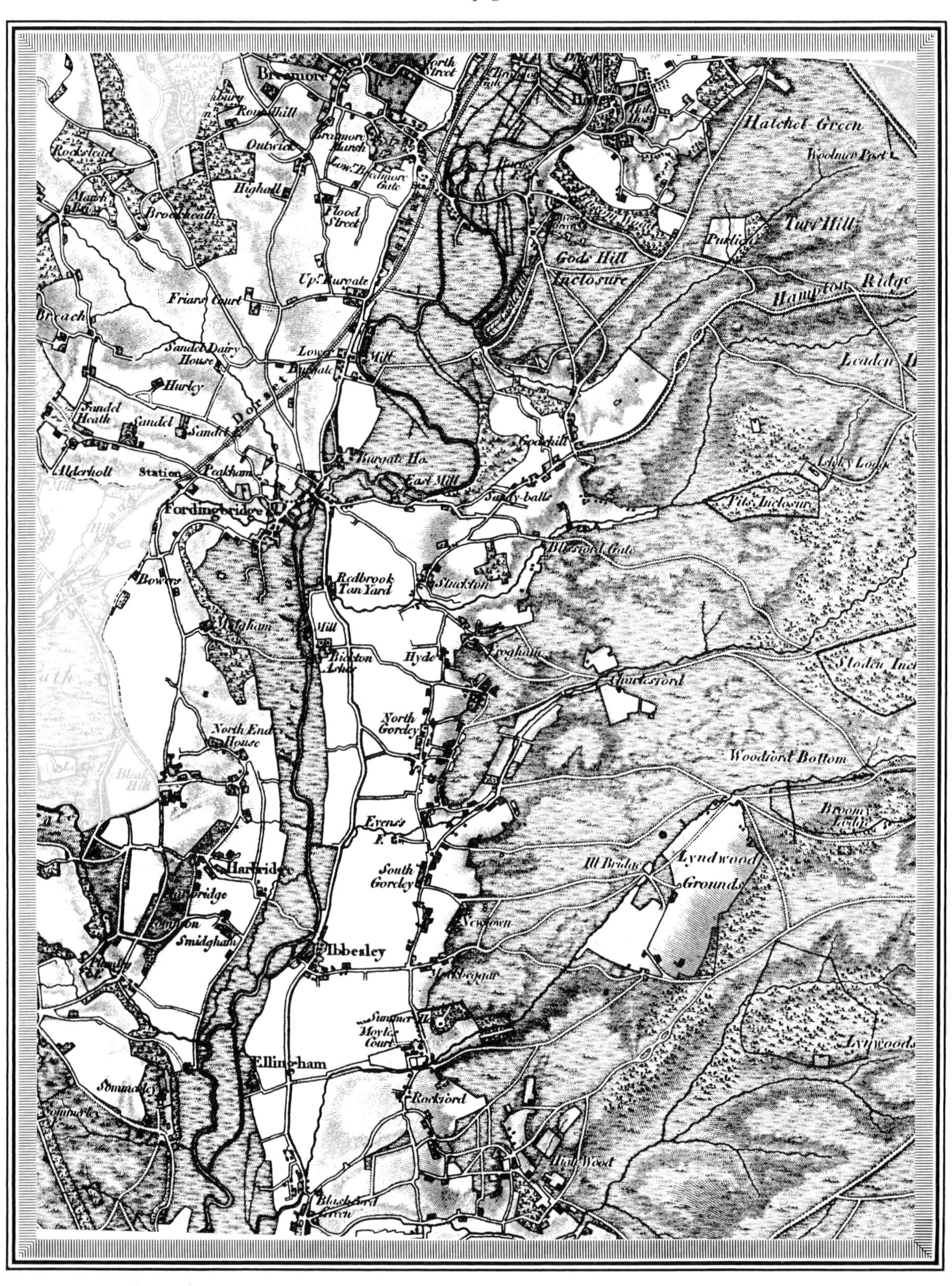
Breamore
North Street
Rockstead
Roundhill
Outwick
Breamore Marsh
Highall
Brookheath
Flood Street
Upr. Burgate
Friars Court
Breach
Sandel Dairy House
Hurley
Sandel Heath
Sandel
Alderholt
Station
Peakham
Dorset
Mill
Burgate Ho.
East Mill
Fordingbridge
Hatchet Green
Woolmer Post
Turf Hill
Gods Hill
Inclosure
Hampton Ridge
Godshill
Sandy balls
Ashley Lodge
Pits Inclosure
Blissford Gate
Bowers
Redbrook
Tan Yard
Stuckton
Mill
Bickton
Ashes
Hyde
Frogham
North End
House
North
Gorcley
Woodford Bottom
Evens's
F.
Broomy
Lodge
Ill Bridge
Lyndwood
Grounds
Harbridge
South
Gorcley
Newtown
Smidgham
Ibbesley
Moyles
Court
Ellingham
Lynwoods
Rockford
Blashford
Green

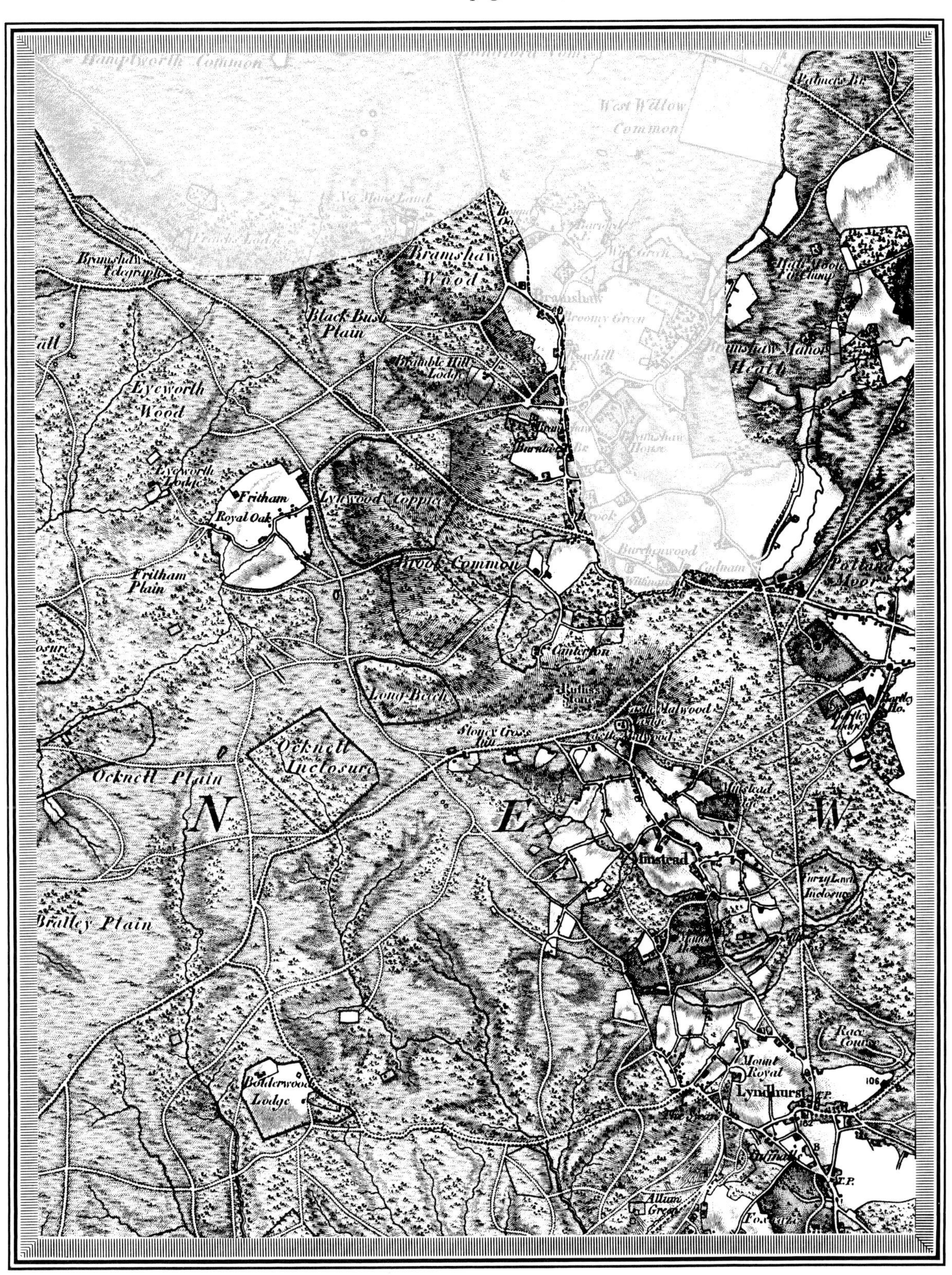
Bramshaw Telegraph
Bramshaw Wood
Black Bush Plain
Eyeworth Wood
Eyeworth Lodge
Fritham
Royal Oak
Fritham Plain
Lynwood Coppice
Brook Common
Long Beech
Canterton
Ocknell Inclosure
Ocknell Plain
Stoney Cross
Castle Malwood
Minstead
Bolderwood Lodge
Mount Royal
Lyndhurst
Allum Green
Bramshaw Manor Heath
N
E
W

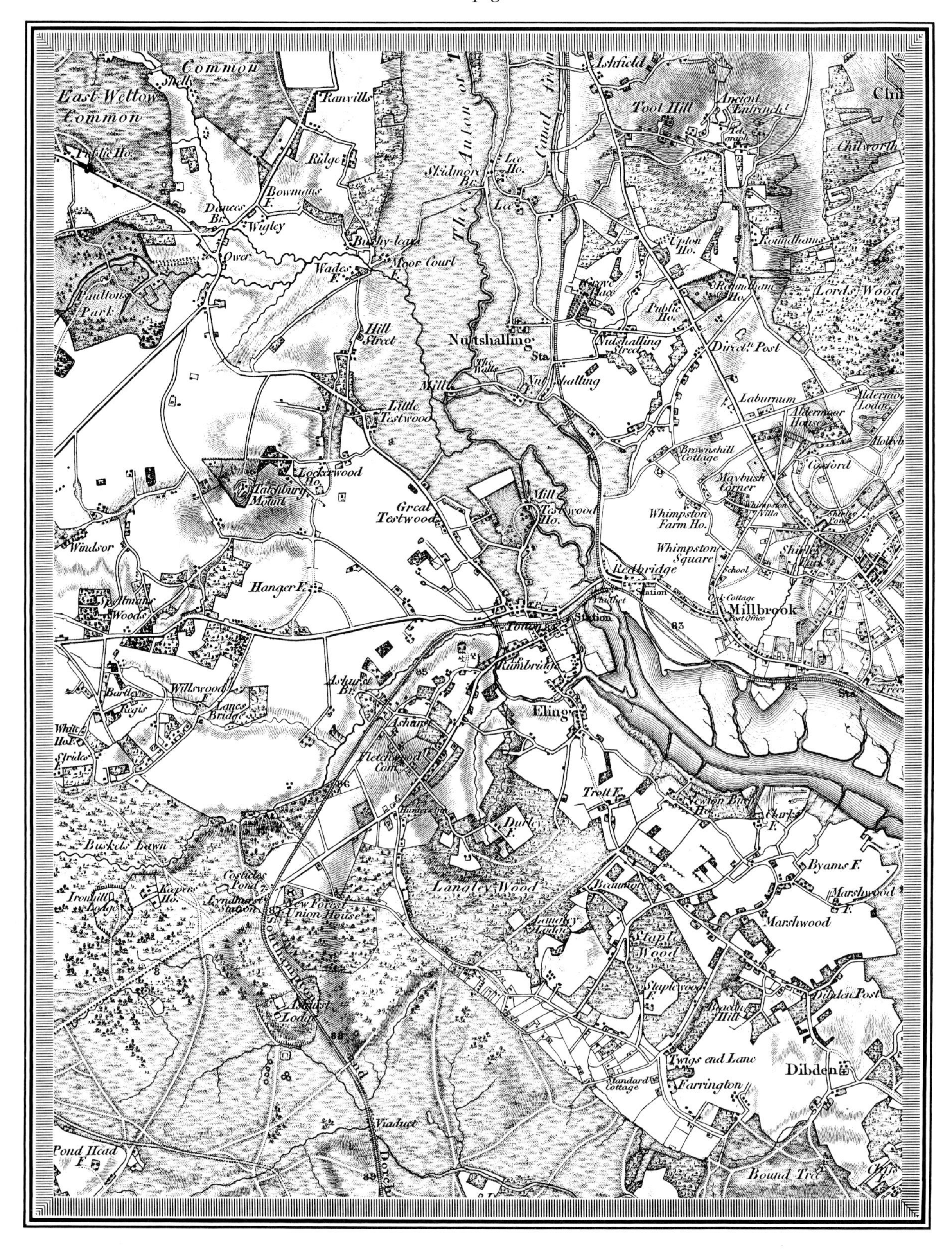
East Wellow Common
Ranvills
Ridge
Bowmans F.
Wigley
Ower
Paultons Park
Moor Court F.
Hill Street
Little Testwood
Lockerwood Ho.
Hatchbury Mount
Great Testwood
Windsor
Hanger F.
Ashurst Br.
Willswood F.
Lanes Bridge
Busket Lawn
Keepers Ho.
Lyndhurst Station
New Forest Union House
Langley Wood
Viaduct
Pond Head F.
Nutshalling
Toot Hill
Chilworth
Upton Ho.
Roundhams
Lords Wood
Public Ho.
Laburnum
Aldermoor House
Brownshill Cottage
Maybush Corner
Whimpston Farm Ho.
Whimpston Square
Redbridge
Station
Millbrook
Totton
Rumbridge
Eling
Trott F.
Newton Bury Ho.
Durley F.
Byams F.
Marshwood F.
Marshwood
Staple Wood
Staplewood F.
Dibden Post
Twigs end Lane
Dibden
Farrington
Standard Cottage
Bound Tree

ROMSEY
Embley Park School
Hall Copse
Burnt Grove
Pauncefoot Ho
Broadlands Ho
Broadlands Fm
Whitenap
Baddesley Common
Nutburn
Great Covert
Ryedown Fm
Warners Fm
Kentford Lake
Embley Wood
Hammonds
Semple Ho
Ranvilles Fm
Yewtree Copse
Cutters Barn
Lee Ho
Ashfield
Hoe Fm
North Baddesley
Telegraph Wood
Toothill
Chilworth Old Village
Chilworth Manor
Chilworth
Fighting Cocks Fm
Shelley Common
Shelley
Ridge
Lee Park Fm
Lee
Moorcourt Copse
Nightingale Wood
Chilworth Tower
Chilworth Common
Home Fm
Hotel
Wigley Country Park
Ower
Wade Park Fm
Wade Hill Fm
Moorcourt
Test Way
Grove Place
Upton
Rownhams
Lord's Wood
Nursling Ho
Colbury Ho
Broadlands Lake
El Sub Sta
Nursling
Hillstreet
Brooke's Hill
Stonyford
Calmore Croft Fm
Copythorne Common
Weir
Nursling Mill
Manor Ho Fm
Testwood Ho
Little Testwood Fm
Hillyfields
Lord's Hill
Sports Centre
Aldermoor
Maybush
Coxford
Shirley Warren
Upper Shirley
Southampton Common
Shorn Hill
Loperwood
Barrow Hill
Copythorne
Calmore
Tatchbury Mount Hospital
Tatchbury Manor Ho
Copied Hall Fm
Winsor
Hammond's Green
Testwood
Redbridge
TOTTON
Civic Centre
Ordnance Survey Office
Wimpson
Old Shirley
Shirley
Hazel Fm
Hanger Fm
Bartley
Bartley Grange
Netley Marsh
Carlton Ho
Ashurst Bridge
Brokenford
Eling Mill
Eling
Millbrook
Freemantle
SOUTHAMPTON
Bartley Manor
Willswood Fm
Bartley Water
Cemy
Fletchwood
Goldenhayes
Woodlands
Fovers
Hotel
Foxhills
Hounsdown
Trotts
Docks
RIVER TEST
Power Station
Woodlands Lodge
Busketts Wood
Busketts Lawn Inclosure
Fletchwood Copse
Hunters Inn Hill
Colbury Fm
Colbury
Langley Fm
Durley Fm
Bury Fm
Works
Cork's Fm
Cracknore Hard
Royal Pier
Town Quay
Ashurst
Pooksgreen
Byam's Ho
Ironshill Lodge
Ironshill Inclosure
Rushpole Wood
LYNDHURST ROAD STA
Deerleap Fm
Langley Lodge
Marchwood
Pumpfield Fm
Churchplace Inclosure
Butterfly Farm
Langley Wood
Lodgehill Cottage
Mallard Wood
Ashurst Wood
Ashurst Lodge
Deerleap Inclosure
Staplewood Hill
Marchwood Park
Veal's Fm
Dunces Arch
Fox Hill
Longdown Inclosure
New Fm
Church Fm
Lock's Fm
West Cliffe Hall (Hotel)
White Moor
Cumulus
Earthwork
Cumuli
Peel Hill
Foxhill Fm
Birchlands Fm
The Old Manor
Dibden
Depedene
Matley Heath
Matley Wood
Ipley Inclosure
Applemore
Park Pale
Beaulieu River
Marchwood Inclosure
Pondhead Inclosure
Parkhill (Hotel)
Matley Bog
Matley Passage
Decoy Pond Fm
Ipley Manor
Sports Centre
Mullin's Fm
Purlieu Ho
Church Place
Yew Tree Heath
Little Holmhill Inclosure
Black Down
Dibden Bottom
Denny Inclosure
BEAULIEU ROAD STA
Hotel
Dibden Purlieu
Park Hill
Denny

winter, keeping frost off the early grass for sheep to eat, and again in the summer to bring on hay crops, water-borne particles from the chalk hills enriching the soil. The railway is the Salisbury branch to connect to the London and South-Western near Wimborne. The area to the west of Ibsley is inset on the map opposite.

Map 31 (page 89) The northern part of the New Forest has large areas of open, boggy moorland, with a number of inclosures of woodland; some stands of oak trees were created by the Crown in the eighteenth century. Fritham and Minsted are instances of small areas of farmland surrounded by the open forest which probably already existed in the eleventh century when Forest Law was imposed. Lyndhurst was a more important place as it had a much-used royal hunting-lodge in the Middle Ages. Another royal connection seems to be The Rufus Stone, supposedly where King William II was shot by an (ill-directed?) arrow in 1100; in fact, his death probably occurred in the southern part of the Forest. Near the stone, the main east-west road is the turnpike of 1758, now the A31.

Map 32 (page 90) The River Test creates a wide valley that opens out into the tidal Southampton Water at Redbridge. (The bridge is actually grey stone. The name was originally 'ford at the reeds'—the change to bridge came at the time of the first of many road improvements there.) 'The Walls' at 'Nutshalling' (Nursling) is a little explored Iron Age fort, and there are others shown at Tatchbury Mount and on Toot Hill. The 'Telegraph' on the latter was one of a line of signalling stations, and was set up in 1806; by semaphore or morse code, messages for military purposes could be sent from London to Plymouth by this system. The streams that met at Shirley produced ponds that supplied an iron-works (some of the streets shown in this area were added to the map after 1811; the railways are also later additions). South of Eling, there is a fringe of coastal marsh, wood and farmland, and then the New Forest's boundary is reached. The location of Eling's famous tide-mill can be seen on the bridge and causeway spanning the creek. 'T.P.' at Totton stands for 'Turn-pike', one of the toll-gates for travellers using the roads improved during the previous hundred years.

Modern map 32 (previous page) The growth of suburbia around Totton is the most obvious change, and it is ironic to see that what had been the new development around Shirley is now called 'Old Shirley'. Motorways have now arrived, and lakes and ponds in the Test Valley show how development has led to large-scale gravel digging, so that The Walls no longer appear, although the forts at Toot Hill and Tatchbury are still recognizable. The north side of Southampton Water has had most of its mud-flats taken up for Millbrook docks, but the south side has fared better, except where Marchwood power station has been built (the earlier 'Marshwood' was more appropriate). Woodland has survived remarkably well, even though not protected by the New Forest, within the boundaries of which little change can be seen. Eling Hill is now marked: it is of course one of the few working mills in the country, a great contrast to the number in the early nineteenth century.

Map 33 (opposite) Southampton had an era as a seaside resort, which only began to give way to industrial developments after the Napoleonic Wars, more rapidly after the coming of the railway in 1840 (the Docks and some of the streets are also additions to this map, as of course is Victoria Hospital). The

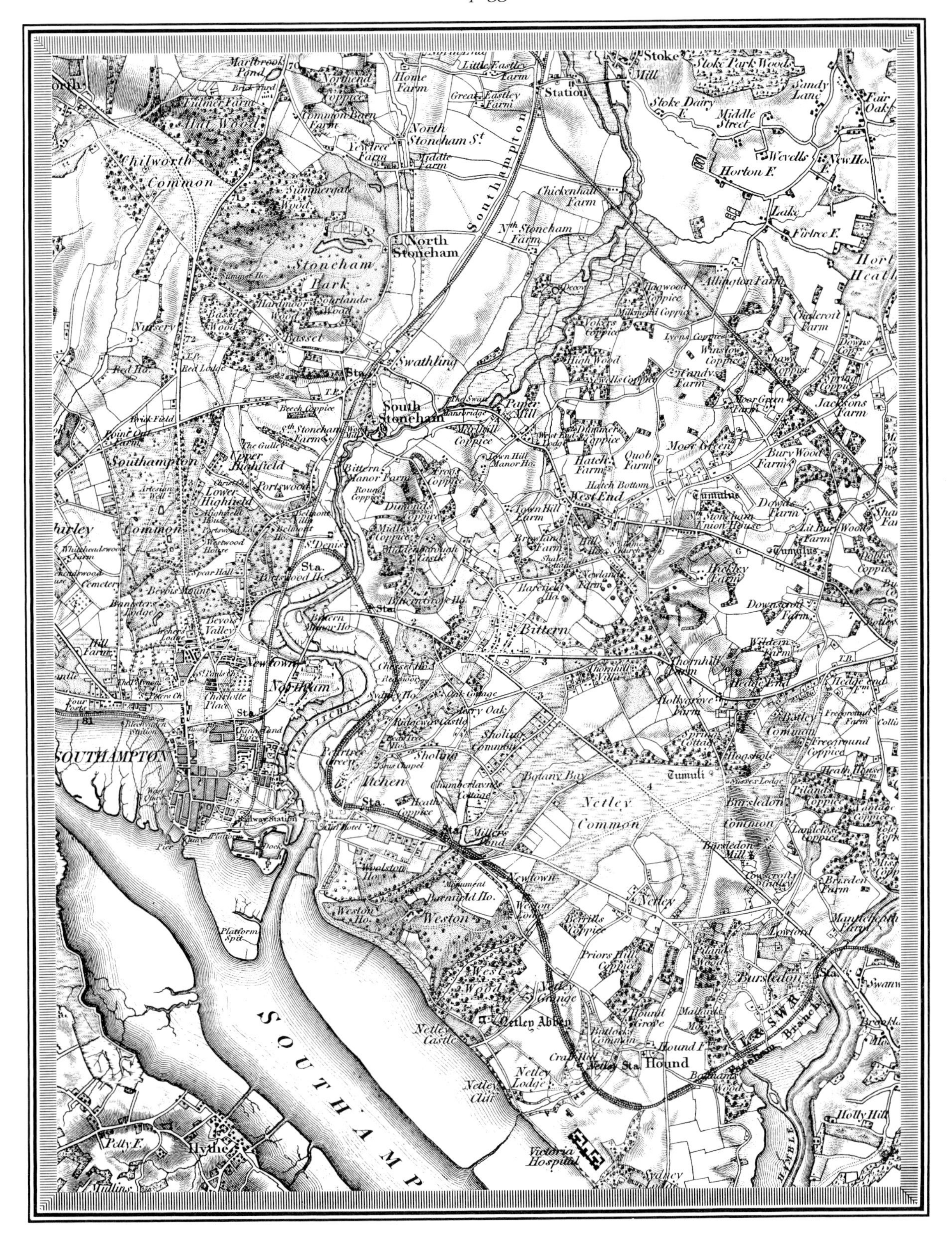
SOUTHAMPTON
Southampton
Chilworth Common
Stoneham Park
North Stoneham
South Stoneham
Swathling
Bassett
Portswood
Highfield
Bevois Valley
Northam
Newtown
St. Denis
Bittern
West End
Moor Green
Hedge End
Netley Common
Sholing
Itchen
Weston
Netley Abbey
Netley Castle
Netley Cliff
Netley Lodge
Hound
Bursledon
Victoria Hospital
Hythe
Stoke Park Woods
Fair Oak
Horton F.
Allington Farm
Chickenhall Farm
Paper Mill
Botany Bay
Miller's Pond
Woolston Ho.
River Itchen
Hamble
L. & S.W.R.

sea still came up to the medieval walls on the west side. A ring of large houses shows that the town was fashionable; most have now gone. Southampton Common is still with us, however, preserved from development by its legal status. At Bitterne, the Roman fort had been built over, but its defences can be recognized from the straight streets across the peninsula. East of the Itchen was poor-quality land, made up of sands, clays and plateau gravel patches, divided into small farms, with much common land and many small woods. Netley Abbey was a thirteenth-century Cistercian foundation, Netley Castle a gunnery fort of Henry VIII's time. Eastleigh did not yet exist, except for a few farms: this 'railway town' was not developed until the 1890s.

Detail map 33 (overleaf) The Ordnance Survey's first large-scale map of Southampton was one in a series of maps of the centres of major towns subject to rapid growth and change in the 1840s. By the end of the nineteenth century, the area north of St Michael's Square had become a notorious slum, and a Clearance Scheme was initiated in 1895: this map shows the density of buildings in that area and in the French Street/Bugle Street sector. The near-circle of streets and buildings north of Simnel Street marks the site of the medieval castle's motte: part of the outer

Sir John Dawtry rebuilt this timber-framed house in Southampton's fish market at the end of the fifteenth century. By the end of the nineteenth century, overcrowding and insanitary conditions had made this area a notorious slum, which in 1895 became an early exercise in town planning, with the St Michael's Improvement Scheme. The buildings that crowd against the big house in this photograph give a good idea of contemporary conditions (see page 116).

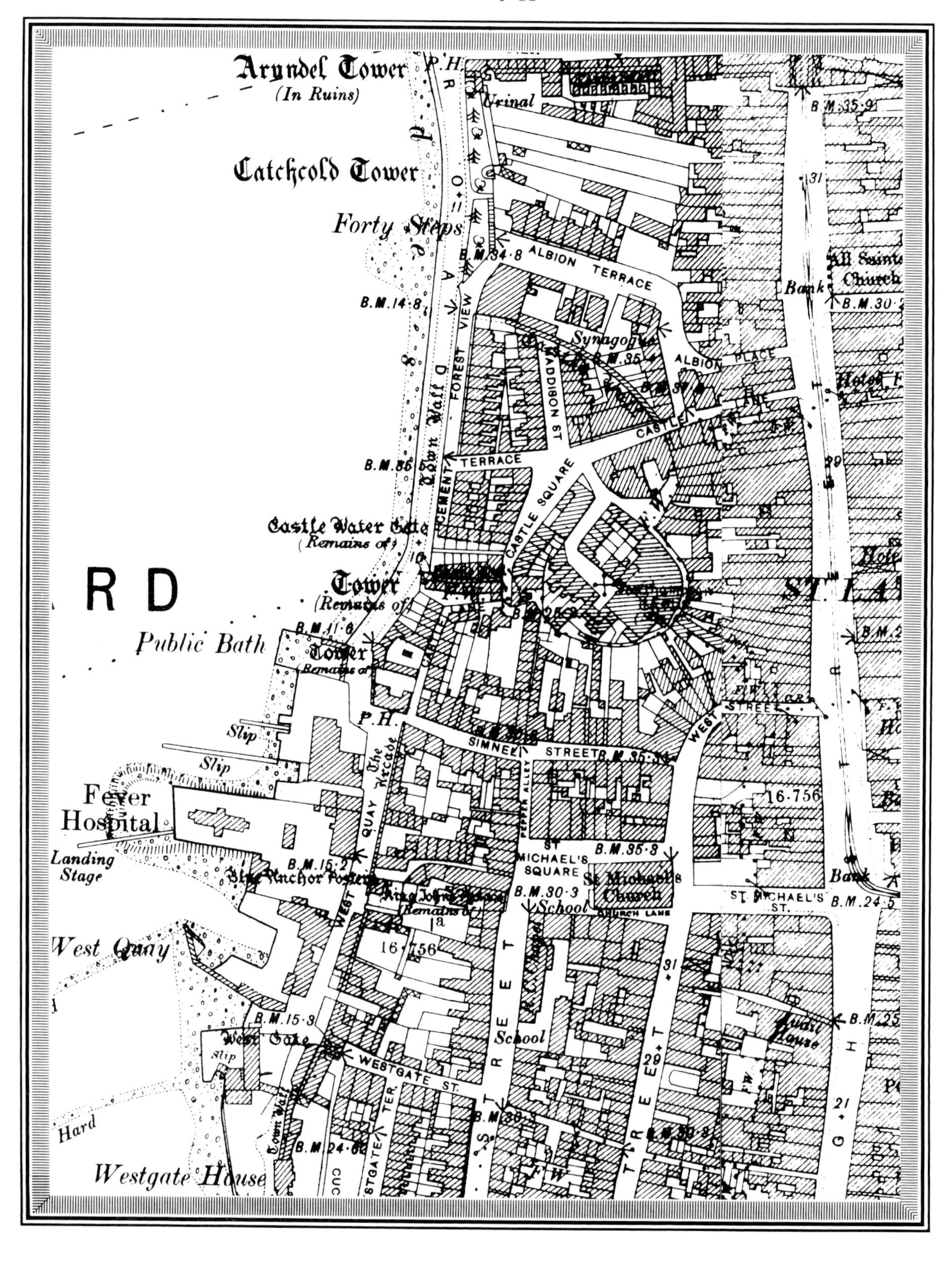
Arundel Tower
(In Ruins)
Catchcold Tower
Forty Steps
Urinal
Albion Terrace
All Saints Church
Bank
Synagogue
Albion Place
Addison St
Forest View
Town Wall
Castle
Terrace
Castle Square
Cement
Castle Water Gate
(Remains of)
Tower
(Remains of)
R D
Public Bath
Tower
Remains of
P.H.
Slip
Slip
The Arcade
Simnel Street
Pepper Alley
West Street
Fever Hospital
Landing Stage
West Quay
St Michael's Square
St Michael's Church
Church Lane
St Michael's St.
School
King John's Palace
(Remains of)
West Quay
Hard
West Gate
Slip
Westgate St.
Westgate Ter.
Town Wall
Westgate House
School
Street
Street
Audit House
High Street
Bank
16·756
16·756
B.M. 34·8
B.M. 14·8
B.M. 35·6
B.M. 11·6
B.M. 15·2
B.M. 15·3
B.M. 35·3
B.M. 30·3
B.M. 24·5
B.M. 35·9
B.M. 30·2

bailey wall is shown, at that time hidden from view by buildings and backyards but now revealed and fronting onto a car park. The only significant changes to Southampton's medieval street layout inside the walls have occurred in this area, with the widening of French Street and its extension northwards as Castle Way.

Along the main High Street, many of the commercial properties had retained their medieval boundaries, narrow on the frontages and with long strips to the rear for outbuildings, privies and gardens; some still do. The tramway ran along the centre of High Street and under the medieval Bargate, the buildings on both sides of which were not demolished until the 1930s. More damage was done by the Blitz in 1940 which destroyed, for instance, All Saints' Church. This was one of the five medieval parish churches in the walled town; none had a graveyard around it, as bodies had to be taken to the ancient Mother-Church of St Mary, outside the town, for burial.

On the west side, the sea still came up to the foot of the town walls at high tide; all this is now dry land, the result of the 1923 Act obtained by the Southern Railway Company. A small reclamation scheme had taken place in 1871, when the Local Board of Health built a hospital in which smallpox cases could be isolated. It is presumably because the health authorities retained their ownership of that land that the site became the city's first crematorium in 1932, and is still a mortuary. North of the hospital, the Public Baths date from 1895, and were another contribution to improving living conditions: they have now become the covered swimming-pool.

The pier at Hythe in 1905 (above), from the end of which the ferry crossed to Southampton. A liner is passing up Southampton Water to the docks. Most of the other working craft were still powered by sail and oar.

Hythe Pier still leads out to the ferry, but ocean liners are now a much rarer sight. On the other side of Southampton Water, the tower blocks of flats show how the city has grown, threatening to become 'Solent City' from Totton to Portsea.

Map 34

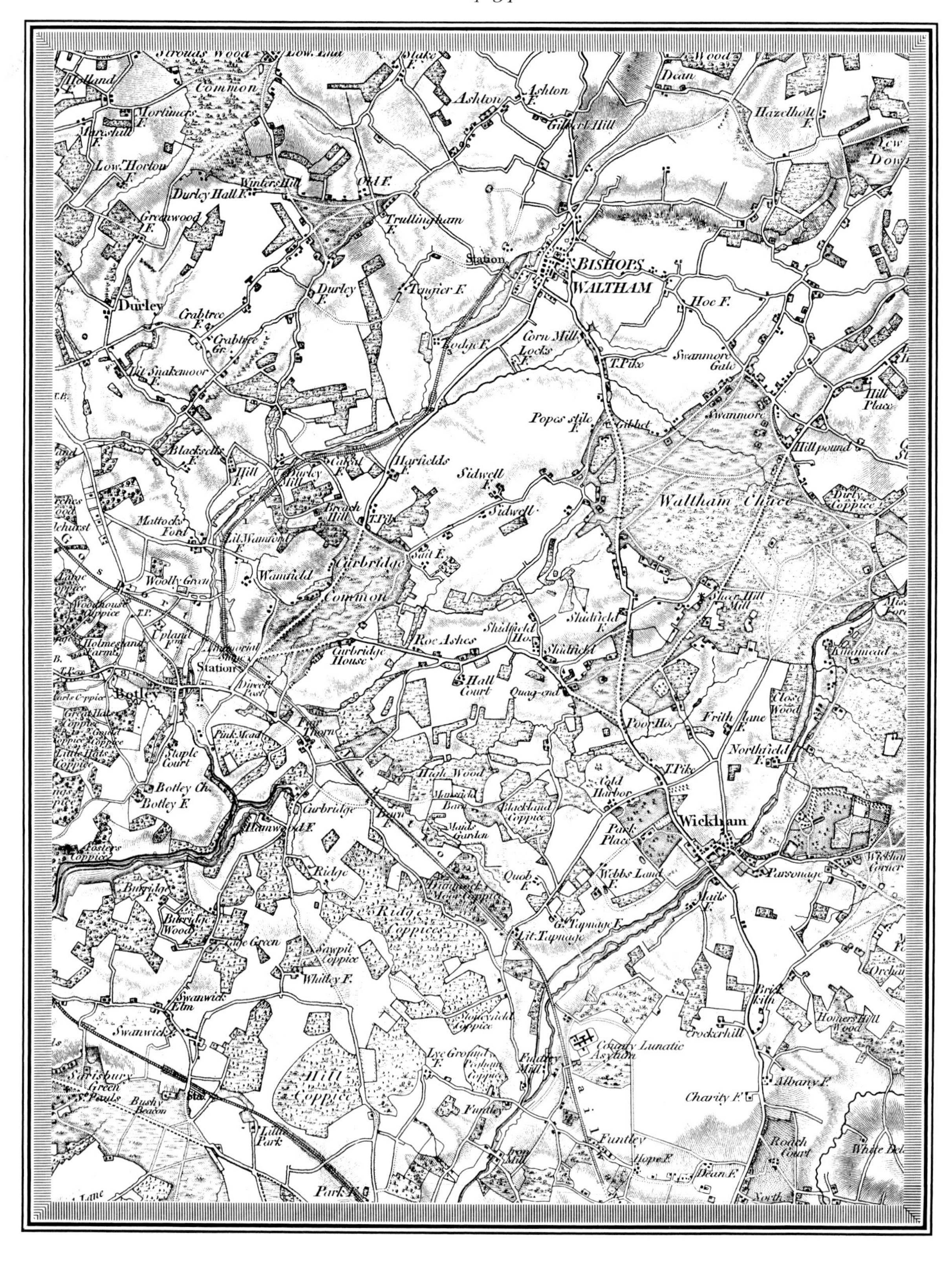

Common
Ashton
Ashton F.
Dean
Hazelholt F.
Mortimers F.
Low Horton F.
Winters Hill
Old F.
Durley Hall F.
Gilbert Hill
Greenwood F.
Trullingham F.
Station
BISHOPS
WALTHAM
Durley
Durley F.
Tangier F.
Hoe F.
Crabtree F.
Crabtree Gr.
Lodge F.
Corn Mill
Locks F.
T.Pike
Swanmore Gate
Lit Snakemoor F.
Popes stile F.
Gibbet
Swanmore
Hill Place
Blacksells F.
Hill F.
Durley Mill
Hartfields
Sidwell F.
Hillpound
Breach Hill
T.Pike
Sidwell
Waltham Chace
Dirty Coppice
Mattocks Ford
Lit.Wamford F.
Curbridge
Wamfield
Woolly Green
Common
Sheer Hill Mill
Woodhouse Coppice
Upland F.
Holmegrand Farm
Roe Ashes
Shidfield Ho.
Shidfield F.
Shidfield
Kingsmead
Station
Curbridge House
Hall Court
Quag-end
Botley
Poor Ho.
Frith lane F.
Close Wood
Northfield F.
Pink Mead
Staple Court
High Wood
T.Pike
Cold Harbor
Botley Ch.
Botley F.
Curbridge
Blackland Coppice
Maids Garden
Wickham
Park Place
Parsonage
Fosters Coppice
Ridge
Quob F.
Webbs Land F.
Burridge F.
Burridge Wood
Ridge Coppices
Gt Tapnage F.
Lit.Tapnage
Sawpit Coppice
Whitley F.
Swanwick Elm
Swanwick
Brick kiln
Homers Hill Wood
Crockerhill
County Lunatic Asylum
Funtley Mill
Hill Coppice
Sarisbury Green
Bushy Beacon
Albany F.
Charity F.
Funtley
Little Park
Funtley
Roach Court
White Del
Hope F.
Dean F.
Park F.
North

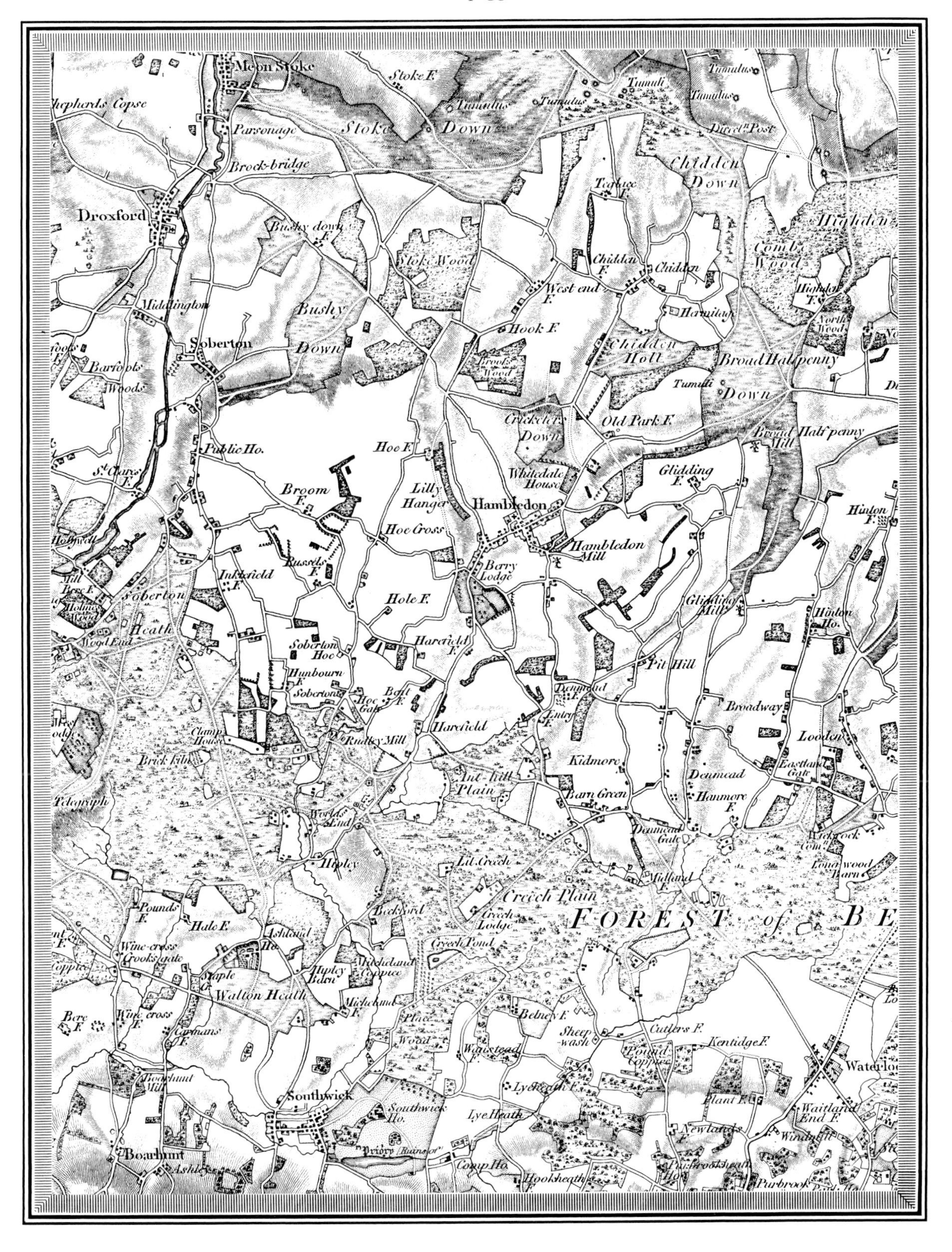
Meon Stoke
Stoke F.
Tumulus
Tumuli
Parsonage
Stoke
Down
Directn Post
Brock-bridge
Chidden
Down
Droxford
Bushy down F.
Stoke Wood
Chidden F.
Chidden
Comb Wood
West end F.
Hermitage
Middlington
Bushy
Down
Hook F.
Soberton
Chidden Holt
Broad Halfpenny
Down
Barfools
Woods
Brooks Wood
Tumuli
Crickleters Down
Old Park F.
Broad Halfpenny Mill
Public Ho.
Hoe F.
St. Clares F.
Whitedale House
Glidding F.
Broom F.
Lilly Hanger
Hambledon
Hinton F.
Hoe Cross
Hambledon Mill
Hollywell
Russels F.
Inkfield F.
Berry Lodge
Soberton
Hole F.
Glidding Mill
Holmes Wood
Heath
Wood End
Hinton Ho.
Soberton Hoe
Harefield F.
Hunbourn F.
Pit Hill
Soberton
Hoe Gate
Bent F.
Denmead
Entry F.
Broadway
Harefield
Rudley Mill
Loden
Clamp House
Brick kiln
Kidmore
Denmead
Eastland Gate
Ant-hill Plain
Barn Green
Hanmore F.
Telegraph
Worlds End
Denmead Gate
Wickrock Com.
Long wood Barn
Hipley
Lit. Creech
Midland
Creech Plain
Pounds F.
Beckford
Creech Lodge
FOREST of BE
Hale F.
Ashland Ho.
Creech Pond
Wine-cross
Crooks gate
Michelands Coppice
Staple
Hipley Bdn
Walton Heath
Michelands F.
Bere F.
Wine cross F.
Carmans F.
Place Wood
Belney F.
Sheep-wash
Cutlers F.
Kentidge F.
Waitstead F.
Pound Coppice
Waterloo
Boarhunt Mill
Lyeheath F.
Plant F.
Southwick
Southwick Ho.
Waitland End F.
Lye Heath
Newlands
Windmill
Boarhunt
Priory (Ruins of)
Ashley
Comp Ho.
Hookheath
Purbrookheath Ho.
Purbrook

There is now a gap where the house's gable-end on to the street stood in 1908 (page 19), but otherwise the houses in Winchester Road, Wickham, are almost exactly as before, though some amalgamation has taken place. The inn is still there at the far end, and even the garden on the left still comes right out to the road.

Map 34 (page 98) Bishop's Waltham became an estate of the Bishops of Winchester in 904, and parts of their great palace survive on the west side of the small town which served it. The pond on the north side was the bishop's fishpond. Waltham Chase suggests a large deer-park, but in fact a much more important park had once surrounded the whole of Bishop's Waltham, although it is scarcely recognizable on the map. Further south, Funtley Iron Mill shows that Portsmouth was nearby, with its demand for munitions, and the brick kiln at Crocker Hill shows growing demand for building materials. The large number of corn mills suggests the supplying of flour to the navy. The gibbet on Waltham Chase is a grim reminder that hangings were still public spectacles.

Map 35 (previous page) The Forest of Bere was one of the great medieval oak forests, and it is perhaps surprising to see how much remained despite the demands of Portsmouth dockyard for the building of England's wooden walls. The brick kiln and clamp house on Soberton Heath were presumably also supplying Portsmouth, but this was still mainly an agricultural area. Broad Halfpenny Down is famous for its late eighteenth-century cricket matches. The windmills on its southern edge show that water power was not available in the immediate area. In the south 'Waterloo' is an addition to the map of the 1890s, as its battle-proud name suggests; the modern 'Waterlooville' is an attempt to be smart. The original name was from an inn, the 'Heroes of Waterloo'.

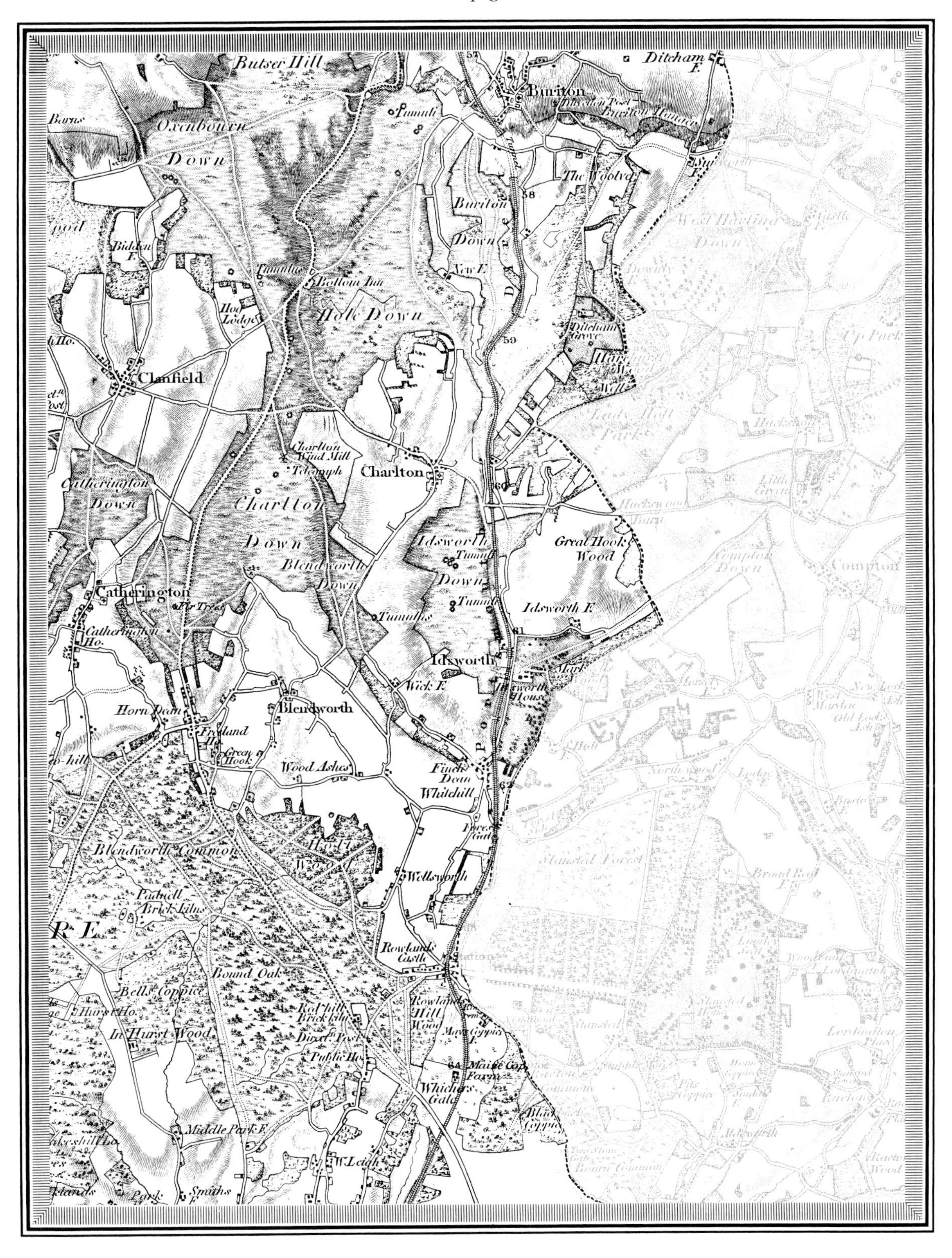
Butser Hill
Ditcham F.
Buriton
Oxenbourn
Down
Tumuli
The Woolve
Buriton
Down
West Harting Down
Bidden F.
Tumulus
Bottom Inn
Hole Down
New F.
Hoe Lodge
Ditcham Grove
Up Park
Clanfield
Lady Holt Park
Charlton Wind Mill
Telegraph
Charlton
Catherington Down
Charlton
Down
Great Hook Wood
Idsworth
Down
Blendworth
Down
Compton Down
Compton
Catherington
Fir Tree
Tumulus
Idsworth F.
Catherington Ho.
Idsworth
Wick F.
Idsworth House
Horn Dam
Blendworth
West Marden
Old Lodge
Frogland
Green Hook
Wood Ashes
Finch Dean
Whitehill
North wood
Lodge F.
Blendworth Common
Holt Wood
Stansted Forest
Wellsworth
Broad Reed F.
Padnell Brick kilns
Rowlands Castle
Bound Oak
Bells Coppice
Hurst Ho.
In Hurst Wood
Red hill Brick kilns
Rowlands Hill Wood
Direct Post
Public Ho.
Maize Coppice
Maize Cop Farm
Whichers Gate
Stansted
Lordington Place
Racton
Black Coppice
Middle Park F.
W. Leigh
Aldsworth
Smiths F.
Park

Map 36 (page 101) The south-east part of Hampshire has countryside much like that of Sussex, and it may well be that this area looked to Chichester as its centre rather than to Winchester, at least in Roman times. Important archaeological work has been done at Charlton: there was a Saxon settlement on top of what in the nineteenth century was the completely open Charlton Down. The many tumuli show Bronze Age activity—one recent theory is that Bronze Age people over-exploited the chalk soils, making them increasingly infertile, and that the early Saxons repeated the same mistake. William Cobbett saw it as happening again in the early nineteenth-century—and some see it repeated with modern 'prairie' farming which relies entirely on applications of nitrates to keep the soil usable.

Map 37 Hampshire lost Ashley Heath and Hurn Common to Dorset in 1974, no great loss, one might think on seeing the huge areas of infertile heathland shown on the nineteenth-century map. But these areas now contain Hurn Airport and parts of north Bournemouth. The gibbet was, typically, in isolated land near the county boundary.

A view of Droxford in 1895 (opposite above) shows a typical downland village, the houses clustering in the stream valley, with the chalk downs almost without buildings. Farming was still almost entirely done by hand—even steam-ploughs and traction engines were uncommon.

Tree growth now obscures the 1895 view of Droxford (opposite below). In the village itself, there are more mature trees than in the last century, despite the loss of elms. Consequently the village looks less raw, and no larger than a hundred years ago. It is rare now to see anyone working in a field: modern machinery demands huge fields like that in the foreground.

Map 37

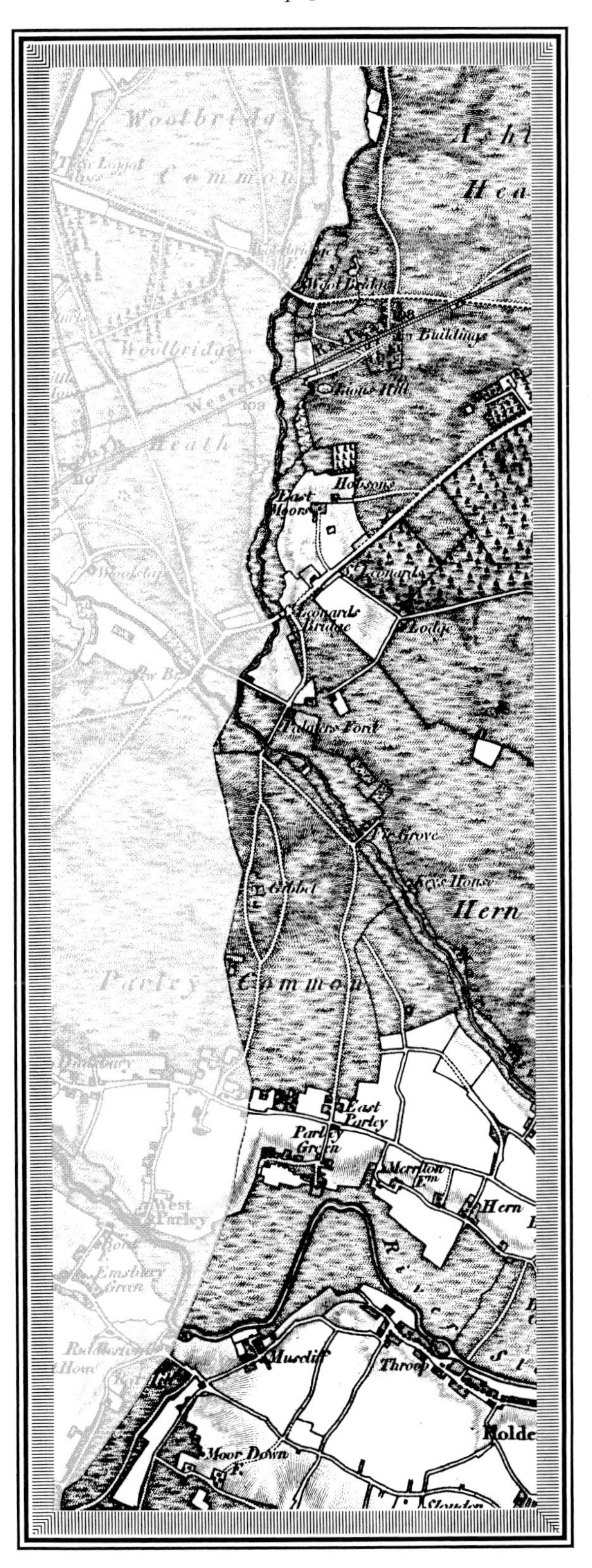

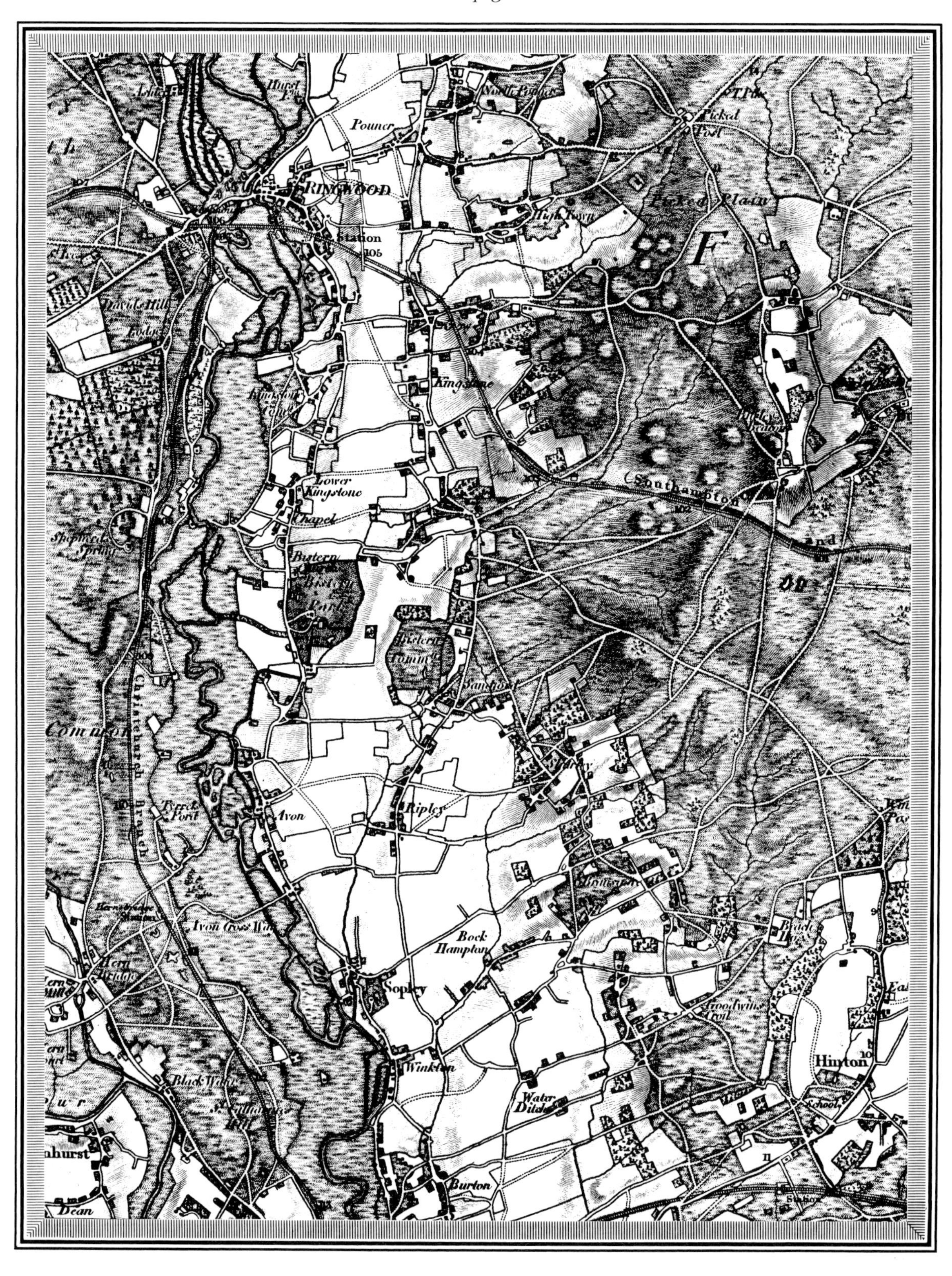
RINGWOOD
Station
Pouner
North Pouner
Picked Post
Picked Plain
High Town
Kingstone
Lower Kingstone
Chapel
Bistern Park
Bistern Common
Southampton
Ripley
Avon
Sopley
Bock Hampton
Winkton
Water Ditch
Burton
Hinton
School
Goodwins Post
Common
Christchurch Branch
Hern Bridge
Dean

Map 39

O
R
E
Inclosure
New Park
Queen Bower
Whitley
Wood
Brockenhurst
Bridge
Over Fm
Station
Wilverley
Inclosure
Wilverley
Lodge
Hinchelsey
Holmsley
Lodge
Holmsley
Inclosure
Wooton
Inclosure
Set Thorns
Wooton
Marlbro
Deep
Marlpit Oak
Roydon
Setley
Common
North
Sway
Station
Arnolds
Pennington
Silver Street
Beck
Hill
Bashley
Station
L.&S.W.R.
Brockenhurst and Christchurch
Milton
Pennington
Common
St Austins

GIVE WAY
ANGLIA
The Raj Doot Tandoori
LICENSED INDIAN RESTAURANT
HOURS OF OPENING SUN-SAT
RINGWOOD (04254) 2196
LICENSED RESTAURANT
4.99

Map 38 (page 104) Ringwood is really *Rimucwude*, probably the 'boundary wood', a reference perhaps to its location on the edge of the New Forest, where a steep slope comes down from the barren uplands into the Avon valley. Ringwood grew during the Middle Ages as a market town close to the river crossing. The Avon itself makes a fringe of more fertile ground between the Forest and the sandy heaths that reach on to and surround Poole Harbour; the river is now the county boundary down to Sopley. The east-west railway was the Southampton–Dorchester line, known because of its twisting route through the Forest as 'Castleman's Corkscrew', Castleman being a Wimborne solicitor and one of the line's promoters. It was used by through trains, rather than the later Christchurch–Bournemouth line, but it was closed in 1964, the branch line south to Christchurch having closed in 1935.

Map 39 (page 105) Because the southern part of this section of the map is outside the New Forest, it has been subject to much more development, particularly around Milton and to a lesser extent Sway. The inclosures within the Forest around Burley and Brockenhurst have also been built up, because land inside them was privately owned. Smaller open inclosures, such as Hincherley Farm, may be medieval 'vaccaries', pastoral farms theoretically specialising in cattle, often recognisable from their partly rounded boundaries. The wooded inclosures may have been planted by the Crown, and were surrounded with hedges and fences in an attempt to keep out the deer—and thus also the commoners' stock, leading to conflict between the graziers' interests and the Crown's.

Map 40 (overleaf) The great Cistercian abbey of Beaulieu once dominated this part of the Forest. King John founded it at the beginning of the thirteenth century, donating the site of a royal hunting-lodge and all the land on the west side of the Beaulieu River (then the Otter) down to the sea, with its western border from Sowley and East End up to Penerley Gate; the northern border is a largely surviving boundary bank. There was already some farmed land, but the monks improved their estate, some of their farms and granges still bearing their medieval names: 'Bouvery' is a corruption of 'Boveria', suggesting oxen or cattle; Sowley was 'South Leigh'. 'Bargery' was 'Bergerie', the centre from which the abbey's flocks of sheep were managed. After the Dissolution, some of this land was not maintained, and the lack of control over the area outside the royal Forest led to squatter development, for example at East End and Beck Heath, where all the houses are on the east side of the road, that is just outside the Forest boundary. Also prominent on the map are post-medieval industrial developments. Sowley Forge was a blast furnace for iron, founded in the late sixteenth century; using

Market day at Ringwood, c1890 (opposite above). The healthy-looking cattle had probably been reared on the lush meadows of the River Avon, which flows past the town. Wide market streets like this are often the result of the original laying-out of a town founded in the Middle Ages, each tenement having a fairly narrow street frontage to maximize the number of rents paid to the landowner.

Market day at Ringwood today (opposite below). Cattle are no longer sold in the town's streets, but otherwise the buying, selling and gossiping go on much as for centuries past. Shop-fronts have changed and windows have been enlarged, but, as in Odiham (page 68), it is remarkable how many of the buildings have survived the last hundred years.

Map 40

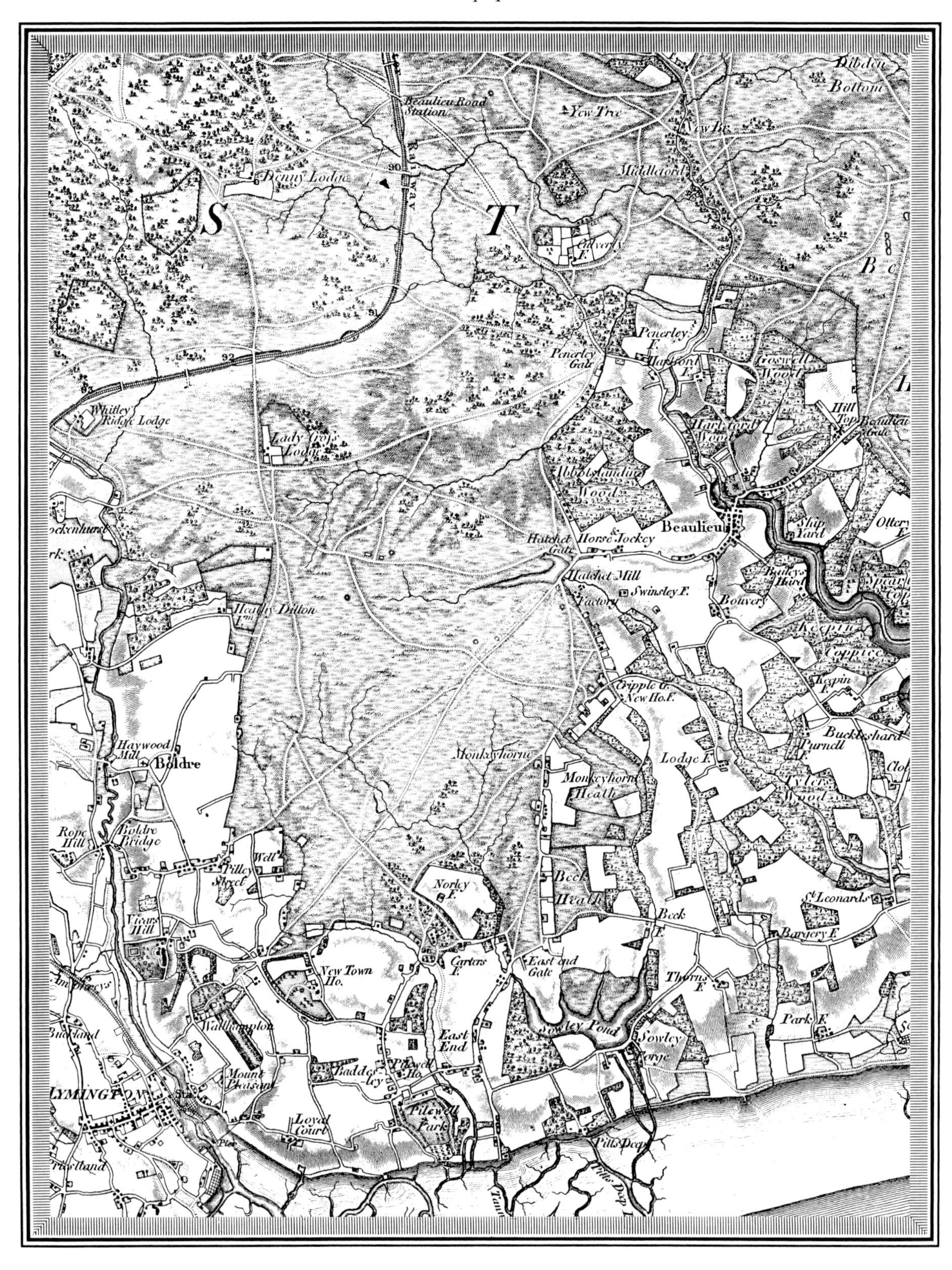
Dibden
Bottom
Beaulieu Road
Station
Yew Tree
Railway
Denny Lodge
S
T
Calvery F.
B
Peuerley F.
Peuerley Gate
Hartford F.
Croswell Wood
Hill Top
Whitley Ridge Lodge
Lady Cross Lodge
Hartford Wood
Wood
Beaulieu
Hatchet Gate
Horse & Jockey
Ship Yard
Hatchet Mill
Swinsley F.
Factory
Heathy Dilton
Coppice
Cripple G.
New Ho. F.
Haywood Mill
Boldre
Monkeyhorne
Lodge F.
Purnell F.
Monkeyhorne Heath
Tylers Wood
Rope Hill
Boldre Bridge
Well
Pilley Street
Norley F.
Beck Heath
St. Leonards
Vicars Hill
Beck F.
Bargery F.
New Town Ho.
Carters F.
East end Gate
Thorns F.
East End
Sowley Pond
Sowley
Park F.
Buckland
Mount Pleasant
Baddesley
Pilewell Ho.
Loyal Court
Pilewell Park
Pitts Deep

TON
WATER
Langdown
Lawn
Bullash F.
Flash Pond
Hardley
Cadland Park
Quay
Little Holbury
Gt. Holbury
Stonyford
Porters Lodge
Lodge
Fawley
Ashlet
Badminston F.
Fields Heath
Rowdown
Blackfield Com.
Owar Green
Oar Creek
Calshot Castle
Mopley
Langley
Gatewood F.
Eaglehurst
Stanswood Mill
Stanswood F.
Whitefield
Up. Exbury
Exbury
Blackland F.
East Hill
Lepe F.
Stone F.
Exbury F.
Lepe
Inchmery Cot.
Stone Point
Beaulieu River
Needs Oar Point
Blackwater
Satchell Farm
Hamble
Hamble Com.
Warsash
GURNET BAY
Egypt
WEST COWES
Debourn
Gurnard

Portsmouth dockyard from a battleship in 1910. In the background are the stone dry docks, the office buildings and the storehouses of the late eighteenth century. Maintaining the British Navy was a huge operation, as the clutter of cranes emphasizes (see page 117).

charcoal from the Forest, it became unprofitable when coal-fired furnaces were invented, but had brief resuscitation to meet the demand for armaments in the Napoleonic War, which is why it was still on the map. Forest timber also supplied the shipyard south of Beaulieu, and the factory at Hatchet produced textiles.

Map 41 (previous page) 'Salterns' are shown at Ginns Farm, Exbury, Calshot, Fawley and at the mouth of the Hamble. These used the tide to bring in seawater, from which salt was extracted by evaporation and by boiling in pans. Since this process was heavily taxed, costly in fuel and fraught with problems in the damp English climate, better transport meant that sea-salt was superseded by rock-salt mined in Cheshire and Worcestershire. Remains of some of the salterns can still be seen today. Bucklers Hard on the Beaulieu River was a ship-building centre with Admiralty contracts, but was to become obsolete during the nineteenth century, particularly as there was no longer any advantage in having timber from the New Forest immediately at hand. There were ironworks at Exbury and Lepe, and bricks were also produced in the area—although this industrialization makes little impact on the map, unlike the oil refinery at Fawley today. Calshot Castle is another of Henry VIII's artillery forts. On Beaulieu Heath several Bronze Age barrows are shown. Beaulieu Gate marks the edge of the Forest and the entry into the enclosed land of Beaulieu Abbey. On the opposite shore of Southampton Water, Warsash was known for its crabs and Hamble was primarily a fishing village.

Map 42 Titchfield is a market town with what is probably Hampshire's oldest surviving church, parts of which date from soon after the arrival of Christianity in this area towards the end of the seventh century. The abbey was a much later, thirteenth-century, foundation; its church was converted into a mansion for Sir Thomas Wriothesley, Earl of Southampton—'Place House' is a corruption of 'Palace'. The brick kilns north of Fareham mark a very significant local product, and the pottery was also exploiting the clays here: there was even an attempt to produce porcelain from the white clay. The railways are the

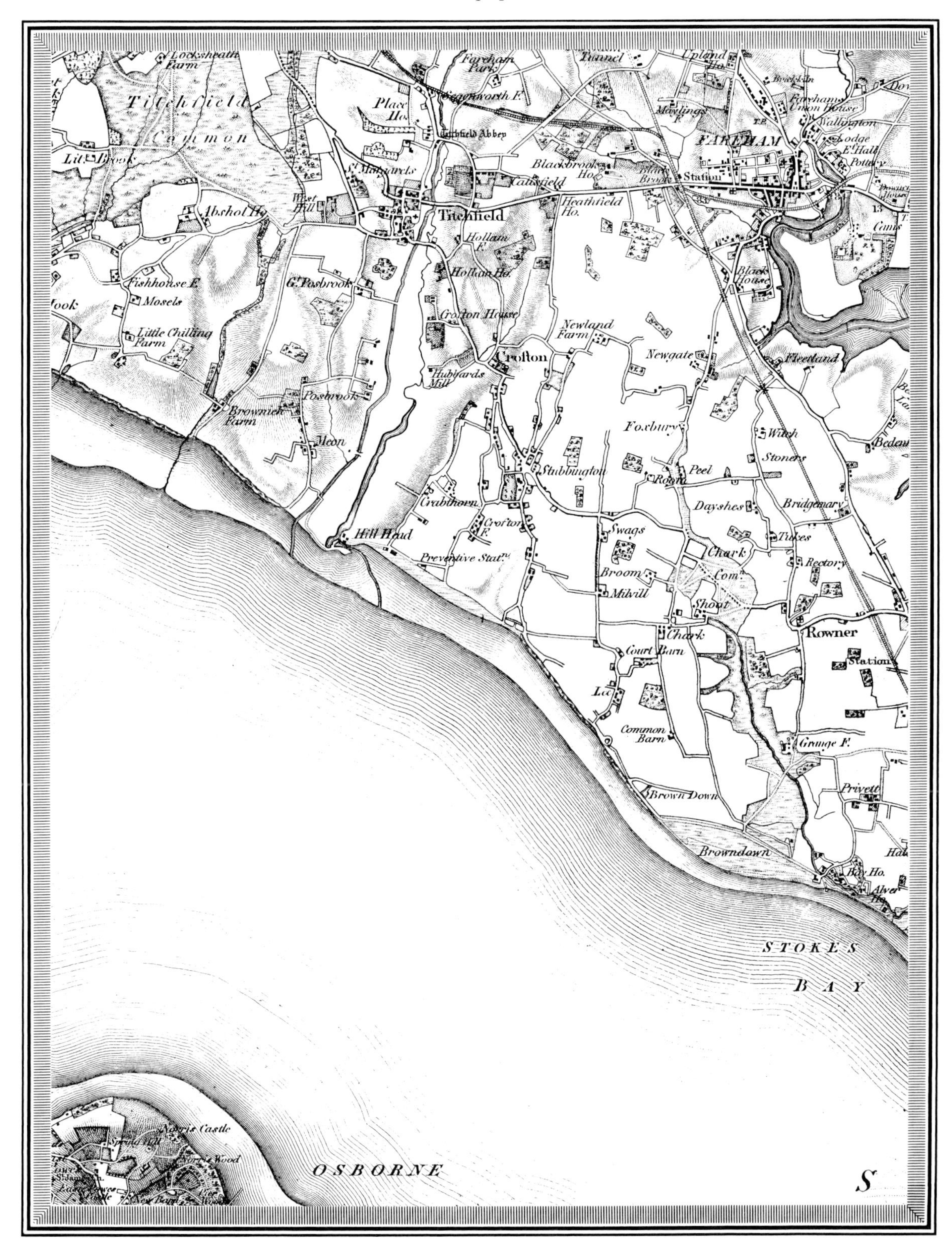
Locksheath Farm
Titchfield Common
Fareham Park
Place Ho.
Titchfield Abbey
Tunnel
Upland Ho.
Maylings F.
Fareham Union House
Wallington
Lodge
FAREHAM
Station
Blackbrook Ho.
Heathfield Ho.
Titchfield
Absholt Ho.
West Hill
Hollam F.
Hollam Ho.
Fishhouse F.
Mosels
Gt. Posbrook
Crofton House
Little Chilling Farm
Newland Farm
Crofton
Newgate
Fleetland
Black House
Hubbards Mill
Posbrook
Brownwich Farm
Meon
Foxbury
Stubbington
Peel
Crabthorn
Dayshes
Bridgemary
Stoners
Hill Head
Crofton F.
Swags
Tukes
Chark
Chark Comn.
Rectory
Preventive Statn.
Broom
Milvill
Shoot
Rowner
Station
Court Barn
Common Barn
Grange F.
Brown Down
Privett
Browndown
Bay Ho.
Alver Ho.
STOKES BAY
Norris Castle
OSBORNE

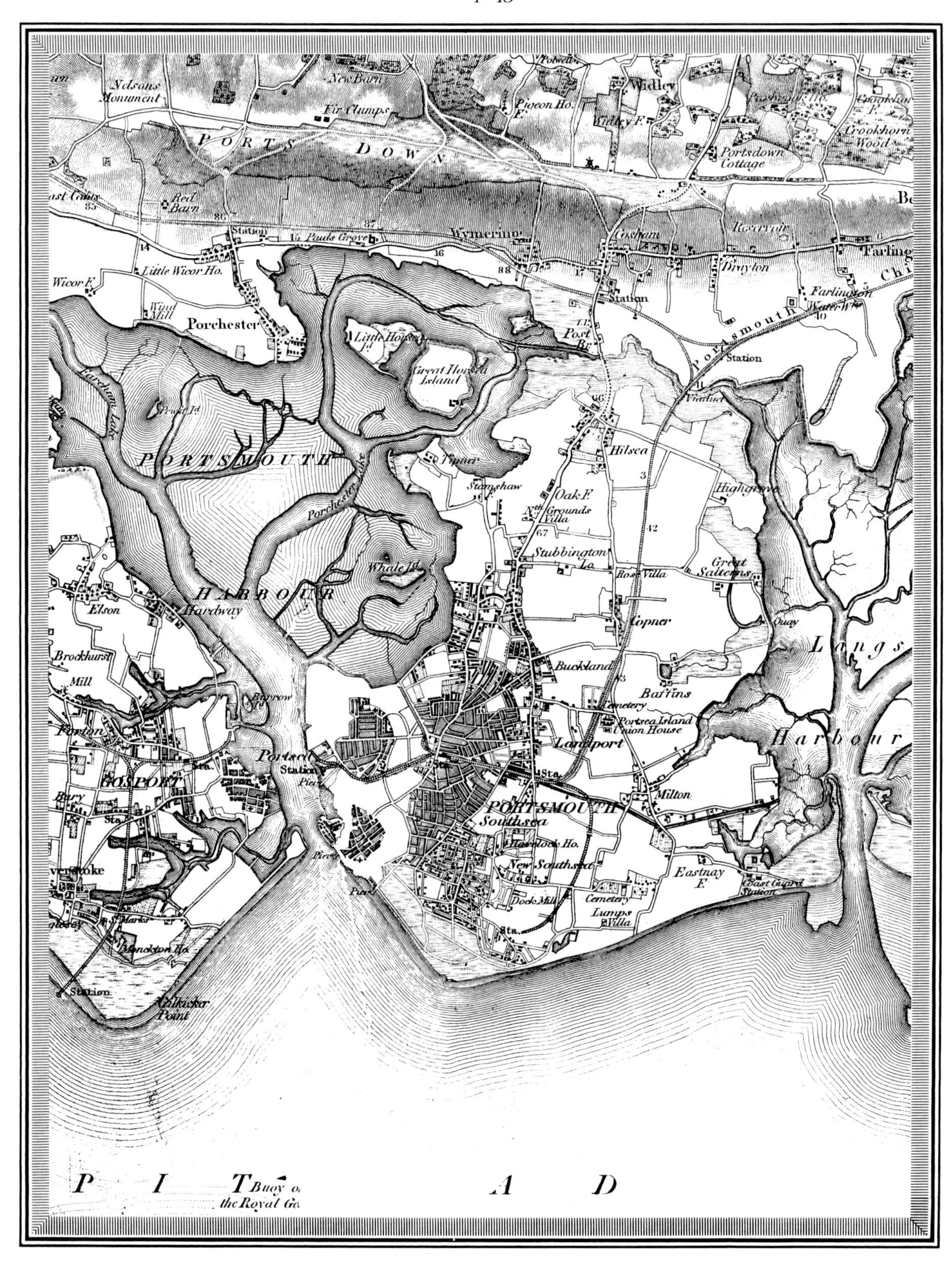
Nelsons Monument
New Barn
Fir Clumps
P O R T S D O W N
Widley
Pigeon Ho. F.
Portsdown Cottage
Crookhorn Wood
Red Barn
Station
Pauls Grove
Wymering
Cosham
Reservoir
Farling
Little Wicor Ho.
Wicor F.
Wind Mill
Porchester
Drayton
Station
Farlington Waterworks
Little Horsea
Great Horsea Island
Post Br.
Station
Viaduct
PORTSMOUTH
Hilsea
Tipner
Stamshaw
Oak F.
Highgrove
Porchester Lake
Whale Id.
Stubbington Lo.
Rose Villa
Great Salterns
HARBOUR
Elson
Hardway
Copner
Quay
Langs
Brockhurst
Mill
Buckland
Barrow
Baffins
Cemetery
Portsea Island Union House
Harbour
Forton
Portsea
Station
Landport
GOSPORT
Sta.
Milton
Bury
PORTSMOUTH
Southsea
Havelock Ho.
New Southsea
Eastnay F.
Coast Guard Station
Dock Mill
Cemetery
Lumps Villa
Monckton Ho.
Station
Gilkicker Point
P I T
Buoy o.
the Royal Ge.
A D

Southwick
HMS Dryad
Boarhunt
Manor Fm
Ashley Down Fm
Offwell Fm
Fort Nelson
Nelson's Monument
Fort Southwick
New Barns
Hookheath Fm
Broomfield Ho
Southwick Ho
Newlands Fm
Plant Fm
Potwell
Pigeon House Fm
Ports Down
Widley Fm
Fort Widley
Wayfarer's Walk
Purbrook
Widley
Fort Purbrook
Bedhampton
Paulsgrove
Wymering
Cosham
Drayton
Farlington
Crem
Portchester
Horsea Island
Highbury Coll
Portchester Castle and remains of ROMAN FORT
Farlington Marshes
North Binness Island
Long Island
Baker's Island
South Binness Island
Pewit Island
Tipner
Hilsea
Industrial Estate
PORTSMOUTH DISTRICT
PORTSMOUTH HARBOUR
Danger Area
Whale Island
Stamshaw
North End
Copnor
LANGSTONE
HARBOUR
PORTSEA ISLAND
Langstone Channel
Broom Channel
Russell's Lake
VEHICLE FERRY FROM PORTSMOUTH TO
Cherbourg 4½ to 6½ hours*
Guernsey 6½ to 7 hours
Jersey 9 to 9½ hours
Le Havre 5½ hours
St Malo 8½ to 10 hours
(Summer only)*
Fort Brockhurst
Elson
Hardway
Brockhurst
HM Naval Base
Mary Rose
HMS Victory
Burrow Island
Landport
Kingston
Baffins
HM Prison
Forton
Annis Hill
Portsea
Fratton
Milton
Newtown
Old Portsmouth
Alverstoke
HMS Dolphin
Haslar Royal Naval Hospital
Clarence Pier
Memorials
Southsea
Southsea Common
Eastney Barracks
Fort Cumberland
Sinah Common
CG Lookout
IRB Sta
West Winner
East Winner
Clayhall
HM Detention Centre
Fort Monckton
Gilkicker Point
Southsea Castle
South Parade Pier
PORTSMOUTH
Spit Bank Fort
HAMPSHIRE
PORTSMOUTH DISTRICT
Hovercraft Ferry
SPITHEAD
Horse Sand Fort
HAMPSHIRE
PORTSMOUTH DISTRICT

Now a museum, Sir John Dawtry's house in St Michael's Square, Southampton (above), has been restored—over-restored in some ways. The alleyway alongside it is now open and wider, and less dangerous at night. Most of the 1895 improvements (page 95) have themselves been swept away in a new renewal scheme, which has resulted in the very attractive brick housing on the right. The area in the foreground, the old fish market, was excavated in 1986.

The naval presence at Portsmouth is diminishing rapidly, and the leisure industry is taking over. The view from from a pleasure launch above shows the masts of Victory *in the background, and the newly-arrived* Wellington *on the right. One of the eighteenth-century buildings in the 1910 picture (page 110) is in the centre here, viewed from a different angle.*

Gosport–Eastleigh line of 1842 and the Southampton–Brighton line of 1848 and later. 'Union House' is also an addition to the map; the workhouses were established after the 1834 Poor Law Amendment Act, and groups of parishes had to form 'unions' to run them.

Map 43 (page 112) The steep chalk ridge of Ports Down overlooks the best natural harbour on the south-east coast, its only serious problem being its narrow mouth. There have been fortifications here at least since the Romans built the shore fort at Portchester. This was used by the Saxons as a strong-point against the Vikings, and the Normans built a castle and a church inside it. In the Napoleonic Wars it was used to house prisoners of war. Deeper water to the south led to present day Portsmouth's establishment at the end of the twelfth century, with dry docks being built in the fifteenth, as were the first of a series of fortifications designed for use with ever more sophisticated guns. A formidable defensive line enclosed both Portsmouth and Gosport in the seventeenth century, which was still regarded as usable in the nineteenth. The earliest editions of the Ordnance Survey maps showed these and other defensive works, but after 1870 no details of the naval establishment were shown, for security reasons. Consequently even Henry VIII's Southsea Castle does not appear, as it still housed guns. Most of the densely packed housing east of the dockyard was built in the nineteenth century, and the map has the railway lines as they were in 1893. The growth of Southsea as a resort in the nineteenth century owes much to the arrival of the railway.

Modern map 43 (page 113) The modern map does at least acknowledge the existence of the navy. It also shows, as well as the inevitable population growth, something of the elaborate provisions that were made to defend the harbour in the nineteenth century, as fears of French iron-clads and long-range artillery grew. Forts Cumberland and Monkton had

been built in the previous century, and could be updated. But to prevent a French army from taking the Ports Down ridge and bombarding the harbour from the heights, Forts Nelson, Southwick, Widley and Purbrook were built to face north, protecting the overland approach to Portsmouth from north and east, while Forts Brockhurst and Rowner faced west, to resist a land attack on Gosport. (Other forts are not on this section of the map.) Out to sea, Spit Bank Fort was built to give further protection to the harbour mouth, and to ships anchored outside it. Some of these forts are now open to the public, and the whole history of Portsmouth and its naval connection can be explored, although unfortunately only a small part of the elaborate seventeenth-century earthwork artillery circuit is intact.

The South Parade Pier at Southsea in August 1910 (top). This has all the ingredients of an Edwardian holiday resort: ladies in long dresses protecting themselves from unbecoming sun-tans; wheeled bathing machines to be towed into the water so that swimmers could enter the sea with due modesty; and the raffish pier hinting at delights like gambling that it could not actually provide.

(Above) Today in late spring the season at Southsea has hardly started, but the contrast with 1910 is not just in the emptiness of the beach. Ladies no longer fear to reveal an ankle, and browning the body in the sun is the object of everybody who would like it to be thought that they had holidayed in Bermuda. Beach huts are still popular, but the wheeled bathing machines are no more. The pier now offers gambling, though not immoderately.

Emsworth in 1890 was a fishing village visited by a few holiday-makers (below). The boats used by the fishermen were small open rowing-boats with masts, for they had to be shallow-draughted for the local creeks and waters, and were not meant for the open sea. Wild-fowling was also an important occupation.

(Far below) Most of the craft in Emsworth today are yachts and small motor boats, and few earn their living from fish. Fishermen's cottages have become holiday flats, though the high dormers show that the most eye-catching building is basically the same structure, as indeed are those by the main road, though much smartened up. No one would stand for long in that road now, for it is the A27, violently yellow-lined.

Map 44 (overleaf) Hayling Island is now a recreational area, partly because of the arrival of the railway in 1867. The road link was passable at low water, and a wooden bridge was built in 1824; there was a ferry as well, which also crossed to Portsea. The salterns show one of the islanders' economic activities, and the coastline also provided fishing and wild-fowling. Shipping was severely restricted by the size of the passage into Langstone Harbour. The castle at Warblington is the ruins of an early sixteenth-century courtyard house within a moat, built by the Countess of Salisbury who was executed by Henry VIII. At Havant, a small medieval town probably overlies a Roman market centre; the east-west road is effectively the Roman line, and there was a temple at North Hayling. Emsworth was a fishing village, with a well-known mill.

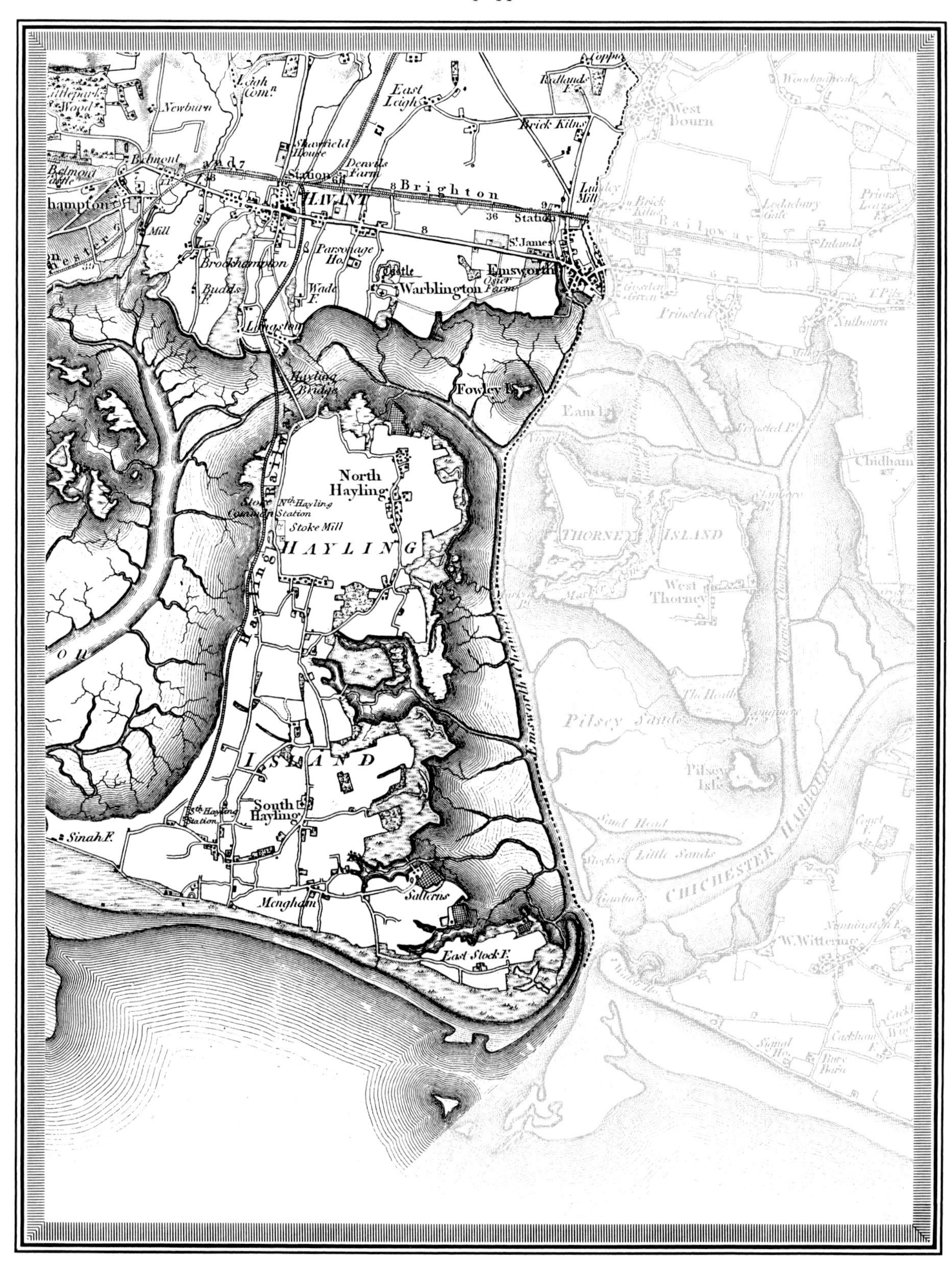
Havant
Brighton
Emsworth
Warblington
North Hayling
Hayling
Island
South Hayling
Mengham
Salterns
East Stock F.
Sinah F.
Fowley I.
Hayling Bridge
Langston
Brockhampton
Bedhampton
Belmont
Newburn
Leigh Com.
East Leigh
Brick Kilns
Redlands F.
West Bourn
Thorney Island
West Thorney
Pilsey Sands
Pilsey Isle
Chichester Harbour
W. Wittering
Chidham
Nutbourn
Prinsted
Stoke Mill
Emsworth Channel
Sand Head
Little Sands
Signal Ho.
Cackham F.

Map 45

Wallis Down
Maze Barrow
Fern Barrow
Little Down
Canford Heath
Bourn Bottom
Poole Heath
Sand Banks
Lodge
Bourne Mouth
Boscomb Mouth
Allum Chine
Durly Chine
North Haven
Staple Cross
Somerford
Barracks
Iford Bridge
Iford
CHRIST CHURCH
Stourfield
Tuckford
Wick
HENGISTBURY HEAD
Studland

The north side of the priory church at Christchurch, viewed from the Wick bank of the River Stour, c1900. The River Avon is on the right, and the two have made Christchurch harbour an attraction for small craft. It is not an easy anchorage to enter, however, and few vessels larger than those in this photograph have ever used Christchurch regularly (see page 126).

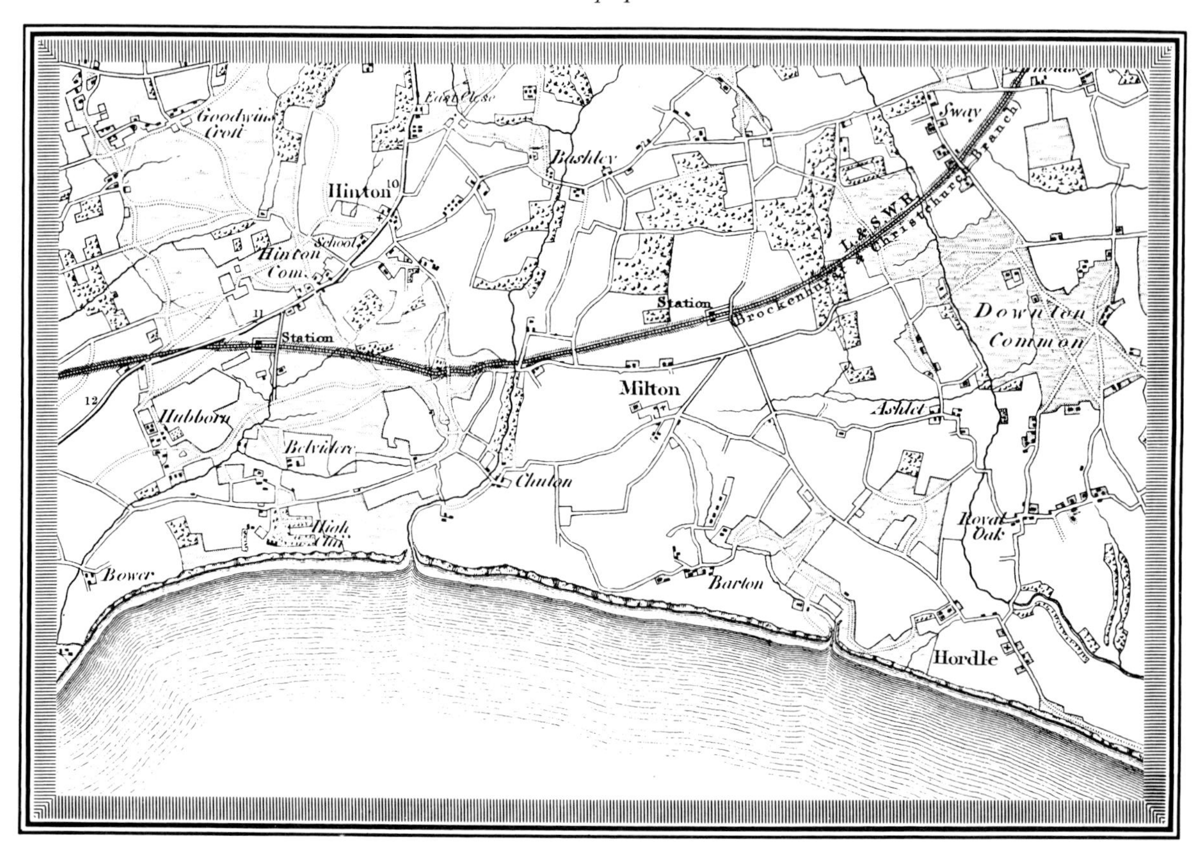

Map 45 (page 121) Hampshire's south-west coastline was severely truncated in 1974, with the loss of Christchurch and Hengistbury Head (inset), and Southbourne and Boscombe, which are now suburbs of Bournemouth. Bournemouth scarcely existed in the early nineteenth century, for it is a resort created by the railways. Hengistbury Head was an important late Iron Age trading-station and industrial centre, protected by earthworks across the peninsula. To some extent, Christchurch took over its role in the Middle Ages, but never became an important port despite a promising start as a Saxon fort, borough and church centre. Apart from two suburbs in Bar End and along the road across the Avon, it was still easily contained within its Saxon defences at the beginning of the nineteenth century.

Map 46 (above) The present-day county boundary is the small stream between Highcliffe and Barton—now entirely built over as seaside resorts, but at the beginning of the nineteenth century farmland with some marshes along the streams that cut through the cliffs. An open stretch remains around Hordwell (a name that alternated with the now invariable Hordle). The cliffs at Barton are clay, famous for their fossils and for their tendency to erode.

Map 47 (opposite) Milford has become Milford on Sea, but Keyhaven marshes still survive, a haven for wild life, protected by Hurst Spit, a narrow ridge of shingle that reaches out to the slightly wider promontory point on which Henry VIII built Hurst

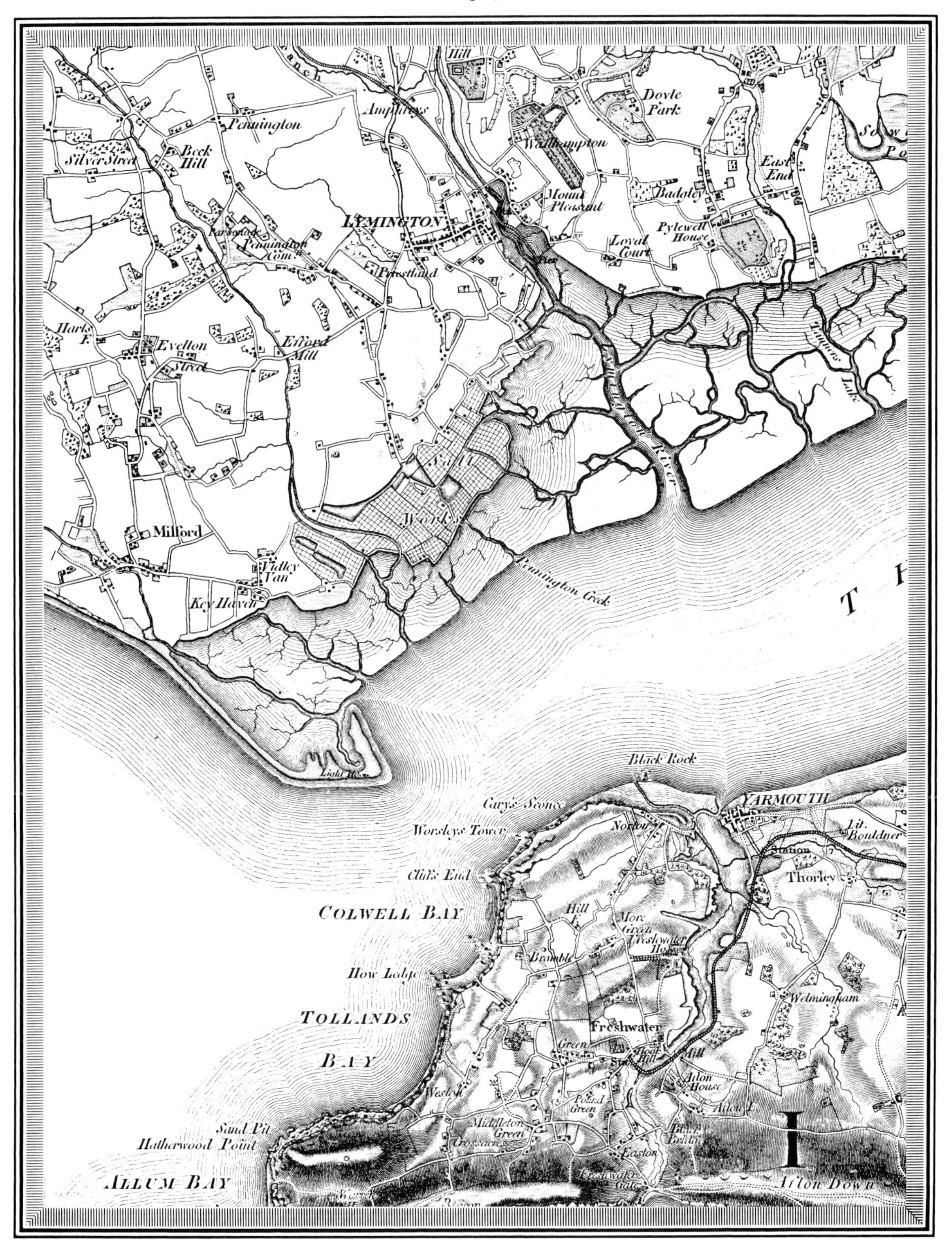

Amplress
Doyle Park
Pennington
Walhampton
Beck Hill
Silver Street
East End
LYMINGTON
Mount Pleasant
Badgley
Pylewell House
Parsonage
Pennington Com.
Loyal Court
Priestland
Harts F.
Evelton Street
Efford Mill
Lymington River
Salt Works
Milford
Vidley Van
Key Haven
Pennington Creek
Light Ho.
Black Rock
YARMOUTH
Cary's Sconce
Worsleys Tower
Norton
Lit. Bouldner
Station
Thorley
Cliff's End
COLWELL BAY
Hill F.
More Green
Freshwater Ho.
Bramble
How Ledge
Welmingham
TOLLANDS
BAY
Freshwater
Green
Mill
Afton House
Weston
Poland Green
Afton F.
Sand Pit
Middleton Green
Hatherwood Point
Crossacres
Easton
ALLUM BAY
Freshwater Gate
Afton Down

(Above) Pleasure boats abound at Christchurch today, though new boat-houses have not completely replaced the mellow brick and stone of 1900 (page 122). This picture, from a slightly different angle, shows the great length of the church, some 325 ft from fifteenth-century west tower to fifteenth-century east end, separated by the twelfth-century nave and transepts which can be seen in the earlier photograph.

(Opposite) The Broadway, Sandown, in about 1895. It is difficult to imagine that this quiet road of a century ago is now an extremely busy thoroughfare, especially in the holiday season. Christchurch was started in 1845 but was not finished until 1874. The fountain, which once stood at the junction of Beachfield Road and The Broadway, disappeared many years ago.

Castle, a fort frequently brought up to date, but from which a big gun has yet to fire a shot in anger. Charles I was brought here from the Isle of Wight on passage to trial in London and thence to his execution.

Across the Solent, on the Isle of Wight, the western Yar rises immediately behind the beach at Freshwater Gate and flows northwards to reach the sea at Yarmouth. As a result the most westerly portion of the island is almost an island in its own right. In the last century much of the area was heathland, sheltered by the high chalk downs to the south. When the survey for this map was made, apart from Yarmouth, settlement consisted of a number of separate hamlets, none of which were of any great size.

Yarmouth was founded as a planned town in the early Middle Ages and developed into an important harbour for the western Wight, although it suffered from competition with other island ports. From the quay were exported corn and livestock while coal and manufactured goods were imported. Yarmouth remained a small compact town because of its situation on an 'island' of solid rock almost entirely surrounded by the sea and low-lying marshes.

The nature of the revisions of the map have provided some rather bizarre anachronisms in this area. While the track of the Freshwater, Yarmouth and Newport Railway, opened in 1888, is shown, none of the modifications to the harbour area, culminating in the opening of the tollbridge over the Yar in 1863, appear. Even stranger is the representation of the military works. The map marks the late medieval structures of Worsley's Tower and Carey's Sconce, even though both of these had disappeared before 1700. It does not show,

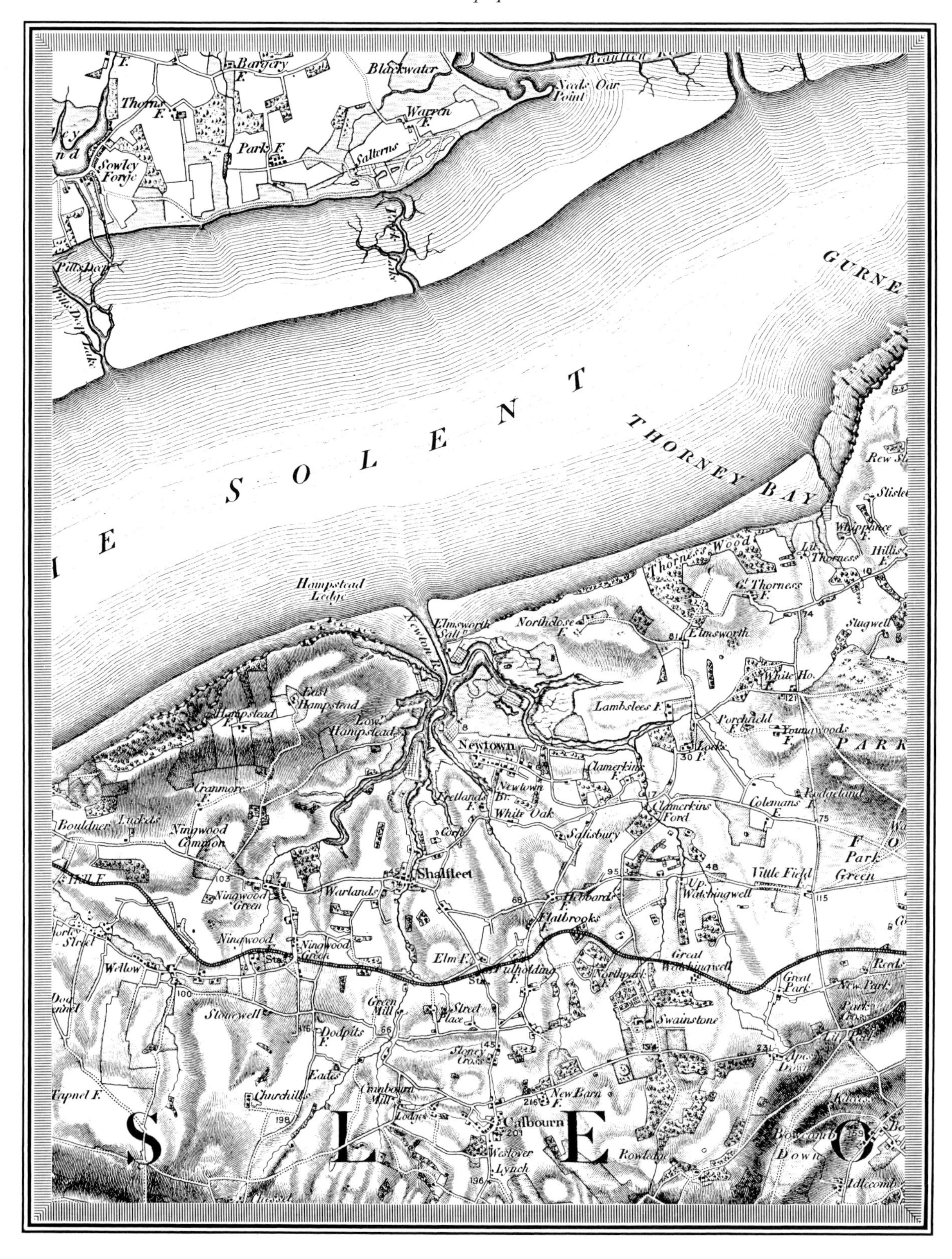
Bargery F.
Blackwater
Needs Oar Point
Thorns F.
Warren F.
Park F.
Salterns
Sowley Forge
Pitts Deep
GURNE
THE SOLENT
THORNEY BAY
Rew
Whippance F.
Thorness Wood
Lit. Thorness
Hillis
Gt. Thorness F.
Hampstead Ledge
Elmsworth Salt
Northclose F.
Elmsworth
Slugwell
White Ho.
East Hampstead
Hampstead
Low Hampstead
Lambslees F.
Porchfield F.
Youngwoods F.
PARK
Newtown
Locks F.
Clamerkins F.
Granmore F.
Newtown Br.
Fretlands F.
White Oak
Clamerkins Ford
Colemans F.
Rodgeland F.
Bouldner
Lucketts
Ningwood Common
Corf
Salisbury
Park Green
Hill F.
Ningwood Green
Warlands
Shalfleet
Hebbard
Up. Watchingwell
Little Field
Flatbrooks
Ningwood
Ningwood Green
Sta.
Wellow
Elm F.
Fulholding F.
Northpark
Great Watchingwell
Great Park
Reeds
New Park
Stonewell
Green Mill
Street Place
Swainstone
Dodpits F.
Stoney Cross
Eades
Churchills
Cranbourn Mill
New Barn F.
Calbourn
Tapnel F.
Westover
Lynch
Rowlidge
Bowcomb Down
Idlecomb
S L E O

Detail map 48

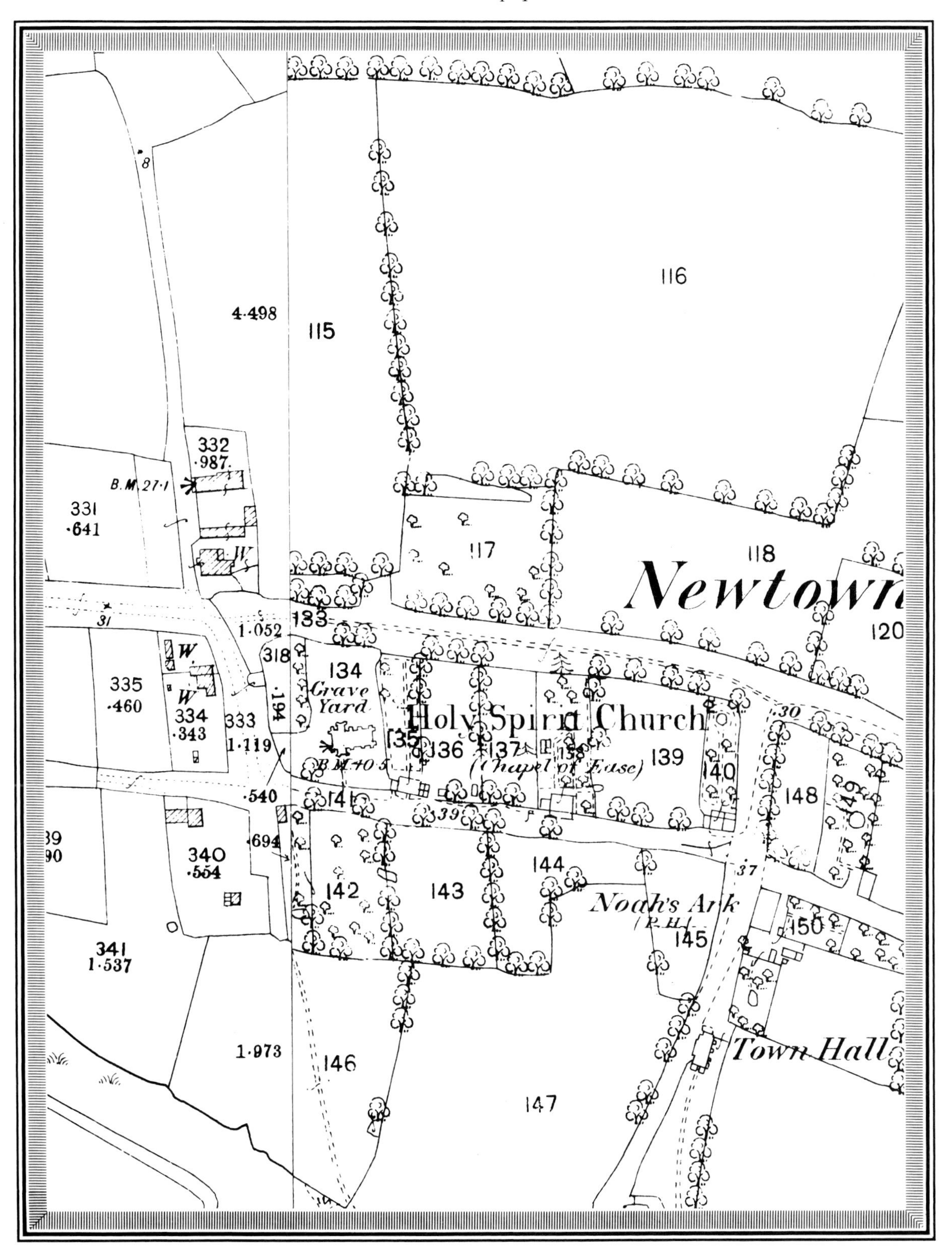

however, any of the mid-Victorian fortifications, even the early ones such as Forts Albert and Victoria. The latter were deleted from the plates following security regulations introduced in about 1870.

Map 48 (page 128) A thousand years ago, the estuary of the Newtown River was much larger than it is today and formed the best natural harbour on the island. It was probably this fact that led to the settlements of Shalfleet and Newtown. In medieval times there was an extensive royal hunting park south of the estuary. By the time of the first Ordnance Survey this park had been broken up into small woods and grazing meadows; only the relatively small area of Parkhurst Forest remained unchanged.

Settlements in the area were generally isolated farms or small hamlets, only Calbourne, Shalfleet and Newtown being of any size. Both Calbourne and Shalfleet were founded in Saxon times. The map shows them to be nucleated villages grouped around their respective churches. Newtown, on the other hand, was a thirteenth-century planned settlement with a grid layout.

The estuary not only dominated the area geographically but also economically. To the north of Shalfleet, a small quay was built in the seventeenth century. This quay was used throughout the eighteenth and nineteenth centuries for the importation of coal. At the time the map was drawn vessels of up to 500 tons could be berthed at the quay. For centuries a salt-producing industry, based on the evaporation of sea water, had operated in the estuary, but in the eighteenth century increasing demand caused an expansion. The six salterns which developed are clearly marked on the map. The salt was shipped out from a small quay which lay north-east of Newtown.

Detail map 48 (previous page) Newtown was a planned settlement, developed in the early thirteenth century by the Bishop of Winchester, within whose manorial lands it lay. The town was originally known as Francheville (literally 'free town'), but later the name was changed to Newtown. The town received borough status in 1256 and by the end of the century it was a thriving market town and port. There appeared to be no reason why it should not continue to expand and prosper, but instead, for a combination of reasons, a decline set in. Firstly, the town seems never to have fully recovered from a French raid in 1377 when it was razed to the ground. Secondly, the economy of the whole area was severely affected by the removal of the wool staple from Winchester to Calais in the fourteenth century. Finally, a local version of 'The Pied Piper of Hamelin' legend tells of the invasion of the town by rats, suggesting that there was an outbreak of the plague at about this time. Whatever the cause, by the mid-sixteenth century Newtown was in a sorry state. Elizabeth I tried to improve the situation by giving parliamentary representation to the town, and, in spite of the very small population, it was to elect two members to Parliament for 250 years until 1832, when it was declared a 'rotten borough' and disenfranchised.

When Ordnance Survey first surveyed the area the original grid pattern of the town was still evident. At this time it had a small population, a public house, a shop and several dairies.

Map 49 (overleaf) Geographically, this area is dominated by the estuary of the River Medina, which penetrates deep into the heart of the island. This waterway has been important since prehistoric times, with four main urban developments growing up along its course. The oldest settlement, Carisbrooke, was founded perhaps as early as the seventh

Town Quay, Newport, in about 1905 (above left). Newport's Town Quay originally developed in the late sixteenth and early seventeenth centuries as the town grew in importance as a port. Stone-built quays and wharves were subsequently added on both sides of the river around the confluence of the Medina with the Lugely Brook. By the middle of the nineteenth century the whole quay had become surrounded by warehouses. On the left is the viaduct, built in 1875 to carry the Ryde & Newport Railway over the Medina and into Newport station.

The Town Quay area of Newport has undergone extensive changes since the Second World War (below left). Many of the warehouses have fallen into disuse and have been demolished as the importance of the port declines. Fortunately a small group (not seen in this view) has been preserved and altered to fit other uses. The railway viaduct was demolished in 1966 and the area is now part of the Newport bypass.

century, and the map shows a nucleated settlement centred on the medieval church and overlooked by the castle. To the north-east of Carisbrooke lies Newport at the confluence of the Medina with its tributary Lukely Brook. The streets have a systematic grid pattern, showing that Newport was a medieval planned town, in face laid out by the de Redvers family in the twelfth century. The growth of East and West Cowes at the mouth of the estuary was a more recent development. While there were small medieval settlements

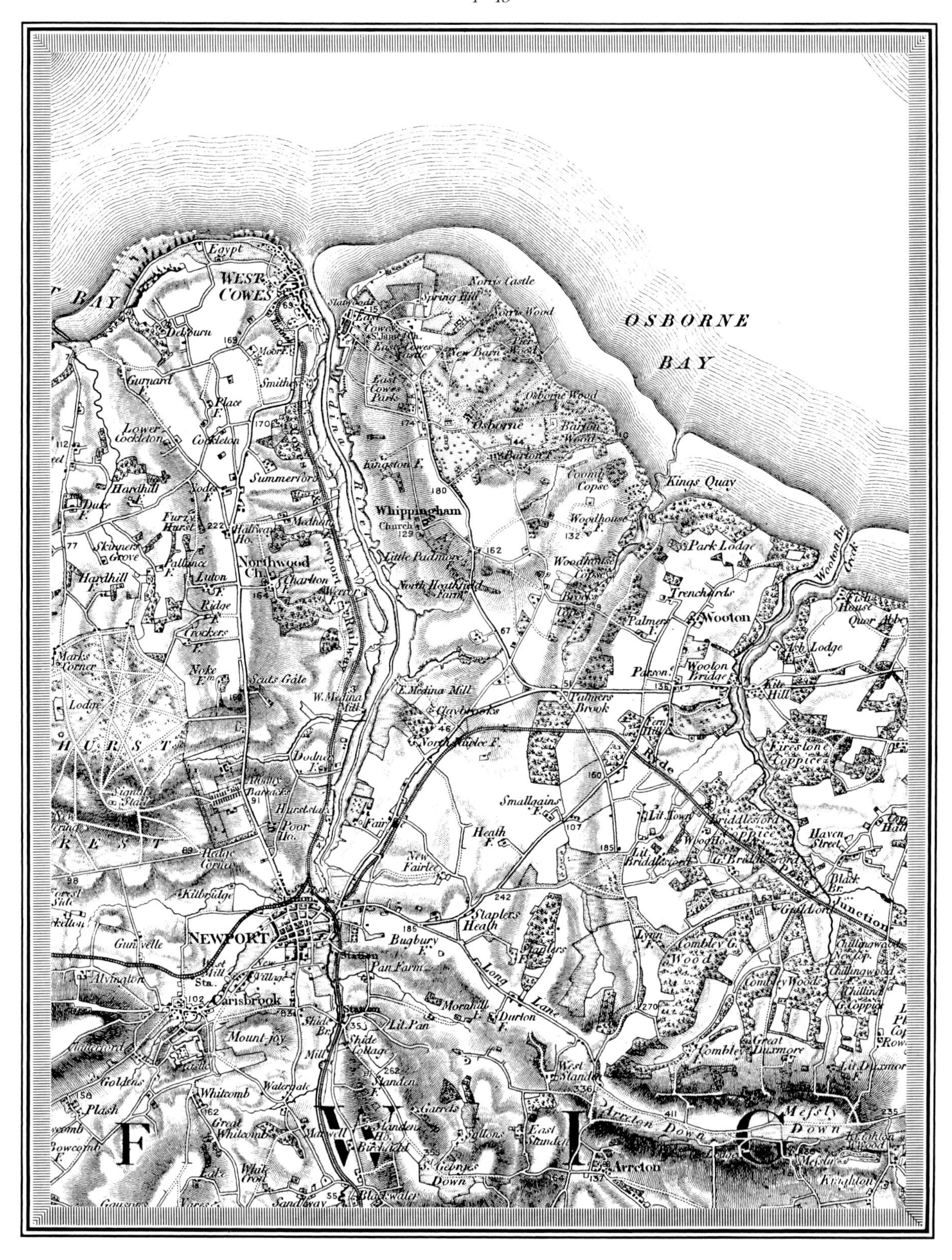
OSBORNE
BAY
Egypt
WEST COWES
Norris Castle
Spring Hill
Norris Wood
East Cowes Park
Osborne Wood
Osborne
Barton Wood
Kingston F.
Kings Quay
Whippingham
Church
Woodhouse F.
Park Lodge
Little Padmore
North Heathfield Farm
Northwood Ch.
Charlton F.
Summerford
Gurnard F.
Lower Cockleton
Cockleton
Place F.
Hardhill F.
Luton F.
Ridge F.
Crockers F.
Noke F.
Marks Corner
Lodge
Scuts Gale
W. Medina Mill
E. Medina Mill
Claybrooks
Trenchards
Wooton
Palmers F.
Parson F.
Wooton Bridge
Kite Hill
Palmers Brook
Fern Hill
Firestone Coppice
Smallgains F.
Heath F.
New Fairlee
Staplers Heath
Bugbury F.
NEWPORT
Station
Pan Farm
Carisbrook
Alvington
Gunville
Kilbridge
Mount-joy
Lit. Pan
Shide Br.
Shide Cottage
Morehall F.
Durton F.
Long Lane
West Standen
East Standen
Arreton
Arreton Down
Mersly Down
Combley Wood
Great Duxmore
Haven Street
Junction
Guildford
Whitcomb
Great Whitcomb
Plash
Garrets
Standen
Blackwater
Sandway
F
W
I
G

SOLENT
Browndown Point
Cowes Roads
COWES
Egypt Point
Castle
Old Castle Point
Breakwater
Norris Castle
Northwood Ho
Marina
Springhill
East Cowes
Osborne Bay
Ferry V&P
Hospl
Osborne
Osborne Ho
Swiss Cott
Barton Wood
Barton Manor
Somerton Fm
Kingston Fm
Northwood
Ruffins Copse
Nodes Fm
RIVER MEDINA
Whippingham
Ludham Cottage
Woodhouse Fm
King's Quay
Mud & Sand
Woodside
Ryde Roads
Medham Ho
Newport Cowes Cycle Way
Padmore Ho (Hotel)
Coastal Path
Dallimores
Holiday Village
Wootton Creek
Pallance Fm
Ridge Copse
Luton Fm
Pallancegate
Werrar Fm
Heathfield Fm
Alverstone Fm
Westwood
Wootton
Fishbourne
Quarr Abbey
Quarr Abbey (rems of)
Ryde Ho
Pelhamfield
Crockers Fm
Noke Fm
Works
Marina
Kite Hill
Quarr Hill
Binstead
Wootton Bridge
Binfield Fm
Crem
dismantled railway
North Fairlee Fm
Puck Ho
Mill Pond
Forest Walk
Firestone Copse
Newnham Fm
Haylands
Parkhurst
Dodnor Ho
Wootton Common
Packsfield
MEDINA DISTRICT
Forest
Parkhurst Prison
Lower St Cross Fm
Butterfly World
Littletown
Blackbridge Brook
Meml
Albany Prison
The Grange
Briddlesford Lodge
Woodhouse Fm
Great Briddlesford Fm
Havenstreet
Upton
Camp Hill Prison
Hospl
Cemy
New Fairlee Fm
Knight's Fm
Doreshill Fm
Steam Railway Centre
Hospital
Pondcast Fm
Forest Walk
Forest Side
Hunny Hill
Coll
Sch
Rowlands Wood
Kitbridge Fm
Barton
Staplers
Blacklands Fm
Guildford Fm
Gatehouse
Deacons
Gunville
Staplers Fm
Lynn Fm
Ashey
Manor
Combley Great Wood
Chillingwood Fm
dismtd rly
NEWPORT
Great Pan Fm
Durton Fm
Robin Hill Country Park
Rowlands Fm
West Ashey Fm
Carisbrooke
Burnt Ho
Duxmore Fm
Little Duxmore
East Ashey Fm
Clatterford
Shide
Nature Trail
Combley Fm
Tumuli
Carisbrooke Castle
Priory
Bembridge Trail
Little East Standen Fm
Hare and Hounds (PH)
Ashey Down
Sea Mark
New Close Ho
Garretts Fm
Downend
Tumulus
Mersley Down
Froglands Fm
Valleys
Shepherds Trail
Standen Ho
Cycle Route
Arreton Down
Mersley Fms
Works
Marvel Fm
Birchfield Ho
Great East Standen Manor
Kern Fm
Great Whitcombe Manor
Arreton Manor
Knighton Fm
Nunwell Trail
St George's Down
Arreton
Bembridge Trail
Blackwater
Vayres Fm
Cemy
Whitecroft Hospital
Stone Fm
Heasley Manor
Langbridge
dismtd rly
Alverstone
Alverstone Nature Trail
Garstons
OF WIGHT
Longdown
Heasley Manor Fm
Stenbury Trail
Merston Manor
Perreton Fm
Horringford
Newchurch
Birchmore Fm
Stickworth Hall (Hotel)
Hill Fm
Gatcombe
Gatcombe Mill
Champion Fm
Wackland
Gatcombe Ho
Merstone
Redway
River Yar
Queen's Bower
Borthwood Fm
Pidford
dismtd rly
Hale Manor Fm
Sheat Manor
Newbarn Down
Long Copse
Five Barrows
Chillerton
Sibdown
Rookley
Pagham Fm
Hale Common
Winford

on both sides of the river to the south of the sites of the modern towns, even the building by Henry VIII of coastal forts on both shores failed to stimulate their growth. It was not until the seventeenth century that both towns developed, West Cowes as a port and East Cowes as a shipbuilding centre. The plans of both towns are irregular, reflecting their haphazard, piecemeal development. Outside the urban areas, the settlement patterns appear for the most part to have remained essentially unaltered since the Middle Ages, a mixture of small nucleated villages, scattered hamlets and single farmsteads.

Newport High Street today (below) has changed remarkably little since the beginning of the century. The streets are much more congested with traffic and this has necessitated the introduction of a one-way system and traffic lights. While shop-fronts, street lighting and signs have been modernized, the upper storeys of the buildings have in many cases changed very little.

(Right) Newport High Street in about 1905, looking west across the junction with St James Street, with the uncongested roads which are so typical of pre-First World War scenes of the island. On the left is the monument to Queen Victoria erected in 1901.

Modern map 49 (previous page) The modern map shows very clearly the great expansion that has taken place over the last century in the urban areas of the island. East Cowes, West Cowes and Newport have all spread out into what had been open country, swallowing up small hamlets and isolated farmsteads in the process. In both East and West Cowes development began with the construction of

large villas in the best situations; the building mostly took place in an unplanned fashion, but in a few cases small villa estates were laid out. Later building consisted of terraced housing for the workers in the local industries. The map shows surprisingly little sign of the shipbuilding industry, upon which much of the prosperity of the area was based. In fact the major shipyards, which developed along the waterfront on both sides of the river, had come and gone between the first and most recent surveys. Most of the large yards have been split into smaller concerns which are not very obvious on the map.

In Newport most of the town's expansion took the form of terraced houses. In recent years relatively large council estates have been built, not only in all three towns, but also in

Until the 1840s the only way to cross the Medina between East and West Cowes was by rowing boat. When Queen Victoria and Prince Albert took up residence at Osborne House, the local council allowed a floating bridge to be winched back and forth across the estuary. In 1854 the first chain ferry was installed. Today, Cowes floating bridge is powered by electricity instead of steam (above), but the overall shape has changed very little since the earlier picture (right) was taken in 1896. The small chapel and the adjacent Crown Inn still stand, but many of the other buildings on the East Cowes side have disappeared, partly as a result of bombing during the Second World War and partly owing to redevelopment in recent years.

some of the villages such as Whippingham and Wootton. A comparison of the two maps shows one major change that has affected the whole island, the loss of the railway network, a casualty of the Beeching axe in the 1950s.

Bay House
Gilkicker Point
Station
S P I T H E A D
Buoy of the Royal George
Pier
Station
Binsted
Ryde Ho.
Stone-pits F.
RYDE
Appley
St. Johns
Puckpool F.
Trouble field F.
Nettlestone Point
Saltern
Pound F.
Play St.
Vinham
Hayland F.
Lit. Small Brook
Preston F.
Sea Grove
Fairy Hill
Nettlestone Green
West Brook F.
Stroud Wood
Aldermoor Heath
Pennyfeathers
Small Brook
Brook Wood
Barnsley F.
Priory
Crooks Heath
Kemphill
G. Upton
Lit. Upton
Little Whitefield
Great Whitefield F.
Whitefield Wood
Park F.
Fivens
St. Helens Church
WATCH HO. P.T
Gate house
Ash Common
Bean Acre F.
Green Lane
Beaper F.
St. Helens Green
Old Ch. Sea Mark
Hill F.
Carpenters
Sta.
Mill
BEMBRIDGE POINT
Round Plat Coppice
Ashley F.
Lit. Harding Shoot
Lit. Nunwell
Rick Hill
Marsh Ho.
Brading Harbour
N. Well F.
Hill Grove
Swains F.
Bembridge Street
Knowles F.
Foreland F.
FORELAN
Ashey Sea Mark Down
Brading Down
Brading
St.
Woolverton F.
Spain
How Gate F.
Bembridge

Map 51

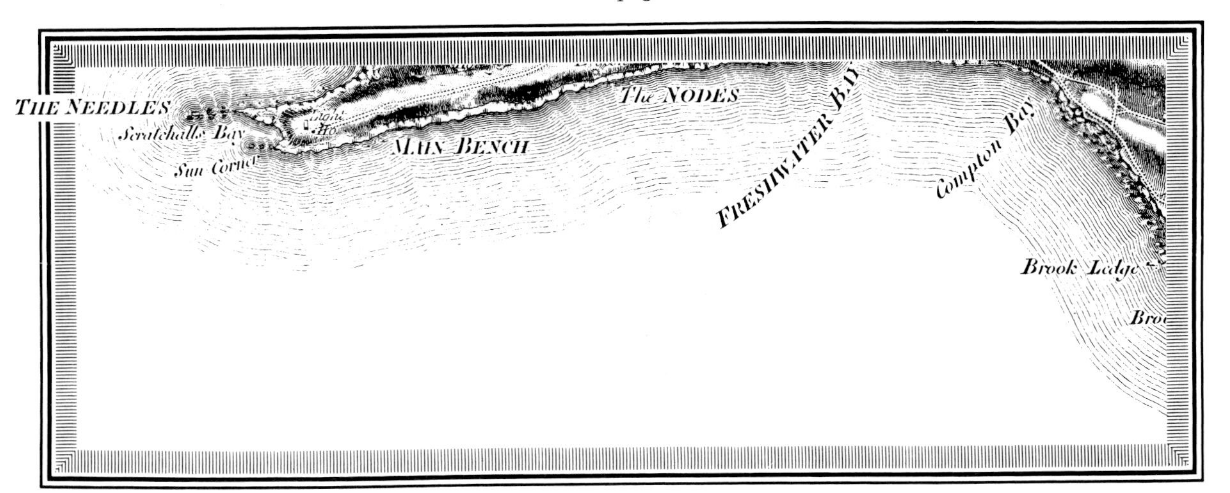

Map 50 (left) In the early nineteenth century the only sizeable towns in the north-eastern corner of the island were Ryde and Brading. Brading was one of the oldest settlements on the island, having its origins in the seventh century. During the Middle Ages it became an important market town and port because of its situation alongside Brading Haven. At the time of the first Ordnance Survey Brading had declined, mainly due to the silting up of the haven. It had developed as a linear town with the parish church at the northern end of the settlement. The quay, east of the church, was probably little used by this time.

Ryde was a major point of entry for visitors to the island from the fourteenth century onwards because of its proximity to Portsmouth. Originally it was two separate settlements, a small fishing hamlet on the shore and a village on the hill above. In the early 1780s the narrow track linking the two was enlarged to form a major thoroughfare, locally called Union Street, and shops and houses began to be built alongside it. In 1813–14 the original pier was constructed and this eased the problems of landing foot passengers, particularly at low tide. Over the years the pier was extended and in 1857–64 a second pier was built a short way to the east. The presence of these piers was a major factor in stimulating visits by tourists.

Brading Haven originally extended through to Sandown Bay, although the southern end was probably very shallow and full of sandbanks. Natural silting combined with various medieval reclamation schemes had, by the seventeenth century, reduced the area flooded by the tide to that shown on the map. It remained though an important natural harbour and was used extensively by the Royal Navy. Ships entering the haven navigated through the narrow channel by lining up the old tower of St Helen Church with the Ashey Down sea-mark built in 1735. It is said that term 'holy-stone' originated here from the habit of sailors to steal the stones from the ancient church to clean the decks.

Map 51 (above) This short section of the coast includes some of the most spectacular scenery on the island. From Compton Bay westwards to The Needles there are high mural chalk cliffs. By the time the first Ordnance Survey was made, the Needles consisted of only three sea-stacks. However, until 1764 there was a fourth stack, a slender pinnacle known as Lot's wife. It is believed that this structure was responsible for the name of the whole group. The map shows the location of the original Needles Lighthouse built in 1785 on the top of the headland.

Map 52 This part of the island, known as the 'Back of the Wight', was, in the last century, very isolated. The northern section of the map is occupied by part of the central chalk downs. In the nineteenth century these downs were open country, used for sheep grazing and largely uninhabited. Only three tracks crossed the downs northwards and only one, that running through Shorwell, went to Newport. For the inhabitants of the villages south of the downland ridge, it was a major undertaking to go to market in Newport.

The area between the downs and the sea comprises a mixture of sandy ridges and clay

Cowes Parade looks very peaceful in this pre-First World War photograph of about 1905 (above left). The only vehicle visible is a small horse-drawn carriage. On the right, the octagonal structures mark the entrance to the Victoria Pier, built in 1901–02. In the distance is New Terrace and beyond that, hidden in the trees, Cowes Castle, the home of the Royal Yacht Squadron.

During the summer months Cowes Parade becomes extremely busy and the road crowded with parked cars (below left). Victoria Pier became unsafe and was demolished in 1960. New Terrace was found to have been built in poor foundations and was demolished in the 1930s. In its place a block of art deco flats was built. Cowes Castle is now much more visible with the removal of all the trees on the southern side.

lowlands. When the survey was carried out, most of the villages lay along a track at the foot of the downs. There was no coastal road and surprisingly little settlement adjacent to the coast. The reason for the latter was probably the extremely exposed nature of this part of the island, with no protection from the prevailing south-west winds.

Along the coast a new road was constructed in the 1860s. This road was designed to allow the rapid passage of troops in the event of a foreign invasion on the south coast of the island. Inevitably it became known as the Military Road.

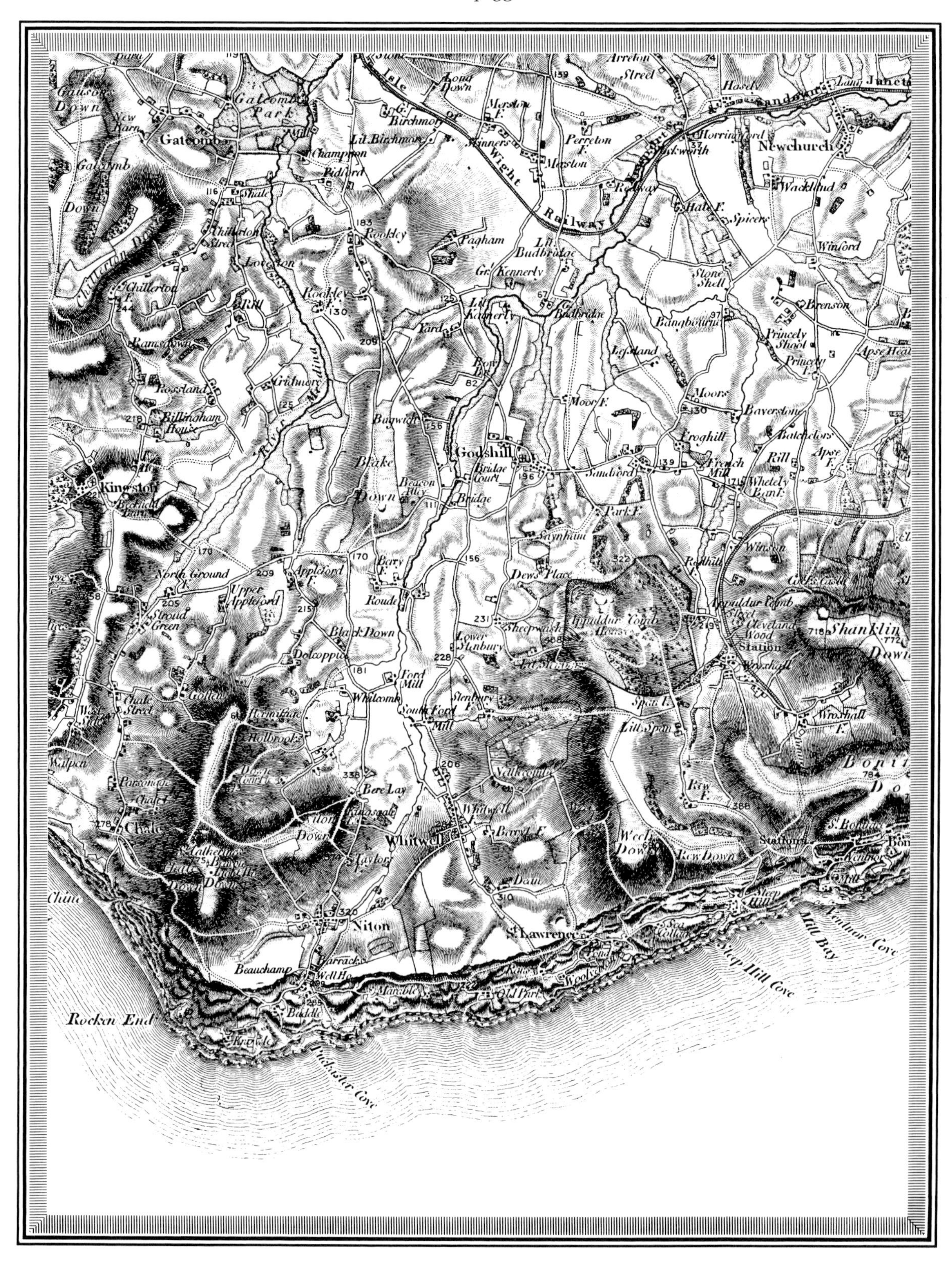
Gatcomb
Gatcomb Park
Champion
Pidford
Lit. Birchmore
Long Down
Isle of Wight Railway
Arreton Street
Merston
Perreton F.
Horringford
Newchurch
Wackland
Hale F.
Spicers
Winford
Shate
Chillerton Street
Rookley
Pagham
Lit. Budbridge
Gr. Kennerly
Lit. Kennerly
Budbridge
Stone Shell
Bangbourne
Brenson
Princely Shool
Princely
Apse Heath
Chillerton F.
Rookley F.
Yard
Ramsdown
Lessland
Moor F.
Moors
Baverstone
Batchelors
Rossland
Gridmore
River Medina
Billingham House
Bagwich
Godshill
Bridge Court
Sandford
Froghill
French Mill
Whetely Bank
Kingston
Blake Down
Beacon Alley
Bridge
Park F.
Saynham
Dews Place
Redhill
Winson
Cooks Castle
North Ground F.
Appleford F.
Upper Appleford
Bury F.
Roude
Stroud Green
Black Down
Sheepwash
Appuldur Comb
Appuldur Comb House
Cleveland Wood
Station
Wroxhall
Shanklin Down
Lower Stenbury
Dolcoppice
Ford Mill
Whitcomb
Chale Street
Gotten
Hermitage
Hollbrook
Stenbury F.
South Ford Mill
Span F.
Litt. Span
Wroxhall F.
Bonchurch Down
Parsonage
Chale
Bere Lay
Walcombe
Whitwell F.
Whitwell
Bury F.
Rew F.
Week Down
Rew Down
Stainford
St. Boniface
Ventnor
Mill
Niton Down
Kingsdale
Taylors
Dam
Chale Down
Niton
St. Lawrence
Steep Hill
Chine
Beauchamp
Barracks
Well Ho.
Marable
Old Park
Woolverton
Steep Hill Cove
Mill Bay
Ventnor Cove
Rocken End
Puckaster Cove

O F W I G H T
OUTH WIGHT DISTRICT
Garstons
Whitecroft Hospital
Stone Fm
Longdown
Stenbury Trail
Cemy
Heasley Manor
Langbridge
Heasley Manor Fm
dismtd rly
Alverstone
Alverstone Nature Trail
Adges
Newchurch
PH
Horringford
Hill Fm
Perreton Fm
Stickworth Hall (Hotel)
Merston Manor
Birchmore Fm
Gatcombe Mill
Champion Fm
Gatcombe
Gatcombe Ho
Pidford
Merstone
Redway
Wackland
Queen's Bower
Borthwood Fm
Hale Manor Fm
River Yar
Winford
Sheat Manor
Rookley
Pagham Fm
Rookley Country Park
Hale Common
Long Copse
Five Barrows Earthwork
Chillerton
Sibdown
Little Budbridge Fm
Isle of Wight Airport
Black Pan
Bohemia Corner
Loverston Fm
Strip Lynchets
Harts Fm
Rookley Green
Kennerley Fm
Great Budbridge Manor
Bathingbourne
Branstone
Bigbury Fm
Cheverton Fm
A 3056
Chillerton Fm
Chillerton Down
River Medina
Lower Rill
Apse Heath
Merrie Gardens
Lower Yard
Lessland Fm
Princelett
Ramsdown Fm
Worsley Trail
Moor Fm
Bobberstone Fm
Ninham
Roslin
Cridmore
Bagwich
Summersbury
Landguard Manor
Bachelors Fm
Apse Manor Fm
Upper Hyde
Shepherds Trail
Billingham Manor
Godshill
Cemy
Natural History Centre
Bridgecourt
Bleak Down
Bridge Fm
North Appleford
Sandford
French Mill
Whiteley Bank
A 3020
Godshill Park
Beacon Alley
Beckfield Cross
Kingston
Sainham Fm
Winstone Fm
Shankli
Leechmore Fm
Worsley Trail
Emmethill
Yard Fm
Redhill Fm
Hospl
North Grounds
Gt Appleford Fm
Holden Fm
Roud
Gatcliff Fm
Obelisk
Sheepwash Fm
Wroxall
St Martin's Down
Shanklin Down
Luccombe Village
Chale Green
Upper Appleford
Wks
Appuldurcombe Ho (ruin)
Dolcoppice
Fairfields
Ford Fm
Itchall
Wroxall Manor Fm
Luccombe
Gotten Manor Fm
Stenbury Manor Fm
Stenbury Down
Span Fm
Nansen Hill
The Landslip
Monument
The Hermitage
Southford
Tumuli
Upper Bonchurch
Westside Fm
St Catherine's Down
Wydcombe
Nettlecombe
Lowtherville
St Boniface Down
DUNNO
Walpan
Downcourt
Bierley
Rew Fm
Strathwell Park
Whitwell
Week Fm
Tumuli
Tumulus
Bonchurch
Monks Bay
Kingates
Head Down
Week Down
Cemy
Rew Down
Horseshoe Bay
Chale
Jobsons Fm
VENTNOR
St Catherine's Oratory
Tumulus
St Catherine's Hill
Dean Fm
Steephill
Pier
Ventnor Bay
Blackgang Chine
St Lawrence
Mus
Botanic Gardens
CG Sta
Blackgang
Niton
Coastal Path
Westcliff
The Undercliff
CG Lookout
The Orchard
Old Park
Tropical Bird Park
Woody Bay
Binnel Point
Rocken End
Knowles Fm
Puckaster Cove
Binnel Bay
Watershoot Bay
Reeth Bay
ST CATHERINE'S POINT
48
49
50
51
52
53
54
55
56
57
58

Gore Cliff, Niton, today (above). The area of land below the Cliff was radically changed by the landslip of 1928 (pages 149 and 150), when extensive areas of woodland were carried away with the old road. The whole area still presents a very rough and tumbled appearance with patches of bare clay marking where small slips have occurred in recent times.

A lane near Godshill in about 1885 (above). This view in the heart of the island shows the peaceful countryside of about a century ago before the appearance of the motor car.

May 53 (page 142) This area divides topographically into three distinct regions: the downs, the northern lowlands and the Undercliff. Most of the downs were open sheep-grazing country with a few scattered farms, and in the valleys cutting through the downs from north to south small villages such as Niton and Whitwell had developed around spring-heads. The northern lowlands show a scatter of small nucleated villages and isolated farmsteads, typical of much of the island.

The most interesting part of the area is the Undercliff, the narrow coastal strip between Bonchurch and Chale. This is the largest region of coastal landslip in northern Europe, where repeated movements over many centuries have produced a distinctive terraced landscape. While the major catastrophic slips appear to have taken place several thousand years ago, movements still occur from time to time. At the time of the first Ordnance Survey, the Undercliff settlements, such as Ventnor, Bonchurch and St Lawrence, were all small hamlets dependent on fishing, a certain amount of agriculture and probably a little smuggling.

Modern map 53 (page 143) The modern map shows that all the settlements in the area have expanded considerably. The most marked development in the last century is that which has taken place in the Undercliff, where the physical geography of the area produces a very distinct moist, equable climate. In the early nineteenth century several doctors recommended the curative properties of this climate, especially in the treatment of pulmonary diseases such as consumption. This stimulated a phase of rapid building, and in a remarkably short period the original hamlet of Ventnor had become the centre of a thriving community. Summer villas were built along the landslip terraces and by the 1880s Bonchurch and St Lawrence had become suburbs of Ventnor. In more recent times terraced housing was built in Upper Ventnor while many of the large villas have been converted into flats. Further development in the Undercliff is largely restricted by the nature of the terrain and the possibility of future land movements.

Ventnor from the sea in 1890. Ventnor grew rapidly from a small fishing hamlet into a fashionable resort in the decades after 1840. It was not built to any plan but plot by plot by speculative developers. By the time that this photograph was taken, a sprawl of large villas extended east and west of the original centre of the town. The pier was built in 1872, but was rebuilt and enlarged after being damaged by a storm in 1882. Today the view from the sea has scarcely altered. The major change has been the growth of trees, especially the covering of the seaward slopes of St Boniface by an evergreen oak wood.

Map 54

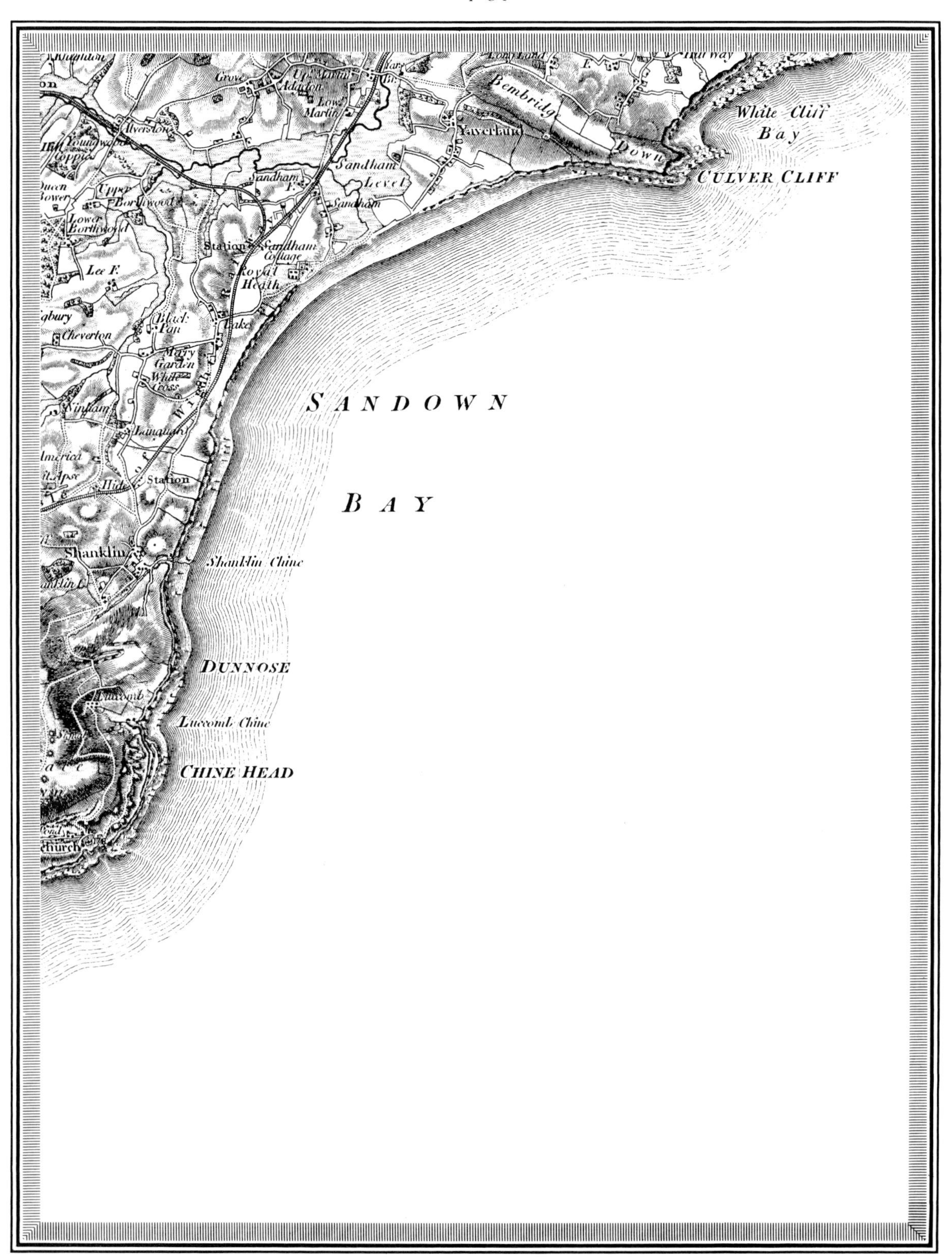
Bembridge Down
Yaverland
White Cliff Bay
CULVER CLIFF
Sandham Level
Sandham
Alverstone
Upper Borthwood
Lower Borthwood
Lee F.
Station
Sandham Cottage
Royal Heath
Black Pan
Cheverton
Lake
Mary Garden
White Cross
Languard
Station
Hide
Shanklin
SANDOWN
BAY
Shanklin Chine
DUNNOSE
Luccomb Chine
CHINE HEAD

Old Blackgang Road, Niton, in about 1895. The original road from Niton west to Blackgang and Chale ran, as shown in this photograph, below Gore Cliff. By the 1880s a popular tourist excursion was to drive along the Undercliff from Ventnor to Blackgang (see pages 144 and 150).

Map 54 The original Ordnance Survey shows just how uninhabited the Sandown Bay area was in the early nineteenth century. At this time Sandown was little more than a tiny fishing hamlet. Shanklin was slightly larger with a small group of buildings near the parish church and a second group clustered round the head of the chine. In 1855 this latter group consisted of small thatched cottages with a few 'cottage orné'. This was destined to become known as the Old Village, when the town expanded later in the century. Both Sandown and Shanklin were surrounded by extensive heathland and there were no adequate roads either to Newport in the west or southwards to Ventnor. On the southern margin of the map is Bonchurch, which at this time consisted of a few cottages along the track heading westwards to Ventnor from the old parish church.

Not all the developments in the area have been residential. Sandown Bay was a potential point of invasion for enemy forces and even in medieval times fortifications had existed here. As a result of a supposed threat of invasion by the French in the 1850s, an extensive series of defensive works was built around the bay.

Old Blackgang Road, Niton, 1928. This cliff fall was photographed as it happened on 26 July, 1928. There had been falls earlier in the year and warning notices were erected on the road as early as February. It is estimated that about 100,000 tonnes of rock fell on this occasion. The road was blocked by the fall and never reopened, and this fall triggered a massive landslip below the cliff in September of the same year which carried away the remains of the old road (see pages 144 and 149).

Bibliography

Hampshire

Bettey, J. H., *Wessex from A.D. 1000* (Longman, 1986)
Proceedings of the Hampshire Field Club and Archaeological Society (annual publication to which all interested in Hampshire's history and natural history should subscribe)
Shennan, S. J. and Schadla-Hall, R. T. (eds), *The Archaeology of Hampshire* (Hampshire Field Club and Archaeological Society, 1981)
Tubbs, C. R., *The New Forest* (Collins, 1986)

Isle of Wight

Barford, H. V., *The Vectis Report*, Isle of Wight County Council, 1980
Dicks, B., *The Isle of Wight*, David and Charles, 1979
Hyland, P., *Wight: Biography of an Island*, Victor Gollancz Ltd, 1984
Sibley, P., *Discovering the Isle of Wight*, Hale, 1977
——, *Isle of Wight Villages*, Hale, 1983
Victoria History of the Counties of England: Hampshire and the Isle of Wight, vols. i–v, 1903–12

Useful Addresses

Hampshire

Cope Collection, University Library, Southampton
Hampshire Record Office, 20 Southgate Street, Winchester
Portsmouth Archive Office, Guildhall, Portsmouth
Southampton Archive Office, Civic Centre, Southampton

Isle of Wight

Carisbrooke Castle Museum, Carisbrooke, Newport
Isle of Wight County Record Office, Hillside, Newport
Isle of Wight County Museum Service, Rylstone Gardens Chalet, Rylstone Gardens, Shanklin
Isle of Wight Natural History and Archaeological Society, 66 Carisbrooke Road, Newport

GAZETTEER INDEX DIAGRAM

174 175 184 185 186 195 196 197

1 2 3 4 5 6
Silchester Kingsclere Bramley
Vernham Dean Hurstbourne Tarrant Sherborne St John BASINGSTOKE Hook FLEET FARNBOROUGH Hartley Wintney
7 8 9 10 11 12 13
Odiham ALDERSHOT Overton Whitchurch Cliddesden Weyhill Hurstbourne Priors ANDOVER S Warnborough Bentley
Thruxton Grateley Preston Candover Lasham Sutton Scotney ALTON
14 15 16 17 18 19 20
Middle Wallop Headley Stockbridge Crawley New Alresford Selborne Broughton
King's Somborne Ropley Liphook Cheriton Bramdean Liss
21 22 23 24 25 26 27 28
Braishfield WINCHESTER Hursley Twyford West Meon East Meon PETERSFIELD ROMSEY Upham Meonstoke
29 Damerham W Wellow EASTLEIGH Bishop's Waltham Bramshaw Hambledon SOUTHAMPTON
Fordingbridge Totton Cadnam 36
30 31 32 33 34 35 HORNDEAN
Minstead Botley Wickham Ibsley Waterlooville Lyndhurst Hythe HAVANT
RINGWOOD Titchfield FAREHAM Brockenhurst Fawley
37 38 39 40 41 42 43 44
Burley Beaulieu Exbury Lee-on-the-Solent Boldre Bucklers Hard GOSPORT S Hayling Sway
Hurn Sopley LYMINGTON COWES PORTSMOUTH New Milton Fishbourne CHRISTCHURCH RYDE Seaview
45 46 47 48 49 50
Milford on Sea Yarmouth Shalfleet St Helens BOURNEMOUTH NEWPORT Bembridge Freshwater Totland Calbourne Brading
Brook SANDOWN Brighstone Shorwell SHANKLIN Godshill
51 52 53 54
Whitwell Chale VENTNOR

KEY

- ONE INCH EDITION MAPS
- 1:50 000 LANDRANGER SHEET LINES

GAZETTEER

This Gazetteer contains the modern names of cities, towns and villages in Hampshire and the Isle of Wight as shown on Ordnance Survey 1:50,000 scale Landranger maps. Each Gazetteer entry gives the place name, the Landranger map number(s) on which it appears and its National Grid reference number. Having identified the place name and the Landranger map number that includes it, references to the diagram on the left will show the page numbers of early Ordnance Survey mapping in this book where the name can be located. By purchasing the relevant Landranger map, the National Grid reference number also included in the Gazetteer will enable you to pinpoint the name and its position in the modern landscape precisely. Ordnance Survey Landranger maps are available from most booksellers, stationers and newsagents.

Ordnance Survey can also supply monochrome copies of a selection of early OS maps held in its Record Map Library. Enquiries on this service should be addressed to Fixed Price Services, Ordnance Survey, Romsey Road, Maybush, Southampton, SO9 4DH. Telephone Southampton (0703) 792338.

Hampshire

A

Place	Map	Grid ref
Abbotstone	185	SU5634
Abbotswood	185	SU3723
Abbotts Ann	185	SU3243
Abshot	196	SU5105
Aldermoor	196	SU3915
Aldershot	186	SU8650
Allbrook	185	SU4521
Alton	186	SU7139
Alverstoke	196	SZ5998
Ampfield	185	SU4023
Amport	185	SU2944
Andover	185	SU3645
Andover Down	185	SU3945
Andwell	186	SU6952
Anmore	196	SU6711
Anna Valley	185	SU3444
Ann's Hill	196	SU5900
Anthill Common	196	SU6412
Applemore	196	SU3907
Appleshaw	185	SU3048
Arford	186	SU8236
Ashansworth	174	SU4157
Ashford	195	SU1314
Ashford Hill	174	SU5562
Ashlett	196	SU4603
Ashley	195	SU1304
Ashley	185	SU3830
Ashley	195	SZ2595
Ashley Heath	195	SU1104
Ashurst	196	SU3310
Ashurst Bridge	196	SU3412
Avington	185	SU5332
Avon	195	SZ1498
Avon Castle	195	SU1303
Awbridge	185	SU3323
Axford	185	SU6143

B

Place	Map	Grid ref
Baffins	196	SU6601
Bagmore	185 186	SU6644
Bailey Green	185 186	SU6627
Ball Hill	174	SU4263
Balmerlawn	196	SU3003
Bank	195	SU2807
Bar End	185	SU4828
Barford	186	SU8537
Bartley	196	SU3013
Barton on Sea	195	SZ2393
Barton Stacey	185	SU4341
Bashley	195	SZ2497
Basing	185 186	SU6652
Basingstoke	185	SU6352
Bassett	185	SU4116
Bassett Green	185	SU4216
Battramsley	196	SZ3099
Battramsley Cross	196	SZ3198
Baughurst	174	SU5860
Beaulieu	196	SU3802
Beauworth	185	SU5726
Beckley	195	SZ2296
Bedhampton	197	SU7006
Beech	185 186	SU6838
Bell Hill	197	SU7424
Bentley	186	SU7844
Bentworth	185 186	SU6640
Bickton	195	SU1412
Bighton	185	SU6134
Binley	185	SU4253
Binstead	186	SU7741
Binstead Place	186	SU7841
Bishop's Sutton	185	SU6031
Bishopstoke	185	SU4619
Bishop's Waltham	185	SU5517
Bisterne	195	SU1401
Bisterne Close	195	SU2202
Bitterne	196	SU4513
Bitterne Park	196	SU4414
Black Dam	185	SU6451
Blackfield	196	SU4401
Blackmoor	186	SU7733
Blacknest	186	SU7941
Blackwater	195	SZ1395
Blackwater	175 186	SU8559
Blashford	195	SU1506
Bleak Hill	195	SU1311
Blendworth	197	SU7113
Blissford	195	SU1713
Blounce	186	SU7145
Boarhunt	196	SU6008
Boldre	196	SZ3298
Boorley Green	196	SU5014
Bordon	186	SU8035
Bordon Camp	186	SU7936
Boscombe	195	SZ1191
Bossington	185	SU3331
Botley	196	SU5113
Bournemouth	195	SZ0891
Bowling Alley	186	SU7949
Bowyer's Common	186 197	SU7626
Bradley	185	SU6341
Braishfield	185	SU3725
Brambridge	185	SU4721
Bramdean	185	SU6128
Bramley	175 186	SU6559
Bramley Corner	175	SU6359
Bramley Green	175 186	SU6658
Bramshaw	184	SU2715
Bramshott	186	SU8432
Bransbury	185	SU4242
Bransgore	195	SZ1897
Breamore	184	SU1518
Bridgemary	196	SU5803
Brighton Hill	185	SU6249
Broad Laying	174	SU4362
Broadmere	185	SU6247
Broadoak	196	SU5013
Brockenhurst	196	SU2902
Brockhampton	197	SU7106
Brockhurst	196	SU5901
Brock's Green	174	SU5061
Brockwood Park	185	SU6226
Brokenford	196	SU3512
Brook	195	SU2714
Brook	185	SU3428
Brook Hill	195	SU2714
Broughton	185	SU3032
Brown Candover	185	SU5739
Browndown	196	SZ5799
Buckland	196	SZ3196
Bucklers Hard	196	SU4000
Bucks Horn Oak	186	SU8041
Buckskin	185	SU6051
Bull Hill	196	SZ3398
Burgates	186 197	SU7728
Burghclere	174	SU4761
Buriton	197	SU7320
Burley	195	SU2103
Burley Lawn	195	SU2203
Burley Street	195	SU2004
Burridge	196	SU5110
Bursledon	196	SU4809
Burton	195	SZ1694
Butlocks Heath	196	SU4608
Buttsash	196	SU4205
Butt's Green	185	SU3026
Butts, The	186	SU7138

C

Place	Map	Grid ref
Cadnam	196	SU2913
Calmore	196	SU3414
Calshot	196	SU4701
Canada	184	SU2817
Carter's Clay	185	SU3024
Catherington	197	SU6914
Catisfield	196	SU5406
Causeway	197	SU6912
Causeway	197	SU7422
Chalton	197	SU7316
Chandler's Ford	185	SU4320
Charlton	185	SU3547
Charminster	195	SZ1094
Charter Alley	174	SU5957
Chawton	186	SU7037
Cheriton	185	SU5828
Chidden	185	SU6617
Chilbolton	185	SU3939
Chilbolton Down	185	SU4136
Chilcomb	185	SU5028
Chilton Candover	185	SU5940
Chilworth	185	SU4118
Chilworth Old Village	185	SU4018
Chineham	185 186	SU6554
Christchurch	195	SZ1592
Church Common	186 197	SU7325
Church Crookham	186	SU8152
Church End	175 186	SU6756
Clanfield	197	SU7016
Clanville	185	SU3149
Clayhall	196	SZ6198
Clayhill	196	SU3007
Cliddesden	185	SU6349
Cold Ash Hill	186	SU8432
Colden Common	185	SU4722
Colemore	186	SU7030
Colt Hill	186	SU7451
Compton	185	SU3429
Compton	185	SU4625
Conford	186	SU8232
Copnor	196	SU6602
Copythorne	196	SU3014
Corhampton	185	SU6120
Cosham	196	SU6605
Court Corner	175	SU6059
Cove	175 186	SU8555
Cowplain	197	SU6911
Coxford	196	SU3914
Crampmoor	185	SU3822
Cranbourne	185	SU6350
Crawley	185	SU4234
Cricket Hill	175 186	SU8260
Criddlestyle	195	SU1514
Crockerhill	196	SU5709

Crondall 186 SU7948
Crookham Village 186 SU7952
Crow 195 SU1603
Crowdhill 185 SU4920
Crux Easton 174 SU4256
Cuckoo's Corner 186 SU7441
Cufaude 175 SU6457
Cupernham 185 SU3622
Curbridge 196 SU5211
Curdridge 196 SU5313
Custards 196 SU2908

D

Damerham 184 SU1015
Daneshill 185 186 SU6553
Darby Green 175 186 SU8360
Deadwater 186 SU8035
Dean 185 SU5619
Denmead 196 SU6511
Denvilles 197 SU7206
Dibden 196 SU4008
Dibden Purlieu 196 SU4106
Dipley 175 186 SU7457
Dogmersfield 186 SU7852
Dora's Green 186 SU8148
Downton 195 SZ2693
Drayton 196 SU6705
Droxford 185 SU6018
Dummer 185 SU5845
Dunbridge 185 SU3126
Dundridge 185 SU5718
Durley 185 SU5116
Durns Town 195 SZ2898
Durrants 197 SU7209

E

Earlstone Common 174 SU4761
East Boldre 196 SU3700
East Cholderton 185 SU2945
East End 174 SU4161
East End 185 SU6424
East End 196 SZ3697
East Green 186 SU7944
East Hill 186 197 SU7827
Eastland Gate 196 SU6712
Eastleigh 185 SU4519
East Liss 186 197 SU7827
East Martin 184 SU0719
East Meon 185 SU6822
Eastney 196 SZ6799
East Oakley 185 SU5750
Eastoke 197 SZ7398
Easton 185 SU5132
East Parley 195 SZ1097
Eastrop 185 SU6451
East Stratton 185 SU5439
East Tisted 186 SU7032
East Tytherley 185 SU2929
East Wellow 185 SU3020
East Woodhay 174 SU4061
East Worldham 186 SU7438
Ecchinswell 174 SU5059
Eling 196 SU3612
Ellingham 195 SU1408
Ellisfield 185 SU6346
Elson 196 SU6001
Emery Down 195 SU2808
Empshott 186 SU7531
Emsworth 197 SU7406
Enham-Alamein 185 SU3649
Eversley 175 186 SU7762
Eversley Centre 175 186 SU7861
Eversley Cross 175 186 SU7961
Everton 195 SZ2894
Everton 196 SZ2994
Ewhurst Ho 174 SU5756
Ewshot 186 SU8149
Exbury 196 SU4200
Exton 185 SU6121

F

Faberstown 184 SU2750
Faccombe 174 SU3858
Fairmile 195 SZ1594
Fair Oak 185 SU4918
Fair Oak 174 SU5561
Fair Oak Green 175 186 SU6660
Fareham 196 SU5606
Farleigh Wallop 185 SU6246
Farlington 196 SU6805
Farnborough 186 SU8754
Farnborough Green 175 186 SU8757
Farnborough Park 175 186 SU8755
Farnborough Street 175 186 SU8756
Fawley 196 SU4503
Filmore Hill 185 186 SU6627
Finchdean 197 SU7312
Fisher's Pond 185 SU4820
Fleet 197 SU7201
Fleet 186 SU8054
Fleetend 196 SU5006
Fleetlands 196 SU5804
Flood Street 184 SU1417
Fordingbridge 195 SU1414
Forest Gate 196 SU6412
Forton 185 SU4143
Forton 196 SU6000
Foulford 195 SU1805
Four Marks 185 186 SU6735
Foxhills 196 SU3411
Fox Lane 175 186 SU8557
Fratton 196 SU6500
Freemantle 196 SU4012
Frenchmoor 184 SU2628
Fritham 195 SU2314
Frithend 186 SU8039
Frogham 195 SU1613
Frogmore 175 186 SU8460
Froxfield Green 186 197 SU7025
Fryern Hill 185 SU4420
Fulflood 185 SU4729
Fullerton 185 SU3739
Funtley 196 SU5608
Furze Hill 195 SU1711
Furzeley Corner 196 SU6510
Furzley 184 SU2816
Fyfield 185 SU2946

G

Gable Head 197 SZ7299
Gilbert Street 185 186 SU6532
Godshill 195 SU1714
Godswinscroft 195 SZ1996
Golden Hill 195 SZ2695
Goodworth Clatford 185 SU3642
Goose Green 196 SU3007
Gore End 174 SU4163
Gosport 196 SU5900
Grange Estate 195 SU1101
Grateley 184 SU2741
Grayshott 186 SU8735
Greatham 186 SU7730
Great Posbrook 196 SU5305
Great Shoddesden 184 SU2748
Green, The 184 SU2729
Greywell 186 SU7151
Griggs Green 186 SU8231

H

Hale 184 SU1919
Halterworth 185 SU3721
Hamble 196 SU4706
Hambledon 196 SU6414
Hammer Bottom 186 SU8632
Hammond's Green 196 SU3413
Hampton Park 196 SU4315
Hangersley 195 SU1706
Hannington 174 185 SU5455
Harbridge 195 SU1410
Harbridge Green 195 SU1410
Hardley 196 SU4304
Hardway 196 SU6001
Harefield 196 SU4613
Harestock 185 SU4631
Hartfordbridge 175 186 SU7757
Hartley Mauditt 186 SU7436
Hartley Wespall 175 186 SU6958
Hartley Wintney 175 186 SU7656
Hatch 185 186 SU6752
Hatch Bottom 196 SU4714
Hatchet Gate 196 SU3701
Hatchet Green 184 SU1919
Hatherden 185 SU3450
Havant 197 SU7106
Hawkley 186 197 SU7429
Hawley 175 186 SU8558
Hawthorn 185 186 SU6733
Hay Place 186 SU7740
Hazeley 175 186 SU7459
Hazeley Bottom 175 186 SU7557
Hazeley Heath 175 186 SU7558
Hazeley Lea 175 186 SU7459
Headbourne Worthy 185 SU4832
Headley 174 SU5162
Headley 186 SU8236
Headley Down 186 SU8336
Hearn 186 SU8337
Heath End 174 SU5862
Heathfield 196 SU5506
Heckfield 175 186 SU7260
Hedge End 196 SU4912
Hensting 185 SU4921
Herriard 185 186 SU6645
Highbury 196 SU6604
Highclere 174 SU4360
Highcliffe 195 SZ2193
High Cross 186 197 SU7126
Highfield 196 SU4214
Hightown 195 SU1604
Hightown 196 SU4711
Hill Head 196 SU5402
Hill Park 196 SU5507
Hillpound 196 SU5815
Hillside 186 SU7550
Hill Side 186 197 SU7827
Hillstreet 185 SU3416
Hill Top 196 SU4003
Hillyfields 196 SU3715
Hilsea 196 SU6503
Hiltingbury 185 SU4322
Hinton 195 SZ2095
Hinton Ampner 185 SU5927
Hinton Ampner Ho 185 SU5927
Hoe 185 SU5617
Holbury 196 SU4303
Holdenhurst 195 SZ1295
Hollywater 186 SU8034
Holmesland 196 SU5013
Holt 186 SU7354
Holt End 185 186 SU6639
Holt Heath 195 SU0604
Holt Pound 186 SU8143
Holybourne 186 SU7340
Hook 196 SU5005
Hook 186 SU7254
Hook Park 196 SU4904
Hordle 195 SZ2795
Horndean 197 SU7013
Horsebridge 185 SU3430
Horton Heath 185 SU4916
Houghton 185 SU3432
Hound 196 SU4708
Hound Green 175 186 SU7259
Houndmills 185 SU6252
Hounsdown 196 SU3512
Hurn 195 SZ1296
Hursley 185 SU4225
Hurstbourne Priors 185 SU4346
Hurstbourne Tarrant 185 SU3853
Hyde 195 SU1612
Hyde 185 SU4830
Hythe 196 SU4207

I

Ibsley 195 SU1509
Ibthorpe 185 SU3753
Ibworth 185 SU5654
Iford 195 SZ1393
Isington 186 SU7842
Island 186 197 SU7325
Itchen 196 SU4411
Itchen Abbas 185 SU5332
Itchen Stoke 185 SU5532

J

Jumpers Common 195 SZ1494

K

Kempshott 185 SU6050
Kents Oak 185 SU3224
Keyhaven 196 SZ3091
Kilmeston 185 SU5926
Kimbridge 185 SU3325
Kimpton 184 SU2846
Kingsclere 174 SU5258
Kingsclere Woodlands 174 SU5361
King's Furlong 185 SU6351
Kingsley 186 SU7838

Rotherwick	175 186	SU7156
Rotten Green	175 186	SU7955
Row Ash	196	SU5413
Rowland's Castle	197	SU7310
Rowner	196	SU5801
Rownhams	185	SU3817

S

St Cross	185	SU4727
St Denys	196	SU4313
St Giles's Hill	185	SU4929
St Ives	195	SU1204
St Leonards	195	SU1103
St Mary Bourne	185	SU4250
St Rose	196	SZ3096
Salters Heath	175	SU6157
Sandford	195	SU1601
Sandleheath	195	SU1214
Sandleheath	184	SU1215
Sandle Manor	195	SU1314
Sandy Down	196	SZ3199
Sarisbury	196	SU5008
Selborne	186	SU7433
Selsmore	197	SZ7399
Setley	196	SU3000
Shalden	186	SU6941
Shalden Green	186	SU6943
Shawford	185	SU4624
Shedfield	196	SU5613
Sheet	197	SU7524
Sherborne St John	175 185	SU6255
Sherfield English	185	SU2922
Sherfield on Loddon	175 186	SU6757
Sherwoods	175 186	SU7457
Shipton Bellinger	184	SU2345
Shirley	196	SU4013
Shirley	195	SZ1798
Shirley holms	196	SZ3098
Shirley Warren	196	SU3914
Shirrell Heath	196	SU5714
Sholing	196	SU4511
Sholing Common	196	SU4512
Shootash	185	SU3222
Shorley	185	SU5726
Shortheath	186	SU7736
Silchester	175	SU6262
Slap	195	SU2002
Sleepers Hill	185	SU4629
Smannell	185	SU3848
Soake	196	SU6611
Soberton	185	SU6116
Soberton Heath	196	SU6014
Soldridge	185 186	SU6534
Solent Breezes	196	SU5004
Somerford	195	SZ1793
Sopley	195	SZ1597
Southampton	196	SU4213
South Baddesley	196	SZ3596
South Bockhampton	195	SZ1795
Southbourne	195	SZ1491
South End	184	SU1015
South Farnborough	186	SU8754
South Gorley	195	SU1610
South Ham	185	SU6151
South Hayling	197	SZ7299
Southrope	185 186	SU6744
Southsea	196	SZ6499
South Tidworth	184	SU2348
South Town	185 186	SU6536
South View	185	SU6352
South Warnborough	186	SU7247
South Weirs	195	SU2801
Southwick	196	SU6208
South Wonston	185	SU4635
Spanish Green	175 186	SU6958
Sparsholt	185	SU4331
Spearywell	185	SU3127
Springbourne	195	SZ1092
Stamshaw	196	SU6402
Standford	186	SU8134
Standon	185	SU4226
Stanmore	185	SU4628
Stanpit	195	SZ1792
Steep	186 197	SU7425
Steep Marsh	186 197	SU7526
Steventon	185	SU5447
Stockbridge	185	SU3535
Stockheath	197	SU7107
Stoke	185	SU4051
Stoke	197	SU7202
Stoke Charity	185	SU4839
Stoke Common	185	SU4720
Stonehills	196	SU4602
Stoner Hill	186 197	SU7225
Stoney Cross	195	SU2511
Stonyford	196	SU3215
Straits, The	186	SU7838
Stratfield Saye	175 186	SU6861
Stratfield Turgis	175 186	SU6959
Stroud	197	SU7223
Strouden	195	SZ1194
Stubbington	196	SU5503
Stuckton	195	SU1613
Summerley	185 186	SU6640
Sutton Scotney	185	SU4639
Swanmore	185	SU5716
Swanwick	196	SU5109
Sway	195	SZ2798
Swaythling	196	SU4315
Swelling Hill	185 186	SU6532

T

Tadley	175	SU6061
Tangley	185	SU3352
Testwood	196	SU3514
Thorney Hill	195	SZ2099
Thornhill	196	SU4612
Thornhill Park	196	SU4713
Three Ashes	175	SU6361
Thruxton	185	SU2945
Tichborne	185	SU5730
Tidpit	184	SU0719
Timsbury	185	SU3424
Tinker's Hill	185	SU3947
Tiptoe	195	SZ2597
Titchfield	196	SU5305
Titchfield Common	196	SU5206
Titchfield Park	196	SU5307
Totton	196	SU3513
Townhill Park	196	SU4514
Townsend	195	SZ1294
Towns End	174	SU5658
Tuckton	195	SZ1492
Tufton	185	SU4546
Tunworth	185 186	SU6748
Turgis Green	175 186	SU6959
Turkey Island	196	SU5613
Turmer	195	SU1309
Twyford	185	SU4824

U

Up Green	175 186	SU7960
Upham	185	SU5320
Up Nately	186	SU6951
Upper Bullington	185	SU4641
Upper Burgate	184	SU1516
Upper Canterton	195	SU2612
Upper Clatford	185	SU3543
Upper Farringdon	186	SU7135
Upper Froyle	186	SU7542
Upper Ratley	185	SU3223
Upper Shirley	196	SU4014
Upper Slackstead	185	SU3926
Upper Street	184	SU1518
Upper Swanmore	185	SU5817
Upper Wield	185	SU6238
Upper Wootton	185	SU5754
Upper Wyke	185	SU4050
Up Somborne	185	SU3932
Upton	174 185	SU3655
Upton	185	SU3717
Upton Grey	186	SU6948

V

Vernham Dean	174	SU3456
Vernham Street	174	SU3457

W

Walhampton	196	SZ3395
Walkford	195	SZ2194
Wallington	196	SU5806
Waltham Chase	196	SU5615
Walton Heath	196	SU6109
Warblington	197	SU7206
Warnborough Green	186	SU7252
Warnford	185	SU6223
Warren Corner	186 197	SU7227
Warren Corner	186	SU8149
Warsash	196	SU4906
Waterditch	195	SZ1896
Water End	186	SU6953
Waterford	196	SZ3394
Waterlooville	196	SU6809
Weeke	185	SU4630
Well	186	SU7646
Westbourne	195	SZ0791
West Common	196	SU4400
West End	196	SU4614
West End	196	SU5605
West End Green	175 186	SU6661
Westfield	197	SZ7199
West Green	175 186	SU7456
West Ham	185	SU6152
West Heath	174	SU5958
West Heath	175 186	SU8556
West Hurn	195	SZ1196
Westlands	186	SU8231
West Leigh	197	SU7208
West Liss	186 197	SU7728
West Meon	185	SU6424
Weston	196	SU4410
Weston	197	SU7221
Weston Common	196	SU4611
Weston Corbett	185 186	SU6847
Weston Patrick	185 186	SU6846
West Southbourne	195	SZ1392
West Tisted	185 186	SU6529
West Town	197	SZ7199
West Tytherley	184	SU2729
West Wellow	185	SU2919
West Worldham	186	SU7436
Weyhill	185	SU3146
Whale Island	196	SU6302
Wheatley	186	SU7840
Wherwell	185	SU3840
Whitchurch	185	SU4648
Whitedown	185	SU5854
Whitehall	186	SU7452
Whitehill	186	SU7934
Whitenap	185	SU3720
Whitsbury	184	SU1219
Wick	195	SZ1591
Wickham	196	SU5711
Widley	196	SU6706
Wildern	196	SU4813
Wildhern	185	SU3550
Wildmoor	175 186	SU6856
Wilsom	186	SU7239
Wimpson	196	SU3814
Winchester	185	SU4829
Winchfield	186	SU7654
Winchfield Hurst	186	SU7753
Winklebury	185	SU6152
Winkton	195	SZ1696
Winkton Common	195	SZ1695
Winnall	185	SU4930
Winslade	185 186	SU6548
Winsor	196	SU3114
Wintershill	185	SU5217
Winton	195	SZ0893
Wittensford	195	SU2813
Wivelrod	185 186	SU6738
Wolverton Common	174	SU5659
Wonston	185	SU4739
Woodcott	185	SU4354
Woodgreen	184	SU1717
Woodlands	196	SU3211
Woodley	185	SU3722
Woodmancott	185	SU5642
Woodmill	196	SU4315
Woodside	196	SZ3294
Woolston	196	SU4310
Woolton Hill	174	SU4261
Wootton	195	SZ2498
Wootton St Lawrence	185	SU5953
Worlds End	196	SU6312
Worting	185	SU6052
Wyck	186	SU7539
Wymering	196	SU6506

Y

Yateley	175 186	SU8160

Isle of Wight

A

Adgestone	196	SZ5985
Afton	196	SZ3486
Alverstone	196	SZ5785
Alverstone Fm	196	SZ5292
Appley	196	SZ6092
Apse Heath	196	SZ5683
Arreton	196	SZ5486
Ashey	196	SZ5789
Atherfield Green	196	SZ4679

B

Barton	196	SZ5089
Bembridge	196	SZ6487
Binstead	196	SZ5792
Blackgang	196	SZ4876
Blackwater	196	SZ5086
Bonchurch	196	SZ5777
Bouldnor	196	SZ3789
Bowcombe	196	SZ4686
Brading	196	SZ6086
Branstone	196	SZ5583
Brighstone	196	SZ4282
Brook	196	SZ3983
Brookgreen	196	SZ3883

C

Calbourne	196	SZ4286
Carisbrooke	196	SZ4888
Chale	196	SZ4877
Chale Green	196	SZ4879
Chillerton	196	SZ4884
Clatterford	196	SZ4887
Cowes	196	SZ4995
Cranmore	196	SZ3990
Cridmore	196	SZ4982

D

Dallimores	196	SZ5293
Downend	196	SZ5387
Dunnose	196	SZ5878

E

East Afton	196	SZ3686
East Cliff	196	SZ6488
East Cowes	196	SZ5095
Easton	196	SZ3486
Elmfield	196	SZ6091

F

Fishbourne	196	SZ5592
Five Houses	196	SZ4287
Foreland	196	SZ6687
Foreland Fields	196	SZ6587
Forest Side	196	SZ4789
Freshwater	196	SZ3486
Freshwater Bay	196	SZ3485

G

Gatcombe	196	SZ4885
Godshill	196	SZ5281
Great Thorness	196	SZ4592
Gunville	196	SZ4789
Gurnard	196	SZ4795

H

Hamstead	196	SZ3991
Havenstreet	196	SZ5690
Haylands	196	SZ5891
Hillis Corner	196	SZ4793
Hillway	196	SZ6386
Hulverstone	196	SZ3984
Hunney Hill	196	SZ4989

K

Kingates	196	SZ5177
Kingston	196	SZ4781
Kite Hill	196	SZ5592

L

Lake	196	SZ5883
Landguard Manor	196	SZ5782
Lane End	196	SZ6587
Limerstone	196	SZ4482
Little Atherfield	196	SZ4680
Littletown	196	SZ5390
Locksgreen	196	SZ4490
Lowtherville	196	SZ5578
Luccombe Village	196	SZ5879

M

Mark's Corner	196	SZ4692
Merrie Gardens	196	SZ5883
Merstone	196	SZ5285
Middleton	196	SZ3386
Moortown	196	SZ4283
Morton	196	SZ6086
Mottistone	196	SZ4083

N

Nettlecombe	196	SZ5278
Nettlestone	196	SZ6290
Nettlestone Point	196	SZ6291
Newbridge	196	SZ4187
Newchurch	196	SZ5585
Newport	196	SZ4988
Newtown	196	SZ4290
Ningwood	196	SZ4088
Ningwood Common	196	SZ3989
Niton	196	SZ5076
Northwood	196	SZ4893
Norton	196	SZ3489
Norton Green	196	SZ3488

O

Oakfield	196	SZ5991

P

Pan	196	SZ5088
Parkhurst	196	SZ4990
Pelhamfield	196	SZ5892
Pilgrims Park	196	SZ4593
Pondwell	196	SZ6191
Porchfield	196	SZ4491
Pound Green	196	SZ3386
Pyle	196	SZ4779

Q

Queen's Bower	196	SZ5784

R

Rew Street	196	SZ4794
Rookley	196	SZ5083
Rookley Green	196	SZ5083
Roud	196	SZ5180
Ryde	196	SZ5992

S

St Helens	196	SZ6289
St John's Park	196	SZ6092
St Lawrence	196	SZ5376
Sandford	196	SZ5481
Sandown	196	SZ5984
Sandy Way	196	SZ4582
School Green	196	SZ3386
Seaview	196	SZ6291
Shalcombe	196	SZ3985
Shalfleet	196	SZ4189
Shanklin	196	SZ5881
Shide	196	SZ5088
Shorwell	196	SZ4582
Southford	196	SZ5178
Springhill	196	SZ5095
Spring Vale	196	SZ6291
Staplers	196	SZ5189
Steephill	196	SZ5577
Steyne Cross	196	SZ6487
Swanmore	196	SZ5991

T

Thorley	196	SZ3788
Thorley Street	196	SZ3788
Thorncross	196	SZ4381
Totland	196	SZ3286

U

Upper Bonchurch	196	SZ5778
Upper Hyde	196	SZ5781
Upper Pennington	196	SZ3095
Upton	196	SZ5890

V

Ventnor	196	SZ5677

W

Warden Point	196	SZ3287
Weeks	196	SZ5991
Wellow	196	SZ3888
Westcliff	196	SZ5076
Weston Manor	196	SZ3286
Westwood	196	SZ5392
Whippingham	196	SZ5193
Whiteley Bank	196	SZ5581
Whitwell	196	SZ5277
Winford	196	SZ5684
Woodlands Vale	196	SZ6191
Woodside	196	SZ5493
Wooton	196	SZ5392
Wootton Bridge	196	SZ5491
Wootton Common	196	SZ5391
Wroxall	196	SZ5579

Y

Yafford	196	SZ4481
Yaldhurst	196	SZ3095
Yarbridge	196	SZ6086
Yarmouth	196	SZ3589
Yaverland	196	SZ6185

GAYLORD S